Social Contexts of Radicalization and Violent Extremism in the MENA and Balkans

Corinne Torrekens • Tasnim Chirchi
Lurdes Vidal Bertran
Editors

Social Contexts of Radicalization and Violent Extremism in the MENA and Balkans

A Multi-Country Analysis

Springer

Editors
Corinne Torrekens
GERME
Université libre de Bruxelles
Brussels, Belgium

Tasnim Chirchi
Ibn Khaldun University
Istanbul, Turkey

Lurdes Vidal Bertran
Blanquerna-Universitat Ramon Llull
Barcelona, Spain

ISBN 978-3-031-84520-8 ISBN 978-3-031-84521-5 (eBook)
https://doi.org/10.1007/978-3-031-84521-5

This Springer imprint is published by the registered company Springer Nature Switzerland AG
The registered company address is: Gewerbestrasse 11, 6330 Cham, Switzerland

Contents

List of Abbreviations

ADS	Social Development Agency
ASDHOM	Association de Défense des Droits de l'Homme au Maroc
AMS	Agency of Sport and Youth of Macedonia
BFI	Macedonian Islamic Community
BFU	Bulgarian Football Union
BiH	Bosnia and Herzegovina
BIK	the Islamic Community of Kosovo
BIRN	Balkan Investigative Reporting Network
BSP	Bulgarian Socialist Party
CBOs	Community-Based Organizations
CEF	Correctional-Educational Facility
CNDH	National Human Rights Council
CoE	Council of Europe
CONNEKT	Contexts of Violent Extremism in MENA and Balkan Societies project
CSD	Center for the Study of Democracy
C/PVE	Countering and Preventing Violent Extremism
CRRCG	Committee on Relations between Religious Communities and Groups' Affiliates
CSOs	Civil Society Organizations
CVE	Countering Violent Extremism
DES	State Directorate for Execution of Sanctions
DUI	Albanian party Democratic Union for Integration
EU	European Union
FATF	Financial Action Task Force
FBiH	Federation of Bosnia and Herzegovina
FGDs	Focus Group Discussions
FFM	Football Federation of Macedonia
GERB	Citizens for European Development of Bulgaria

ICM	Islamic Religious Community of North Macedonia
INDH	National Initiative for Human Development
IOM	International Organization for Migration
KCS	Kosovo Correctional Services
KII	Key Informant Interviewee
KIA	Kosovo Intelligence Agency
KP	Kosovo Police
KFOR	Kosovo Force
KSC	Kosovo Security Council
KUBN	Katibat Uqba Bin Nafi
LMCDH	Ligue Marocaine pour la Citoyenneté et les Droits de l'Homme
MB	Muslim Brotherhood
MENA	Middle East and North Africa
MEST	Ministry of Education, Science and Technology
MIA	Ministry of Internal Affairs
MMA	Mixed Martial Arts
MLSW	Ministry of Labor and Social Welfare
MoD	Ministry of Defense
MoI	Ministry of Interior
MoJ	Ministry of Justice
MONEYVAL	Committee of Experts on the Evaluation of Anti-Money Laundering Measures and the Financing of Terrorism
NATO	North Atlantic Treaty Organization
NCCVECT	National Committee for Prevention of Violent Extremism and Counterterrorism
NCoCVECT	Office of the National Coordinator for CVE and CT
NGO	Non-Governmental Organizations
NLA	National Liberation Army
NSCT	National Strategies for Counterterrorism
NSCVE	National Strategies for Countering Violent Extremism
NSPVE	National Strategy for Prevention of Violent Extremism
OFA	Ohrid Framework Agreement
OHR	Office of the High Representative
OPM	Office of the Prime Minister
OSCE	Organization for Security and Cooperation in Europe
PF	Patriotic Front
PJD	Party of Justice and Development
PVE	Prevention of Violent Extremism
RS	Republika Srpska
RNM	Republic of North Macedonia
SCK	Security Council of Kosovo
SPVERLT	Strategy on the Prevention of Violent Extremism and Radicalism Leading to Terrorism 2015-2020
UNDP	United Nations Development Program

UNODC	United Nations Office on Drugs and Crime
US	United States of America
USAID	United States Agency for International Development
VE	Violent Extremism
VEOs	Violent Extremist Organizations

Introduction: Conducting Fieldwork on Radicalization and Violent Extremism in the MENA and the Balkans—Some Conceptual and Methodological Considerations

Tasnim Chirchi, Lurdes Vidal Bertran, and Corinne Torrekens

The case studies presented in this book have been gathered through the project CONNEKT (Contexts of Violent Extremism in MENA and Balkan Societies) which is a Horizon 2020 EU-funded research proposal exploring the drivers of radicalization and violent extremism among young people aged from 12 to 30 in eight countries: Bosnia and Herzegovina, Bulgaria, Egypt, Jordan, Kosovo, Morocco, North Macedonia, and Tunisia.[1] The project was led by the European Institute of the Mediterranean (IEMed) and engaged 14 partners from 12 countries, including universities and think tanks, but also civil society actors and local authorities.[2]

[1] For more information, see the website of the project https://h2020connekt.eu/the-project/

[2] Partners included the American University Cairo (Egypt), Generations For Peace (Jordan), the Jasmine Foundation (Tunisia), the University Moulay Ismail (Morocco), the University of Sarajevo (Bosnia and Herzegovina), the Kosovar Institute for Policy Research and Development (Kosovo), the Macedonian Academy of Sciences (Republic of North Macedonia), the Islamic Youth Forum (Macedonia), the Center for the Study of Democracy (Bulgaria), the Université libre de Bruxelles (Belgium), the University of Graz (Austria), the Universitat Rovira i Virgili (Spain) and the Euromed Cities Network.

T. Chirchi (✉)
Ibn Khaldun University, Istanbul, Turkey
e-mail: director@jasminefoundation.org

L. Vidal Bertran
Blanquerna-Universitat Ramon Llull, Barcelona, Spain
e-mail: LourdesVB@blanquerna.url.edu

C. Torrekens
Université libre de Bruxelles, Brussels, Belgium
e-mail: corinne.torrekens@ulb.be

C. Torrekens et al. (eds.), *Social Contexts of Radicalization and Violent Extremism in the MENA and Balkans*,
https://doi.org/10.1007/978-3-031-84521-5_1

The contexts of the emergence of radicalization and violent extremism (VE) in the MENA region and the Balkans are studied in relation to seven pre-identified drivers: religion, economic deprivation, political grievances, education, culture and leisure opportunities, digital socialization, territorial inequalities, and transnational dynamics (Vidal Bertran, 2020). The project maps and establishes interrelationships and specific significance of these seven potential drivers within three different levels of analysis (macro level, meso level and micro level). This framework aimed to build a cumulative knowledge of the complex phenomenon of radicalization: going from macro to meso to micro levels of social reality, findings are each time included at the next stage as a starting point, and their interaction with the next analysis level is studied. This book is especially based on the meso-level analysis while making reference to major contextual findings of macro-level investigations in each country under study.

The project thus developed innovative research bringing a multilevel and multidisciplinary study of radicalization by adopting a dynamic approach embracing the complexity of the social/political/economic contexts studied. Moving away from unidimensional and security-centered research on the topic, the project adopts a participatory and inclusive approach engaging communities/youth/women as significant stakeholders in building an accurate understanding of the dynamics of the radicalization of youth in the Balkans and the MENA regions.

The large geographical scope of the project, covering eight countries, necessitated a flexible methodological framework including data collection and analysis of case studies in relation to the subject matter of the research project. Hence the drivers are considered according to each country and each specific social context, taking into consideration the multiplicity of stakeholders and narratives on radicalization and VE.

1 Why Studying Radicalisation in the MENA and the Balkans Matters

Radicalization is certainly a buzzword (Neumann & Kleinmann, 2013) that is the target of severe criticism from well-established and respected scholars specializing in terrorism studies who are sometimes quite negative when assessing the results of four decades of research on the topic (Van de Voorde, 2011). For more than a decade now, many scientists have indeed pointed out the serious empirical weakness of studies in the field (Jackson et al., 2015; Sageman, 2014; Vergani et al., 2018). One of the fragilities of the concept is its lack of common definition. In the frame of the CONNEKT project, the term radicalization has been defined as “the process of developing extremist ideologies and beliefs” and violent extremism (VE) as “ideologies which oppose a society’s core values and principles”. This practical conceptualization addresses the fact that VE is a diverse phenomenon with no universal agreement as acknowledged by the United Nations (UN) Secretary-General’s

Action Plan at the UN, which in order to enable international cooperation in this field, adopts a practical approach to the prevention of violent extremism (PVE), without venturing to address definitional issues (Torrekens & De le Vingne, 2020). However, it is stated that in the absence of an agreed definition, countries should define VE in their national context but warns, in parallel, that such definitions should be consistent with obligations under international law, in particular international human rights law (Feve & Dews, 2019). This lack of a common definition has been criticized by some authors (Bakker, 2015; Ganor, 2002) who have highlighted that its existence would limit governmental abuses that take advantage of its absence to silence political opposition. Comparing the MENA and the Balkans regions thus offers the opportunity to decenter the European/Western focus of radicalization literature in order to analyze how radicalization is defined and interpreted in various contexts, by either authoritarian state apparatus or polarized and ethnically fragmented societies having faced civil wars. Indeed, post-communist nationalism, the conflicts of the early 1990s and revived ethnic and religious passions have produced social divisions within and between Western Balkan countries (Becirevic et al., 2017).

When it comes to the Maghreb countries, they have adopted a broad definition of terrorism that includes political dissent (Tamburini, 2018). Egypt was the first one to come up with a definition in 1992 and described terrorism "in such vague terms that it could jeopardize political and civil freedoms, as well as human rights" (Tamburini, 2018, p. 1237), an approach copied by the other anti-terrorist laws in the Maghreb. As for Tunisia, the incitement to hatred or racial or religious fanaticism is also condemned as 'terrorist'" but the law allows for a wide interpretation of what can fall into "fanatic religiosity". Indeed, the word used in Arabic is *'al-ta sub* which means intolerance, opening a wide array of possibilities to implement the law on social and political protest. In a similar vein, the Jordanian judicial order outs a list of terrorist acts that can be used as a justification to curb freedoms in the kingdom (Chirchi & Jrad, 2021). The Moroccan Penal Code is no exception to this rule since the list of terrorist acts includes broad and vague definitions likely to result in violations of freedom of association, sanctioned by the need to protect public order and state security (Chirchi & Jrad, 2021).

Regarding the Balkan region, the term "terrorism" was already heavily used in former Yugoslavia in the 1990s by political elites "to either describe the opponents on the other side of the ethnic divide—often employed to describe a whole nation—or to portray threats in general against the respective nation" and terrorism acts were mainly "motivated by ethnicity and/or national identity" (Bieber, 2003, p. 40). For example, Kosovo introduced some changes to the UNMIK Regulation 2001/12, which was the regulation prohibiting terrorism after the former 1977 Yugoslav Criminal Law. The changes modified the former definition of terrorism as "a threat to public order", to a "destabilization or destruction of basic political, economic or social structures of Kosovo, of a country or international organization" (Demolli, 2008, p. 118), making the definition more subjective. Also in Bulgaria, the definition of 'terrorism' remains "vague and overly broad" (Amnesty International, 2016) facilitating the targeting of "political opponents, ethnic and religious minorities, human rights defenders, and environmental, LGBTQ, and other activists" (Amnesty

International, 2016). In brief, contemporary counter-terrorism policies "cannot be separated from the historical legacies of imperial agendas in the Balkans" (Sadriu, 2019). This reminds us that the concept of radicalization is a social construction. In political contexts where interests and values of different groups are confronted, definitions of VE often reflect the interests of the defining powers. How terrorism is defined directly affects the response to it and therefore can impact a particular situation and affect the whole society and politics. Indeed, counterterrorist measures change enormously if one understands terrorism not as perpetrated only by non-state actors and acknowledges that states can be terrorists too. These measures change also when the definition of terrorism does not distinguish resistance to occupation movements from terrorist organizations. To paraphrase Schmid (2004, p. 402), the question of defining terms like radicalization and terrorism can therefore not be detached from the question of who is the defining agency.

Another advantage to introducing the Balkans in comparison with the MENA relies on distancing the analysis from an over-focalization on Islam and Islamism by taking into account the challenges posed by the activism of extreme-right and nationalist groups. Indeed, a very important part of the literature on radicalization focuses on Islamism and Salafism, reflecting Western interests and the domination and power relations existing in the production of the most prominent academic literature on the topic that moslty neglects non-Muslim forms of violent extremism. Consequently, our concern here is to raise a comparative and historical perspective between distinct forms of radical engagement in space and time across the two regions. This comparative approach also benefits from several important methodological shifts in security analysis from macro-level, state-focused approaches towards acknowledging and capturing the complexity of social realities and the plurality of contexts.

2 Shifting Paradigms in a Changing Security Landscape

The case studies presented in this book, have been conducted following an approach building on the contextual (Ciută, 2009, 2016) and vernacular (Bubandt, 2005; Jarvis, 2019) "turns" in Security Studies. Those theoretical paradigms view the understanding and practice of security to be dependent on context and amenable to change (Balzacq, 2011; Ciută, 2009, 2016; Floyd, 2010; Hansen, 2006; Huysmans, 2006). From this perspective, classical security studies have been questioned on several key aspects, including the focus, methodology, and underlying assumptions.

Classical Security Studies (Buzan, 1983; Mearsheimer, 2001; Walt, 1987; Waltz, 1978) have a state-centric focus as the main actors considered in international security are the states, while their main concerns are national security, military threats, and interstate conflicts. In this perspective, the main emphasis is placed on military capabilities, strategic alliances, and geopolitical strategies.

The analytical paradigm privileged in these classic approaches is often grounded in positivist epistemology, seeking objective, universal truths about security. For this reason, the favored methodology commonly used to analyze security issues is quantitative methods and formal modeling following a top-down approach. Additionally, this approach is focused on the decisions and policies of the state leaders and institutions (macro-level analysis) and mobilizes an understanding of security which is mostly viewed from the perspective of political and military elites.

The approach privileged in classical security studies is thus static and predictable based on the assumption that the international system is relatively static and predictable, while security threats are seen as tangible and quantifiable, often external to the state. Offering a narrow scope of security and excluding non-state actors, and the everyday experiences of citizens, the classical approach to security has been increasingly questioned with the dynamics of globalization and the emergence of new threats and interdependencies in the world.

The end of the Cold War (Fukuyama, 1992; Gaddis, 2005), as well as the dynamics of globalization (Held & McGrew, 2002; Nye & Goldsmith, 2011), shifted the focus from the traditional military threats and the state-centric security concerns towards new security issues such as transnational crime, terrorism, and other threats in an emerging multipolar and complex architecture of the international system. The old static paradigms seemed inefficient also in addressing the rise of non-state actors (Kaldor, 1999; Stern, 2003) including terrorist groups, multinational corporations, and international organizations, which have become increasingly influential in global politics.

Consequently, a gradual shift away from the classical approach in security studies occurs, reflecting broader changes in the international system and the nature of security threats. The transformations of the global landscape have brought the need for more inclusive, multilevel, and context-specific approaches to understanding and addressing security.

This shift included not only epistemological and paradigmatic changes in dealing with security but also contributed to re-conceptualizing security by acknowledging that it is not limited to protecting states from military threats but also includes the well-being of individuals and communities in an increasingly complex and interconnected world (Buzan & Waever, 2003). This is how we have seen the rise of the "human security paradigm" (Sen, 1999; Ul Haq, 1995) where the classical concept of security is expanded to include the protection of individuals and not just states. This paradigm emphasizes the focus on human well-being and rights and the critical nature of security threats such as poverty, disease, and the absence of human rights.

In addition to this, other transformations posed new security threats that needed to be addressed. For example, the emergence of new information and communication technologies (Floridi, 2014; Singer, 2014) has transformed how security threats emerge and are managed, thus requiring new frameworks of analysis and action. Ciută (2009, 2016) for instance advocates for a contextual approach in security studies because it offers a more comprehensive, nuanced, and adaptable framework for understanding and addressing security issues. By incorporating local contexts and broadening the concept of security, this approach overcomes the limitations of classical security studies and provides more relevant and effective policy recommendations.

In the same vein, Huysmans (2006) adopts an approach that helps him highlight the social construction of security issues. He argues that security practices are embedded in everyday life. According to him, social and political contexts are key in analyzing and understanding security issues. Hansen (2006) also highlights the construction of security issues through discourse and identity. Security is framed and practiced through narratives, which can be objectively analyzed using the method of discourse analysis. Floyd (2010) emphasizes how constructed and contested security is in specific contexts. She looks more specifically into the emerging threats related to environmental issues. Vallet (2014, 2015) addresses the material and discursive practices concerning border security that construct borders as security issues.

But this shift from the classical perspectives on security has also been advocated through a pragmatic perspective. Balzacq (2011) calls, in this regard, for approaching security with a pragmatic perspective that helps take into account practices, technologies, and contextual factors.

The situated approach to studying security thus moves away from the static and universal explanatory models and definitions characteristic of the classical security studies, as well as from conceptual frameworks primarily focused on state-centric and military threats, because they can oversimplify complex security dynamics. Moreover, classical approaches to security lack the specific historical, cultural, and social contexts of the regions or issues being studied, which may lead to misinterpretations and ineffective policy recommendations.

Considering specific contexts and the diverse perspectives and experiences of individuals and communities is one of the main recommendations formulated by the situated approaches to security. They aim to produce a more comprehensive and nuanced understanding of security issues by incorporating some methodological considerations that help enhance the relevance and impact of security research but also empower communities and promote more inclusive and effective security practices.

3 The Focus on Communities: The "Vernacular Turn"

The move away from the classical approaches to security studies has also been taking place through the focus on communities and everyday practices as part of the expansion of the understanding of security to the concept of human security. The "vernacular turn" challenges traditional, top-down notions of security by emphasizing how ordinary people understand and navigate security in their daily lives (Bourbeau, 2015; de Almagro & Krause, 2021; Schafer et al., 2019).

Research adopting this perspective thus seeks to understand how people perceive and articulate security in their specific local contexts. They are considered "experts" of their reality, of its challenges, and having the agency to develop strategies to face them. From this point of view, rather than seeking to form universal knowledge, this approach values local knowledge and insights. This bottom-up approach enriches the top-down approach focusing on elite actors and state institutions by bringing in the voices and experiences of ordinary people. Also, this helps include the cultural, social, and historical contexts that shape these experiences.

The post-positivist approach to security thus helps enrich the concept of security and recognize its plurality by acknowledging that it is experienced and interpreted differently across communities and societies and at the various levels of the complex social reality from the macro, to the meso and to the micro-level.

Re-conceptualizing security towards such a plural, and inclusive understanding can lead to a more comprehensive and nuanced perspective that includes various dimensions such as personal safety, community well-being, and economic stability. Such an approach can enhance the relevance and effectiveness of security policies and interventions by helping address the actual needs and concerns of communities while also fostering greater community resilience and participation by acknowledging their agency in navigating and addressing security challenges.

In this perspective, Bourbeau (2015) explores how local perspectives are important in understanding the various security approaches by analyzing how it is understood and practiced in different cultural and social contexts. Schafer et al. (2019) emphasize the role of local knowledge and practices by examining how people in fragile states navigate security in their daily lives. On their side, de Almagro and Krause (2021) challenge conventional state-centric security narratives by investigating how African communities understand and practice security.

4 Methodological Considerations

To be able to capture the complexity of security experiences and representations across the various levels of social reality, the situated or contextual approaches vary their methodological lenses and include a range of research methods allowing the production of comprehensive and inclusive insights into the role of communities, social contexts, as well as into the interactions between the various levels of social reality. In this frame, we want to especially stress six methodological considerations:

1. Empirical Research: Balzacq (2011) advocates for the importance of empirical research for a situated and nuanced analysis of security. He recommends in-depth case studies and fieldwork to understand how security is practiced and experienced in different contexts.
2. Methodological Pluralism: Moving away from the classical methodological dichotomies like subjective versus objective methods or qualitative versus quantitative methods, Balzacq (2011) recommends the adoption of methodological pluralism, or the use of diverse research methods, including qualitative, quantitative, and mixed methods. Such methodological pluralism allows us to capture the complexity of security issues.

3. Ethnographic Methods: whether in dealing with institutions or with communities, ethnographic methods, such as participant observation, and in-depth interviews allow researchers to gain a thorough understanding of both institutional and local security practices and perspectives.
4. Participatory Research: Situated analysis can be produced through active engagement with communities through participatory research methods that seeks to meaningfully involve them in the research process. Adopting participatory research approaches can include co-designing research questions, collecting data collaboratively, and involving participants in data analysis and dissemination. Research methods not only help to build more representative and relevant knowledge by addressing the concerns and needs of local communities but also can empower them.
5. Comparative Analysis: The focus on social contexts and communities helps to build comparative perspectives that provide insights into how security practices and experiences vary across regions and contexts by identifying common patterns and differences.
6. Interdisciplinary Approaches: For a more comprehensive and holistic understanding of security issues, research needs to incorporate insights from various disciplines, including sociology, anthropology, political science, geography, and cultural studies.

5 Focusing on Communities in the CONNEKT Project Through Meso-Level Research

CONNEKT aimed to study the contexts of the emergence of radicalization and violent extremism in the MENA region and the Balkans in relation to seven pre-identified drivers: religion, economic deprivation, political issues, education, culture and leisure opportunities, digital socialization, territorial inequalities, and transnational dynamics.

The meso-level research objectives were as follows:

- Analyze three sub-national community-level environments identified as conducive or at risk of violent extremism.
- Determine the factors of the social environment that feed violent extremism patterns and the flows of relations established among the national, community, and individual dimensions.
- Improve expertise on preventing violent extremism in target countries (local authorities and CSOs) and EU policy groups

In this framework, meso-level research tackles two main issues: firstly, how the drivers identified in CONNEKT interact with social entities and local stakeholders and, secondly, how to translate research at the meso level into preventive actions by taking a distinct approach beyond the security-driven approaches. With this aim, the important role of communities is underlined and methodological practices to create meaningful spaces for dialogue and consultation are explored.

Data collection mobilized ethnographic methods such as non-participant observation, in-depth interviews, and fieldwork to gain a deep understanding of local security practices and experiences. Ethnography allows researchers to immerse themselves in the community and gather rich, contextual data. The research activities included 24 case studies (3 case studies in each country) mobilizing 39 focus groups, 74 in-depth interviews and 2 online observations of public social media groups. The main target population of these research activities were young people from 12 to 30 years old (208 youth).

5.1 Defining and Operationalizing Community

Throughout the case studies covered in this book, the focus is placed on the social contexts where the individual relates to her/his family, neighborhood, school, peer group, religious and ethnic communities, etc. In this framework, meso-level research tackles two key issues: firstly, how the drivers identified in CONNEKT interact with social entities and local stakeholders and, secondly, how to translate research at the meso level into preventive actions by taking a distinct approach beyond the security-driven approaches. The chapters in this book will mostly focus on the first issue and examine the significant role of communities and local social contexts.

The focus on meso-level research necessitated a shared understanding of the concept of community. Within CONNEKT, community as a concept has been dealt with as an entity whose characteristics are: physical or non-physical, functional, and symbolic. Within CONNEKT, "community" is defined as a "social context", "cultural construct", and a "network of individual and collective interrelations". In this social context, we observe interactions between the members of the community; interactions between individuals and meso-level institutions that are significant for their lives (family, neighborhood, school, local authorities, etc.) and collective practices for achieving common goals, both discursive and behavioral.

While community is usually defined and operationalized as linked to a geographical location, the concept of community in our project allows both for a geographical definition when applicable, and for conceptualizing community regardless of physical location, when relevant. This definition of the social context means it is not specifically tied to geographical location in general, although it can be. However, in a context where territorial inequalities are a significant driver at the macro-level analysis, geography continues to be a major defining element of community.

As communication technologies play a more significant role in today's societies, especially resulting from the COVID-19 pandemic, CONNEKT also covered digital communities (as part of observing the driver of digital socialization). Undoubtedly, considering online communities made community detection and analysis more challenging and necessitated special methodological and ethical adaptations. The methodological guidelines document shared with all research partners specified that the concept of community can be operationalized as a social context that allows the observation of collective and individual practices (behaviors) for achieving common goals.

Community thus refers to a relational network focused on interactions and interrelations between individuals, but also between individuals and meso-level institutions, as well as to a discursive reality: perceptions, values, and beliefs shared in communicative contexts.

5.2 The Case Studies

In this framework, the case studies consisted of "sub-national community-level contexts" that allowed the research teams to "determine the social factors that feed VE patterns and the relations between national, community, and individual dimensions". Each country team initially selected five case studies, i.e., five meso contexts in which they considered that research might bring relevant results. These were narrowed down to three final case studies per country. The cases were selected according to the following criteria:

- Relevance: with respect to each national context, attention was given to those cases that were indicative in each country, seeking to bring added and improved understanding of the social contexts of radicalization in the country.
- Comparability: the empirical content obtained from the case studies was selected based on its potential for being susceptible to comparison between the different national realities. Although not all countries needed to cover all types of contexts and issues relevant to the project, there was a minimum comparability between more than one country.
- Feasibility: the case studies were selected considering the practical considerations related to fieldwork implementation.
- Prevention: each analysis contained insights that were relevant to further research on prevention. Consequently, the conclusion of this book provide several recommendations for stakeholders to implement efficient policies at different levels for countering radicalization and violent extremism.

Ethical considerations in terms of obtaining consent and/or assent from participants (or their parents/guardians) and data collection were respected for all the case studies. To collect comparable research results from the 24 case studies, all the research teams used the same questionnaire, which they were, nonetheless, able to adapt to their contexts. The questionnaire contained nine sections of questions covering indicators of the social drivers and contexts tested by CONNEKT.

This questionnaire was formulated based on the results of the previous project phase (macro level) and designed from the broadest societal field (local community) to the narrowest (family), ending with a question directly about VE. As this stage of the CONNEKT project is centered on the identification of meso-level drivers, the research focused on the meso-level institutions (family, school, local associations, local branches of political parties, local mosques, local social groups, etc.) with which individuals (young people) interact and their perceptions of these interactions, as well as their thoughts and perception on the drivers of radicalization and VE in their context.

5.3 Social Contexts

Following the results of the macro-level research (Kapidžić et al., 2021), the meso-level data collection focused on variable and different contexts of social interaction such as:

Socialization/education: Educational contexts in society, both formal and informal, are mechanisms of transmission of ideas, values and identities.

Employment and labor relations: Unemployment as a factor that limits access to a decent level of social welfare.

Urban and peri-urban spaces: Urban areas where social interactions take place in a dimension of daily relationships.

Cultural and leisure activities: Artistic and cultural expressions as mechanisms of intervention and reflection on social realities. Leisure activities of a diverse nature (cultural, educational, sports, artistic, etc.) are specific contexts of social interaction for young people.

Punitive justice system: Institutions, mechanisms, and practices that apply punitive measures on individuals who have committed crimes.

Ethnic community: The activation of ethnic belonging implies sharing a certain identity, which can transcend national borders.

Political and social participation: The dimensions in which a society articulates the participation of its citizens, whose deficit calls into question the democratic quality of that society.

The cases selected in the eight countries were expected to help observe the interaction of several social factors in each of these contexts, which they have done to variable degrees. Comparative analysis showed that these social contexts appear to be more significant in activating/deactivating the drivers of radicalization. Moreover, the drivers being tested have accumulated effects that prevent us from considering any mechanical causality between one factor and the occurrence of VE.

5.4 Explanatory Statement on Methodological Limitations

We would like to highlight that data collection in the MENA region was an arduous task as the process was fraught with difficulties due to the variable limitations in access to communities. Below is the list of such limitations reported by the local partners:

- Target group members belonging to a religious group did not want to take part in the discussions and consultations (Morocco).
- Access to target group (prisoners) was denied by central authorities after initial acceptance (Jordan).
- Target group members were overcautious because of harsh security measures in the target community (Tunisia).
- Case study selection did not go through the participatory consultative process followed in choosing all the other case studies and hence did not benefit from the input of experts (Egypt).

It is also worth noting that the human rights/freedoms situation in the four countries is variable, allowing for different degrees of intellectual freedom and freedom of expression. The selection of case studies as well as the degree of local and official engagement have been subject to significant limitations in the three other countries, such as being denied access to the target group (prisoners in Jordan), difficulties getting clearance or permission to do fieldwork (Jordan and Egypt), and difficulties to communicate with some target groups (Morocco).

6 Structure of the Book

After this introduction, the following four chapters will present the different case studies researched in each Middle Eastern and North African country under the scope of CONNEKT. Starting in Tunisia, the three contexts under analysis share high rates of underemployment, poor access to social services and high levels of perception of reltive deprivation and inequality, as well as low levels of political participation. In the three locations—Hammam Lif, Feriana, and Sidi Abdelhamid— structural territorial inequalities intersect with socioeconomic and political grievances, as well as persistent underdevelopment. This is what the Tunisian authors denominate the "Triangle of Anger". The commonalities and specificities of each context provide useful insights into the potential avenues for prevention and enhancing community resilience to radicalization and violent extremism.

Jordan's research focuses on economic deprivation as the most prominent driver, present in the three cases under study: unemployed and vulnerable youth in Karak, refugees in Northern Jordan, and female preachers in Ma'an. While all of them experience economic deprivation, the prominent tribal context of Karak offers a stronger platform against the spread of violent extremism. In the case of refugee camps, the family plays the primary role, while showing the relevance of access to education, culture, and leisure opportunities and the increasing dependence on online socialization due to limitations in mobility and access to leisure and physical socialization spaces. The case of female preachers in Ma'an is particularly revealing as it contributed to the understanding of both gendered dynamics within the community as well as the role of religion as a potential driver or prevention factor of radicalization and VE.

In Egypt, the research team focuses on two communities, Al-Warraq and Bahtim, as well as in a completely different context, the community of students at Alexandria University. In the case of students at Alexandria University, even though they are more politically aware than their peers in more deprived areas, they offer a fragmented knowledge of their recent political events while focusing much more on socioeconomic problems as their political interest. Both in Al-Warraq and Bahtim the importance of community institutions such as the Coptic church or the former charitable associations—currently outlawed due to their links with the Muslim Brotherhood—play an important role in replacing the gaps left by the state public services in deprived communities. The absence of such institutions in certain areas creates a vacuum, fostering vulnerability to radicalization.

Finally, in Morocco, research with the members of *Amal*, a well-known organization for its activism in the fight against violence, especially against women, and its promotion of human rights, will present insights regarding how they promote the transformation of violence into new discourses of tolerance and acceptance. The second case study will focus on the Ultras "Siempre Paloma" football supporters in the Tanger region. This case is crucial to identify how sports is transformed into a channel to claim rights as well as a potential ground for violence, and at the same time, it allows for a comparative approach as the football hooligans' environment is also explored in several Balkan chapters. The third case study in Morocco is centered on *Adl wal Ihsane*, an Islamist movement that does not recognize the political and religious legitimacy of the Monarch and is located within the realm of political Islam.

Then, the following four chapters move to the Balkan region where, despite the stark differences with the MENA region, many of the same drivers are present and intersect in similar ways across countries and regions. While religion is, as in MENA, seen as a prominent driver from the macro/state perspective, in both regions the community perspectives turn out to be much more nuanced. However, the Balkan case studies will reveal a more relevant role and complex intersections with identity beyond religion, such as ethnic and national belonging. The case of "two schools under one roof" in Bosnia and Herzegovina shows how the education system encourages exclusive worldviews, insisting on artificial divisions that can become fertile ground for the development of extreme behaviors. As in Morocco, a second case study focuses on organized football fan groups, where animosity towards the political system and institutions is pointed out as a driver of radicalization. The online context will be highlighted in the case of the online Salafi influencers in BiH, comparable with the research of online groups carried out, for example, in Bulgaria, showing the intersection between transnational dynamics with local political grievances. While territorial inequalities are not seen as a driving force, the sentiment of injustice linked to deep ethnic divisions increases the perceptions of inequality.

In Bulgaria, research focuses on ultraconservative communities online and on football supporters groups. Being the rise of far-right extremis a concern in Bulgaria, the first case study focuses on the intersections between far-right narratives and actions within online communities, focused on the protection of traditional family values and opposition to COVID-19 restrictions. The research on football supporters in Bulgaria is conducted within online and offline communities and the results show more radical expressions online than offline, revealing the impact of digital socialization as a driver of radicalization.

Football fans are also targeted in North Macedonia, both in Tetovo and Skopje identifying youth non-engagement as the factor preventing them from personal and professional growth, which combined with the political context excludes them from active participation in decision-making processes. On the other hand, the political driver is also very present in the other case study, the Commemorations of the 2001 Macedonian conflict in Tetovo, that witness how commemorative events are used as platforms for promoting exclusivist and ethnocentric agendas which, in turn, mobilize individuals and, eventually, can fire up interethnic tensions. The chapter highlights how the memory of cultures and practices related to the 2001 North Macedonian conflict influence public discourse and interethnic relations, identified as dominant drivers of radicalization and violent extremism. The third case deals with correctional-educational facilities for juveniles in Volkovija, near Totovo, and highlights the strong role played by education and the urgent need for resocialization, rehabilitation, and reintegration programs.

The last set of case studies comes from Kosovo, where three municipalities are researched: Mitrovica South, Gjilan and Gjakova. Having carried out important efforts in countering radicalization and violent extremism, state government and security actors view religion as the most prominent factor for radicalization, in strong connection with digital socialization and transnational dynamics. Despite the complex national, ethnic, and religious divides existing in the country, radicalization does not root in local interreligious conflicts but stems from the import of extremist Islamist currents elsewhere. On the contrary, research results show how education and employment ensuring social mobility are crucial to building social resilience.

Finally, the conclusion reviews the results of all case studies carried out in the eight countries and analyses them to identify the complex interplay among drivers, across countries, regions and a variety of community contexts. Thus, common cross-regional patterns such as online socialization replacing traditional educational and leisure spaces for youth are evident across countries. The same dynamics of opposition to state institutions and security actors coincide across football fans' clubs, which become spaces for youth participation in the absence of traditional ones. The complex interplay between religion, political grievances, and governance models is discussed thoroughly. All case studies feature crucial elements linked to youth alienation and underrepresentation, as well as to the impact of external actors and digital communities. The chapter concludes with a detailed list of recommendations addressed to different institutional actors at the local, national, and international levels.

References

Amnesty International. (2016). *Bulgaria: Proposed counter-terrorism bill would be a serious step back for human rights*. Retrieved September 2024, from https://www.amnesty.nl/actueel/bulgaria-proposed-counter-terrorism-bill-wouldbe-a-serious-step-back-for-human-rights

Bakker, E. (2015). *Terrorism and counterterrorism studies: Comparing theory and practice*. Leiden University Press.

Balzacq, T. (2011). *Securitization theory: How security problems emerge and dissolve*. Routledge.

Becirevic, E., Halilovic, M., & Azinovic, V. (2017). *Literature review. Radicalisation and violent extremism in the Western Balkans*. Extremism Research Forum. Foreign and Commonwealth Office British Council. Retrieved September 2024, from https://www.britishcouncil.al/sites/default/files/erf_literature_review_2017_radicalisation_and_violent_extremism.pdf

Bieber, F. (2003). Approaches to political violence and terrorism in former Yugoslavia. *Journal of Southern Europe and the Balkans, 5*(1), 39–51.

Booth, K. (2007). *Theory of world security*. Cambridge University Press.

Bourbeau, P. (2015). *Security: Dialogue across disciplines*. Cambridge University Press.

Bubandt, N. (2005). *The vernacular turn in security studies: Norms, ethics and society*. Routledge.

Buzan, B. (1983). *People, states and fear: The national security problem in international relations*. University of North Carolina Press.

Buzan, B., & Waever, O. (2003). *Regions and powers: The structure of international security*. Cambridge University Press.

Chirchi, T., & Jrad, E. (2021). *CONNEKT regional report: Perspectives on radicalisation and violent extremism*. The European Institute of the Mediterranean (IEMED). Retrieved September 2024, from https://h2020connekt.eu/publications/radicalisation-and-violent-extremism-in-the-mena

Ciută, F. (2009). Security and the problem of context: A configurational analysis of security studies. *Security Dialogue, 40*(6), 591–614.

Ciută, F. (2016). *The contextual turn in security studies*. Routledge.

de Almagro, M., & Krause, J. (2021). *Vernacular security: Statecraft, security, and subjectivity in Africa*. Oxford University Press.

Demolli, H. (2008). Terrorism in Kosovo and measures against it. In I. Prezelj (Ed.), *The fight against terrorism and crisis management in the Western Balkans* (pp. 114–131). IOS Press Ebooks. Retrieved March 2020, from http://ebooks.iospress.nl/volume/the-fight-against-terrorism-and-crisis-management-in-the-western-balkans

Feve, S., & Dews, D. (2019). *National strategies to prevent and counter violent extremism: An independent review*. Global Center on Cooperative Security. https://doi.org/10.2307/resrep20256

Floridi, L. (2014). *The fourth revolution: How the infosphere is reshaping human reality*. Oxford University Press.

Floyd, R. (2010). *Security and the environment: Securitisation theory and US environmental security policy*. Cambridge University Press.

Fukuyama, F. (1992). *The end of history and the last man*. Free Press.

Gaddis, J. L. (2005). *The cold war: A new history*. Penguin Books.

Ganor, B. (2002). Defining terrorism: Is one man's terrorist another man's freedom fighter? *The International Policy Institute for Counter-Terrorism, Police Practice and Research, 3*(4), 287–304.

Hansen, L. (2006). *Security as practice: Discourse analysis and the Bosnian war*. Routledge.

Held, D., & McGrew, A. (2002). *Globalization/anti-globalization: Beyond the great divide*. Polity Press.

Huysmans, J. (2006). *The politics of insecurity: Fear, migration and asylum in the EU*. Routledge.

Jackson, R., Breen-Smyth, M., & Gunning, J. (2015). *Critical studies on terrorism: A new research agenda*. Routledge.

Jarvis, L. (2019). *Security studies: A reader*. Routledge.

Kaldor, M. (1999). *New and old wars: Organized violence in a global era*. Polity Press.

Kapidžić, D., Hirkić, M., Dudić, A., Turčalo, S., Bašić, S., & Bakić, S. (2021). *Drivers of radicalization and violent extremism in the light of state dynamics in MENA and the Balkans - Bosnia and Herzegovina*. The European Institute of the Mediterranean (IEMed). Retrieved February 2022, from https://h2020connekt.eu/wp-content/uploads/2021/09/Bosnia_Herzegovina_CONNEKT_Macro_Drivers.pdf

Mearsheimer, J. J. (2001). *The tragedy of great power politics*. Norton & Company.

Mouna, K., & Erryfai, A. (2021). *CONNEKT regional report on macro approaches to the study of radicalisation and violent extremism: A view from the MENA region*. European Institute of the Mediterranean. Retrieved February 2022, from https://h2020connekt.eu/publications/mena_macro_approaches_to_the_study_of_radicalisatio_and_violent_extremism/

Neumann, P., & Kleinmann, S. (2013). How rigorous is radicalization research? *Democracy and Security, 9*(4), 360–382.

Nye, J., & Goldsmith, J. (2011). The future of power. *Bulletin of the American Academy of Arts and Sciences, 64*(3), 45–52.

Sadriu, B. (2019). Rebranding the war on terror and remaking Muslim subjectivities. *East European Politics, 35*(4), 433–456.

Sageman, M. (2014). The stagnation in terrorism research. *Terrorism and Political Violence, 26*(4), 565–580.

Schafer, M., Martin, M., & Chandler, D. (2019). *The vernacular security turn: Security and everyday life*. Routledge.

Schmid, A. (2004). Terrorism - The definitional problem. *Case Western Reserve Journal of International Law, 36*, 375. Retrieved March 2020, from https://scholarlycommons.law.case.edu/jil/vol36/iss2/8

Sen, A. (1999). *Development as freedom*. Oxford University Press.

Singer, P. W. (2014). *Cybersecurity and cyberwar: What everyone needs to know*. Oxford University Press.

Stern, J. (2003). *Terror in the name of god: Why religious militants kill*. HarperCollins.

Tamburini, F. (2018). Anti-terrorism laws in the Maghreb countries: The mirror of a democratic transition that never was. *Journal of Asian and African Studies, 53*(8), 1235–1250.

Torrekens, C., & De le Vingne, D. (2020). *Concepts and analytical framework. Debating notions and approaches to radicalisation and violent extremism*. European Institute of the Mediterranean. Retrieved February 2022, from https://south.euneighbours.eu/publication/connekt-papers-concepts-and-analytical-framework-debating-notions/

Ul Haq, M. (1995). *Reflections on human development*. Oxford University Press.

Vallet, E. (2014). Borders, fences and walls: State of insecurity? *Journal of Borderlands Studies, 29*(2), 201–218.

Vallet, E. (2015). Border walls and their impact on legal and illegal migration. *Revue Européenne des Migrations Internationales, 31*(2), 15–31.

Van de Voorde, T. (2011). 'Terrorism studies': A critical appraisal. In R. Coolsaet (Ed.), *Jihadi terrorism and the radicalisation challenge: European and American experiences*. Ashgate.

Vergani, M., Iqbal, M., Ilbahar, E., & Barton, G. (2018). The three Ps of radicalization: Push, pull and personal. A systematic scoping review of the scientific evidence about radicalization into violent extremism. *Studies in Conflict & Terrorism, 43*, 854. https://doi.org/10.1080/1057610X.2018.1505686

Vidal Bertran, L. (2020). *Mapping the drivers of radicalization and violent extremism in MENA and the Balkans*. IEMED Publications. Retrieved October 2020 from, https://h2020connekt.eu/publications/mapping-thedrivers-of-radicalization-and-violent-extremism-in-mena-and-the-balkans/

Walt, S. M. (1987). *The origins of alliances*. Cornell University Press.

Waltz, K. N. (1978). *Theory of international politics*. Addison-Wesley.

Meso-Level Approach to the Social Contexts of Radicalization and Violent Extremism in Tunisia

Tasnim Chirchi, Khaoula Ghribi, and Ramzi Aloui

1 Introduction

Previous institutional macro-level research has shown that while Tunisia has improved its counterterrorist technical and operational capacities, between 2011 and 2021, thus achieving important successes in facing terrorist security threats, institutional impediments remained noteworthy (Chirchi et al., 2021). The existing approaches focusing mostly on enhancing technical capacities and hard security measures do not provide sustainable solutions to radicalization and VE. Moreover, little attention has been given to the role of local dynamics in either strengthening the drivers of radicalization or weakening them (Chirchi et al., 2021). For example, the Tunisian Center for Research and Studies on Terrorism (TFESR, 2016) shares in "Terrorism in Tunisia: An Analysis of Judicial Cases" the result of the analysis of 1000 judicial cases of individuals tried for terrorist offenses between 2013 and 2016. The study notes that 40% of those brought before an examining magistrate during the same period have a university degree, 36.33% have secondary education, 13% have vocational training, and 4% have a baccalaureate (TFESR, 2016). However, the study focuses on individual characteristics without considering the individuals' social environment or geographical origin, limiting its analysis to the micro-level. Meddeb (2016) calls for a differentiated and situated approach that helps avoid the homogenization of youth in Tunisia as a social group. Focusing on youth necessitates that we go beyond both the discourse of euphoria and that of disenchantment, which are characteristic of the increased focus on youth since

T. Chirchi (✉)
Ibn Khaldun University, Istanbul, Turkey
e-mail: director@jasminefoundation.org

K. Ghribi · R. Aloui
Independent Researcher, Tunis, Tunisia

C. Torrekens et al. (eds.), *Social Contexts of Radicalization and Violent Extremism in the MENA and Balkans*,
https://doi.org/10.1007/978-3-031-84521-5_2

2011. He emphasizes the importance of focusing on case studies to understand the specific characteristics of youth as a social group across Tunisia as well as to capture the diversity of this social group and its many facets. In the same vein, Sterman and Rosenblatt (2018) urge that for efficient prevention efforts, a situated and context-sensitive analysis of radicalization and VE in the MENA region is needed. They highlight that "grand theories" and models of explanation on radicalization fail to account for crucial local distinctions.

To fill these gaps in the current literature, our research team in Tunisia has engaged in a multilevel analysis at the macro, meso and micro levels of the relevant social realities in relation to radicalization and VE in the country over a period of 4 years. This paper will focus on sharing the meso-level research findings and analysis of three case studies. The cumulative methodology of the research necessitates that we first take stock of the findings on the macro level, then our paper will describe the three case studies and summarize the findings from the meso level, while highlighting the interactions between social contexts and drivers of radicalization as well as potential prevention avenues.

2 The Contexts of Radicalization and Violent Extremism in Tunisia

Violent extremism and radicalization in Tunisia have been notable issues since 2002 with reports of citizens joining ISIS and other VE groups both within and outside the country (Wolf, 2013). In 2012, it was estimated that around 500 Tunisians had received military training within Salafi Jihadist groups (CSIS, 2016), although no recent official numbers are available. The prominent violent extremist group, *Ansar al-Sharia*, had between 10,000 and 20,000 Tunisian members in 2012 (CSIS, 2016) However, not all members were involved in violent activities, with many supporting the organization's cause for social, economic, and psychological reasons.

In the past decade, between 6000 and 7000 Tunisians were reported to have joined ISIS and Al-Qaeda in Iraq, Syria, and Libya (The Soufan Group, 2020; UNHR, 2015), although Tunisian authorities dispute these figures, claiming the actual number was between 2800 and 3000, with around 12,000 prevented from joining ISIS (Marsad Tunisie, 2015).[1]

Before 2011, the "scientific Salafist" (*Salafiyya 'Ilmiyya*) movement had been classified as an extremist group, but remained doctrinal and devotional, advocating for leaving political affairs to "the ruler" (Braham, 2014; Zoghlami & Toumi, 2019). The post-revolution period saw, however, the emergence of the "jihadi salafist"

[1] The Washington Institute for Near East Policy estimated that 27,000 Tunisians were prevented from joining violent extremist groups in Libya and Syria, with 1000 to 1500 believed to have joined VE organizations in Libya (Zelin, 2018).

(*Salafiyya Jihadiyya*) movement, particularly after a general amnesty in 2011 (Petré, 2015). *Ansar al-Sharia*, established in April 2011, gained popularity in popular neighborhoods especially among young people, offering a puritanical discourse and a lifestyle based on an idealized Islamic caliphate (Cavatorta, 2015; Petré, 2015).

Ansar al-Sharia was classified as a terrorist organization in 2013 following its involvement in political assassinations and other terrorist incidents. Many of its leaders then went to fight outside the country, especially in Libya, Syria, and Iraq. The *Uqba Bin Nafi* Brigade became the main domestic terrorist organization, focusing on attacking Tunisian security and military personnel (Cavatorta, 2015; Petré, 2015). Tunisia also witnessed a rise in the activities of local terrorist groups and ISIS members in Jabal Chambi on the Tunisian-Algerian border and the Tunisian-Libyan border, often overlapping with criminal and smuggling networks (Ayari, 2017; Boukhars, 2017). Most violent extremist groups claim affiliation with wider, supranational groups like ISIS and Al-Qaeda (Cavatorta, 2015; Petré, 2015). Neo-institutional macro-level analysis of radicalization and VE in Tunisia showed that violent extremism in Tunisia is a multifaceted issue lacking a universal definition (Chirchi et al., 2021). Tunisia's official approach to combating radicalization is focused on enhancing technical capacities while heavily relying on hard security without clear, unified definitions in policy documents, leading to confusion and inconsistency in addressing extremism. This absence of precise definitions hinders the development of effective strategies and highlights the need for collaboration among national actors, both governmental and non-governmental, to establish a coherent understanding of violent extremism. Moreover, terms like radicalization and extremism are often politically instrumentalized, like in the rest of the region, to discredit political opposition,[2] thus diminishing their value and legitimacy (Anzil et al., 2022; Chirchi & Ghribi, 2023).

Institutional barriers impede efforts to address radicalization and violent extremism in Tunisia like in the rest of the MENA region. Political instability further complicates the development of coherent P/CVE strategies (Mouna & Er-Rifayi, 2021), and limited resources impact the consistency and sustainability of these efforts (Anzil et al., 2022; Mouna & Er-Rifaiy, 2021). The prevention and countering of violent extremism (P/CVE) in Tunisia, like the rest of the region, are indeed significantly influenced by state security bodies, which often operate in hierarchical structures with limited communication, hindering a unified approach to VE (Bieber & Pollozhani, 2021; Mouna & Er-Rifaiy, 2021). Collaboration between state agencies

[2] The Bureau of Counterterrorism at the American State Department in its 2022 report mentions that "Tunisia continued to professionalize its security apparatus in partnership with the United States. Its commitment to joint Ministries of Interior (MOI) and Defense (MOD) CT operations steadily degraded Violent Extremist Organization capacity within the country. However, the Government of Tunisia misused terrorism-related charges to arrest and prosecute individuals for expression and peaceful activism." (Country Reports on Terrorism 2022: Tunisia, available at: https://www.state.gov/reports/country-reports-on-terrorism-2022/tunisia), This is confirmed by several human rights organizations such Human Rights Watch and Amnesty International.

and civil society organizations (CSOs) in PVE is poor, with minimal CSO involvement, and limited information sharing among state agencies, which hampers CSOs' ability to evaluate P/CVE strategies (Anzil et al., 2022; Chirchi & Ghribi 2023).

Furthermore, the ineffectiveness of central governments in addressing local challenges contributes to regional disparities and indirectly fuels radicalization, while cooperation between central and local authorities and communities on P/CVE approaches is lacking, deepening perceptions of marginalization within local communities.

These contexts have an impact on citizens' participation which is weakened by the absence or lack of channels for communication and engagement, leading to apathy and a lack of hope in affecting institutional reform (Chirchi et al., 2021; Chirchi & Ghribi 2023).

Macro-level research also identified failures in the governance and developmental model, particularly concerning regional and class disparities, as well as political grievances resulting from the exclusion of individuals, groups, and regions, as key drivers of VE in Tunisia. The findings at this level also noted limitations in the institutions' ability to combat these drivers, citing slow progress in adopting innovative approaches during the country's democratic transition due to several factors such as the duplication of programs, the lack of coordination between state agencies and a notable resistance to change in some institutional practices (Chirchi et al., 2021).

These findings also pointed to central structural factors in understanding the social contexts of radicalization and VE in Tunisia from a macro-level perspective. The authors of the report emphasize a triangular relationship between regional disparities, economic and political grievances, and the implementation of an unequal developmental model as playing a significant role in fueling frustration and anger within youth and local communities. This "triangle of anger" lies at the heart of persistent social and economic challenges, with youth social, economic, and political grievances often unaddressed over the past decades, highlighting the need for comprehensive and sustainable solutions (Chirchi et al., 2021).

The current chapter will examine the consequences of this structural correlation between the drivers of radicalization and VE and social contexts from a meso-level perspective, investigating in a more detailed way the perceptions of youth and local community dynamics to build a nuanced understanding of the drivers of radicalization in their interaction with local social contexts.

3 Case-Studies and Methodologies

In Tunisia, our research team selected three case studies based on macro-level research findings which have highlighted territorial inequalities as a central issue, forming what researchers describe as a triangle of asymmetric development/governance, economic and political grievances, and regional disparities. This triangle is identified as a significant combination of drivers for both criminal violence and violent extremism (VE). The geographical distribution of developmental indicators mirrors that of VE networks and hotspots, with areas lacking in development, employment opportunities, and infrastructure, and experiencing higher rates of crime, street violence, and school dropouts. These findings suggest that internal regions in Tunisia face deep-rooted economic challenges and limited opportunities, contributing to a heightened vulnerability to radicalization, particularly in marginalized communities within these regions (Chirchi et al., 2021).

These dynamics can be observed in the case study of Feriana, a sub-governorate with a high poverty rate and youth unemployment rate, located along the Algerian border. Such geographical location is also a relevant context to analyze the impact of transnational dynamics as a driver. Deep territorial inequalities and political, social and economic grievances are also present.

Such deep social and economic grievances as well as other vulnerability factors are not however only found in the internal regions in Tunisia. The governance and development model adopted in the country (Chirchi et al., 2021) has created vulnerabilities that can also be found in urban and peri-urban contexts close to the capital Tunis, or to the second most important urban center in Tunis, the city of Sousse.

Fieldwork has been conducted in Hammam Lif as the second case study. This northern suburb faces economic and social marginalization and prominent levels of crime and delinquency among its youth. It has been a hotspot for violent extremist networks, with several arrests of individuals linked to terrorist groups. Interviews and workshops identified in Hammam Lif several vulnerability factors to VE narratives.

Sidi Abdelhamid, a delegation in the Sousse governorate of Tunisia, was selected as a third case study due to its deep socio-economic polarization. Despite being part of the prosperous city of Sousse, Sidi Abdelhamid experiences urban and peri-urban dynamics of informality and marginalization, like those found in the capital, Tunis. This polarization creates conditions favoring vulnerability to radicalization, despite the area's proximity to economic opportunities.

The following section provides a more detailed description of the relevant social contexts in these three case studies.

3.1 Feriana

Our research on the drivers of violent extremism at the macro-level demonstrated the impacts of the collective social and economic grievances and strong feelings of exclusion and marginalization by the state experienced in some regions suffering from a lack of opportunities and a serious absence of basic economic and social rights (employment, good public services, infrastructure, etc.). Data collection revealed Kasserine, a governorate in the center-west of Tunisia, as one of the most affected regions by the drivers and dynamics of radicalization and VE.

Feriana, which is a delegation in the Southwest of the governorate of Kasserine, one of the largest governorates in the center-west region of Tunisia, features several of the vulnerability factors and drivers of radicalization identified in previous macro-level research in Tunisia.

In 2020, the poverty rate in Kasserine was 33.6%, more than twice the national rate (15.2%). The unemployment rate in 2020 was 22.1%, which is substantial compared not only to the national rate (17.4%) but also to the regional rate in the center-west (17.5%). In addition, the illiteracy rate in Kasserine is high, reaching 32.6% in 2018, while the national average was only 19.15% (ORD, 2020). Feriana is one of the most populated sub-governorates in Kasserine (the third in terms of population after Kasserine North and Sbeitla) with 55,137 inhabitants (Institut National de Statistiques, 2020).

The youth (15–29 years) unemployment rate in Feriana is extremely high: 60.79% (ORD, 2020). Other socioeconomic indicators show that youth have limited access to education and social and cultural activities. Data from 2017 show a high secondary school dropout rate at 181 out of 1955 youth (almost 10%) and low baccalaureate success rate (34.3%), in comparison with the national average (50.28%). The household connection to the internet is extremely low, at 8.58%, compared with the governorate rate of about 30%. There is also a lack of spaces for youth to express themselves or explore their talents, with only one youth center for the entire community. Moreover, access remains a challenge, as 37.12% of youth live more than 2 km away (ORD, 2020).

Feriana's proximity to the mountainous border area with Algeria constitutes an additional vulnerability factor, given the presence of violent extremist organizations (VEOs) and VEO activity linked to smuggling (Boukhars, 2017; Meddeb, 2016). Located around 20 km from Bouchebka, a commercial border crossing, Feriana is an important passage for the informal economic activities of smuggling of cigarettes, alcohol, and other illicit goods.

Not only militant groups, but also Tunisian and Algerian paramilitary groups have taken refuge in this border area. These groups are closely linked by their networks of fighters and the smuggling economy (Meddeb, 2016). In terms of violent extremist organizations' presence, since 2012, *Katibat Uqba Bin Nafi* (KUBN) has been based in and around the Jabal Chambi and Jabal Samamma mountainous border zones in the Kasserine governorate. By 2014, the group had begun to fracture and became scattered between various mountain locations in Kasserine and Kef. For the past 7 years, groups including KUBN and *Jund al-Khilafah-Tunisia* have been engaged in a protracted insurgency against the Tunisian army, in which 127 militants and 118 Tunisian security personnel have been killed (Herbert, 2018).

Qualitative field research in Feriana was conducted by the research team in Tunisia over a period of 5 months (from November 2021 to March 2022) through data collection activities including three in-depth interviews with youth from the region, two interviews with local stakeholders, and three focus groups. The sample for the research activities in Feriana included 35 young people aged from 16 to 30 years old (26 males and 9 females), in addition to three young local leaders with a close and influential relationship with adolescents and young adults. The participants in the activities have varied profiles, including school dropouts, university students, university degree holders, vocational training certificate holders, unemployed youth, workers in the informal economy, etc.

3.2 Hammam Lif

Hammam Lif is a coastal city in the southern suburbs of Greater Tunis, located between sea and mountains, 16 km south of the capital. Hammam Lif is administratively attached to the governorate of Ben Arous and constituted a municipality of 44,018 inhabitants in 2020 (General Commission for Regional Development, 2020).

Despite its location and proximity to the capital Tunis, Hammam Lif suffers from multi-level economic, social and political marginalization, especially in the poorer neighborhoods. Socioeconomic gaps are clearly noticeable when compared with other nearby well-to-do areas. Despite the low rates of the governorate in terms of unemployment compared to the national level (General Commission for Regional Development, 2020), the area of Hammam Lif al-Chaabia has one of the highest rates of unemployment in Tunisia. Many families live under the poverty line. Demographically, those between the age range of 20 and 29 constitute 14.98% of the overall population of the region (Institut National de Statistiques, 2016). Youth—especially university graduates—struggle with high rates of unemployment and lack training opportunities to develop their employability skills. The popular neighborhoods of Hammam Lif, such as Al-Chaabia, are stigmatized areas with high criminality rates, mid-level activity of violent extremist groups, and high youth unemployment. Hammam Lif's local community overall also struggles with other challenges, including declining family and social ties and issues related to internal domestic migration to the community.[3]

It is worth noting that Hammam Lif is one of the neighborhoods where VE networks have erupted in Tunisia since before 2011. In 2006, Tunisian security forces arrested several young people accused of having joined terrorist groups involved in the attacks in Slimene (Cavatorta, 2015; ISS, 2008; Wolf, 2013), and the majority of

[3] Over two decades (1994–2004 and 2004–2014), three million Tunisians changed their place of residence within the country (Institut National de Statistiques, 2014). More than two thirds of this mobility took place within the same governorate, while for the remaining third, i.e. approximately one million people, this mobility led to a change of governorate. These migratory movements have mainly benefited the coastal regions which are now home to 68.4% of the total population, three-quarters of the urban population and 80% of industrial employment and hotel units. Inland regions (West and South) are the main points of departure for internal migrants to attractive regions of the East and North-East coast. Since the mid-1960s, and with rare exceptions, all interior and southern areas have been continuously shrinking in terms of population, and still are, while all the coastal regions have been, and still are, growing. Given that 80–90% of internal migratory flows have cities as their destination (Institut National de Statistiques, 2014), the consequences and impacts of these flows manifest through spontaneous or informal housing, inadequate infrastructure, and marginalisation and exclusion of the most vulnerable urban social groups: the working poor, the unemployed, women, disabled people, single parent families, and others (Boubakri, 2020).

those accused came from Hammam Lif. The same neighborhood was also home to Abu Yadh, the leader of the group *Ansar al-Sharia* in Tunisia (Cavatorta, 2015; Wolf, 2013).

In the Hammam Lif case study, the main target population included youth from 12–30 from the poor neighborhoods of the area, children or/and young people at risk of delinquency and drug addiction, as well as young members of the football Ultras of Hammam Lif. Qualitative field research consisted of two focus groups (13 participants, 5 from 13–17, 8 from 19–30, 4 females and 9 males), five in-depth individual interviews with three local youth (12–30 years old, 2 males and 1 female) and two local stakeholders working with youth.

3.3 Sidi Abdelhamid

Sidi Abdelhamid is another place with popular neighborhoods close to urban centers in Tunisia where social and urban marginalization prevails vulnerability to VE drivers has also been recorded. This peripheral area of the urban agglomeration of Sousse, the third most important urban center in Tunisia, is interesting for research on the topic of radicalization and VE because it presents a significant paradox: although it is situated in a governorate that is a highly privileged coastal city, Sousse (having been the home region of the former President Ben Ali), Sidi Abdelhamid has produced a significant number of Tunisian foreign fighters (ICG, 2017). Focusing on this case study can help explain this paradox and understand the local context and dynamics facilitating vulnerability to radical beliefs of violent extremism in this region.

Sousse is a coastal city in Tunisia located 140 km south of the capital Tunis and is home to 271,428 inhabitants (2014) and is the third most important city in Tunisia (after Tunis and Sfax).[4] The governorate of Sousse has a rich cultural heritage and natural resources. Its economic fabric is characterized by its diversity and dependence on the services sector, which attracts 53.7% of active workers, most of whom are in tourism, which provides 21% of the national accommodation capacity (General Commission for Regional Development, 2020). It also has an active industrial sector, particularly in textiles, clothing, and mechanical and electrical industries.

The major public projects implemented in the areas of transportation infrastructure, industrial zones, the technological pole of mechanics, electricity, electronics, media, and university institutions attract internal migration from different regions of Tunisia to this governorate. The city thus has undergone several waves of expansion since independence. Due to this expansion, Sousse today covers 11 delegations.

Sousse has also 8 industrial zones covering 226 hectares of its territory. Sidi Abdelhamid covers two of those zones (the two biggest ones covering respectively

[4] It is the most important Sahel region metropolis, with 1,634,611 inhabitants (Institut National de Statistiques, 2014). 43.7% of the 547,403 (Institut National de Statistiques, 2014) inhabitants of the governorate of Sousse live in urban areas. See also Boubakri (2020).

49 and 48 hectares) (General Commission for Regional Development, 2020). It has a population of 55,553 inhabitants (Institut national de Statistiques, 2020). Young people aged between 20 and 29 years represent 19.04% of its population. Over 52% of youth in general, and 18% of undergraduate youth, are unemployed (Institut national de Statistiques, 2020).

Early school dropout is a key area of concern for youth since Sidi Abdelhamid has a high school dropouts' rate according to official figures (GCRD, 2020). Previous studies (Lamloum, 2016; Meddeb, 2016; Zoghlami & Toumi, 2019) indicate that particularly vulnerable groups, including the VE threat, are school dropouts, marginalized youth, and individuals who are not in a stable family environment. For the governorate of Sousse, there is a direct proportionality between the poverty rate and school dropout. The poorest delegations are characterized by the highest dropout rates (Institut National de Statistiques and World Bank, 2020). For Sidi Abdelhamid the poverty rate is 17.7%, higher than the governorate rate (14.3%) and the national rate (152%) (Institut National de Statistiques and World Bank, 2020).

The local community also faces deteriorating infrastructure and a lack of recreational, sports, cultural, and civic activities. Some of these issues were further exacerbated due to the impact of COVID-19, as many people lost their livelihood, and the period of confinement added considerable stress that has contributed to a rise in domestic violence.

Grievances tied to unemployment and deteriorating economic conditions are key sources of vulnerability in Sidi Abdelhamid, which are especially problematic when combined with an intense sense of marginalization and relative deprivation compared with other more well-off areas in the governorate. According to the report "All Jihad is Local", the governorate of Sousse produced 7% of Tunisian foreign fighters (Sterman & Rosenblatt, 2018) but 89% of foreign fighters originating from Sousse came from peripheral urban communities, such as Sidi Abdelhamid. There are some concerns that since the fall of ISIS, these foreign fighters could return and pose a renewed threat (ICG, 2017). The June 2015 Sousse attack is the major terrorist incident to take place in the governorate and claimed the lives of 38 tourists.

Field research consisted of qualitative research activities implemented between May 2021 and May 2022. This involved two focus groups (11 participants, 2 from 16 to 18 and 9 from 19 to 30; 5 females and 6 males) and five in-depth interviews (2 females and 3 males). In addition to these activities, the research team relied on data collected through field observations, informal interviews with several local inhabitants, as well as unstructured interviews with young activists from the region.[5] These activities involved youth who dropped out of school, unemployed university graduates, and youth and teenagers active in local civil society.

[5]All quotes from the focus groups and interviews were originally in the Arabic-Tunisian dialect and were translated to English by the research team.

4 Results

The various research outcomes in Tunisia validate the project's initial hypothesis on radicalization factors as they highlight the complex interplay between macro-level (large-scale), meso-level (intermediate), and individual factors (micro level). These findings emphasize the multidimensional nature of radicalization drivers, highlighting the necessity of moving beyond simplistic interpretations and embracing a nuanced understanding of these drivers. Data analysis results confirm the significance of contextual elements in comprehending the dynamics of radicalization and violence, contrasting with the classical mono-dimensional and non-contextualized explanations.

The contexts of the emergence of radicalization and VE in Tunisia are studied in relation to seven pre-identified drivers: economic deprivation, territorial inequalities, political issues, education, culture and leisure opportunities, religion, digital socialization, and transnational dynamics. This chapter maps and investigates the interrelationships and specific significance of these seven potential drivers within communities at the local level (meso level). Macro-level findings in Tunisia have emphasized the significance of some combinations of drivers. That is why the drivers will be mostly described in their interactions with other drivers and social contexts in the three case studies.

4.1 The Role of Social and Economic Grievances in Combination with Territorial Inequalities

Findings in Feriana highlight the significant role of territorial inequalities and economic and social grievances, in combination with transitional dynamics. The results of the macro-level research already showed that highly centralized and unbalanced state policies resulted in the marginalization of governorates in the center-west region, the largest of which is Kasserine, to which the Feriana region belongs. Participants emphasized the great sense of injustice regarding this marginalization of their region and unequal opportunities (education, employment, leisure) available to its youth.

In response to the absence of economic opportunities and basic services or any development initiatives by the central government for more than six decades, participants repeatedly expressed their deep feelings of resentment against the state. They insisted that while their city is rich in historical and natural wealth, it had been neglected by successive political regimes, which deprived the region of all opportunities for economic development. This has weakened and polarized the relationship between the Feriana communities and the state.

Geographically, Feriana's proximity to the Algerian border has facilitated informal trade, with many residents relying on the informal economy for their livelihoods. The participants view their engagement with the informal economy, whether as consumers or workers, as a necessity. They do not see this as an illegal activity or a crime. Focus group participants over the age of 18 talked about the absence of the state in their region, which contributes to the region's economy being based on informal trade. They describe it as "the economy of luck" where risk creates wealth. The region's border location has contributed to the intertwining of informal trade and illicit activities. Despite this, participants observed a level of tolerance from authorities towards the informal economy, suggesting an informal agreement between the state and these regions where the absence of development is compensated for by some tolerance towards the informal economy and informal activities.

Closer to the capital, Hammam Lif is a low-income neighborhood suffering from social inequality and marginalization, which caused various community tensions. This provides fertile ground for perceptions of marginalization and injustice which are exacerbated by exclusion despite the proximity to the center (the capital) and despite the availability of the natural and geographical assets of the city. Respondents reported that they felt that their city was excluded from state policies and programs, firmly convinced that it is systematically subjected to marginalization despite its high potential and resources for economic development (natural resources, the beach and mountain as well as the existence of an established middle class). Altough it has a high touristic potential, its beaches are neglected and polluted because of bad waste management policies (domestic waste and industrial waste). According to the inhabitants of Hammam Lif, their city was prosperous in the past but was targeted and punished by the Ben Ali regime. Its youth hold a narrative that explains the marginalization of their city as a deliberate political decision by the Ben Ali regime against their area. As a result of this marginalisation, their city is lacking in economic projects and thus in employment opportunities. Their socioeconomic grievances are mostly centered on the high level of unemployment in Hammam Lif. Young people typically spend long hours in cafes until the early hours of the morning.

In Sousse, economic opportunities are not lacking, but young people from poorer backgrounds feel stigmatized by wealthier residents. This sense of discrimination is particularly strong among second-generation internal migrants who moved to Sousse from poor interior regions. The participants talked about profound and strong class differentiation in Sousse. The wealthy class includes those who have been able to benefit from the opportunities of economic investment since independence, the various generations of the historical local bourgeoisie including the old migrants from outside of Sousse[6] who managed to make money, became rich

[6]The city of Sousse mainly attracts three categories of migrants, namely, Tunisian migrants from the interior regions, Tunisian migrants who return from abroad and foreign migrants mainly from sub-Saharan Africa, other Maghreb countries, and Europe. In 10 years (1999–2004 and 2009–2014) the city of Sousse received 73,351 internal migrants, which represents 61.5% of all 119,952 migrants who came to the governorate of Sousse during the same period. Internal migration to Sousse has significant consequences for the living conditions of the inhabitants. A remarkable urban-social divide marks the city due to this migration. This divide separates the city between the rich or middle-class neighborhoods, located mainly west and north of the city center, and informal housing districts, located mainly to the south of the city center and occupied by poor or with low

and moved to the more well-off areas of the governorate. Those still belonging to the working class and their children suffer from what the participants reported as being strong social discrimination as real social barriers separate the classes and are deeply entrenched in unwritten local norms. This is illustrated according to them by the fact that "marriage customs and many other social customs enforce social discrimination against class intermarriage", which strengthens the isolation of the lower working classes as well as feelings of *hogra* (contempt) by the upper classes towards the working class and the internal migrants who moved more recently to the city, and settled in the popular neighborhoods of Sousse, such as Sidi Abdelhamid.

Unlike their parents, who worked (or continue to work) in the industrial zones of Sousse, the youth of Sidi Abdelhamid, even when they find jobs "are not happy with the low wages offered by local factories". The minimum (450 Tunisian dinars) or even medium wage (850 dinars) is in their eyes insufficient as it "keeps them in an inferior position in comparison with youth from the more privileged neighborhoods", and it does not give them access to the social spheres that those youth have access to.

They are thus led to work in the informal economy and in delinquent and criminal activities that bring them more money and faster through existing networks of criminality, such as robbery, drug dealing, etc. Neighborhoods in Sidi Abdelhamid such as Taffela, for example, are known for such activities and Sidi Abdelhamid often features in the news for such criminal activity.

4.2 Education, Leisure, and Socialization

Discussing the high rate of school dropouts in Feriana, focus group participants insisted that young people in Feriana suffer from the absence of support structures, be it from state or other socializing institutions (family, associations), that could encourage them to continue their education. Some participants stated that even their families do not encourage them to continue their studies but rather consider work in the informal sector as a better garantee of social success. Especially for young males, this is considered as confirmation of their capacities to take risks and be prepared to be a daring and strong adult. Those who do more advanced studies are not seen as successful as that does not allow them to find jobs later and they will have to migrate to other regions to make a living.

In relation to the education system, young participants in Feriana talked about being exposed to verbal abuse, and sometimes physical violence by teachers,

---

incomes, mostly from interior regions. The development of informal housing, inherited from the internal migration of Tunisians from the interior, causes challenges for the public authorities, including municipalities, in the provision of road services, sanitation, urban infrastructure, transport, health, education, and social services in the neighborhoods concerned. The informal neighborhoods continue to receive new migrant communities from the interior of the country annually. There are 19 informal settlements in the city of Sousse.

administrative staff or fellow students at school. In a region where education does not lead to better job opportunities, teenagers and young people are prepared for the harsh conditions of living, from the family to the school, by accepting violence as a way of resolving conflicts and achieving social status. It is also a necessary passage rite for young men coming of age.

Teenagers expressed extreme frustration at many incidents of verbal abuse by the teachers, without the possibility of reporting those incidents to parents. The victims are seen as weak if they choose to complain to the school or even to parents. There is no clear institutional or legal mechanism to combat this violence, leading the majority to normalize it and confront it with similar violent responses. Neither the school administration nor the teachers intervene in settling conflicts between youth, or even sanction violence.

Adolescents as well as older participants emphasized, in addition to this, the absence of spaces for entertainment that young people can use in Feriana. Teenagers and young males spend most of their free time in the local cafés or on digital social media platforms when the Internet is available. As for girls, they said that they had nowhere to go for recreative activities. The area thus does not provide any opportunities for entertainment for teenagers and young people, inside and outside schools and institutions, which exacerbates their feelings of injustice and between them and other regions in the country.

The lack of recreational spaces in the city makes young people live in a vacuum where risky behaviors (drugs use, drugs dealing) and stories about them are one of the few forms of entertainment, along with stories of "bravery" related to illegal activities such as smuggling. Most of the participants spoke about drugs and reported widespread use of drugs amongst youth, explaining this by the need to escape the harsh local reality marked by the lack of job opportunities and decent living, in addition to the scarcity of spaces for leisure and self-expression.

In Hammam lif also, youth in the most underprivileged neighborhoods are reluctant to pursue their education, and this is confirmed by the high school dropout rates in the region. Focus group discussions reveal that schools are unpleasant environments for youth in these neighborhoods. Even more concerning is that the education system no longer offers a real chance of social mobility for children of these youth as it reproduces the same inequalities and discrimination as the ones existing outside of school.

Participants reported a tense relationship with the educational staff (teachers, administration) at school who do not intervene in the students' conflicts and do not provide any kind of protection for the vulnerable or for those who do not choose violence as a response to conflict. Some of them talked about violence between classmates as a daily adventure as teenagers sometimes turn to violence as a means of entertainment and energy release for lack of constructive spaces to invest their immense energy.

Neither at school nor in their families, can young participants coming from more marginalized and poorer neighborhoods sense that they can express their feelings or engage in calm dialogue with adults and authority figures (parents, school). Only some participants (from a middle-class background) reported that they could discuss their issues with their parents. However, they also reported that due to the ever-increasing costs of life, their middle-class families are under tremendous financial constraints and can no longer pay for them to join clubs and recreational activities as they wish.

Most participants in Hammam Lif also complained of the absence of entertainment and cultural opportunities. Some participants in the teenagers' focus group said they used to spend their free time at football clubs. However, over the past few years, participating in these clubs has become too costly for families. While the older youth reported the absence of entertainment opportunities other than cafes, teenagers reported spending most of their time in arcades (electronic and digital gaming places) or on digital games on their phones when internet access is available.

Focus group discussions additionally showed that local group subcultures, like the football fans (the ultras), or underground rap music groups, appear as spaces and platforms for alternative socialization. Hammam Lif has developed distinctive subculture groups, with whom local youth strongly identify and feel an intense sense of belonging. Within these groups, young people spend "an enjoyable time with friends", often consuming drugs but also sharing a deep sense of fraternity and solidarity, which bonds them in opposition to power and authority figures (the police, the state, the school).

For teenagers and young males especially, these groups are spaces of self-expression in the absence of such spaces in the family, at school or in the cultural sphere. However, these groups also contribute to socializing them into oppositional discursive and social identifications. Both the widespread underground rap culture in Hammam Lif and the Ultras fan groups mobilize violent verbal repertoires that often convey rejection of authority as well as messages about the grievances of their neighborhood and their constant battle with the "police" in response to their perceived severe brutality.

The opposition to power and authority figures amongst youth in Hammam Lif is also evident during football games as the young public chants slogans and songs against "the system" and for freedom and rights. The young participants considered that stadiums are the only space for entertainment and an outlet for expressing their frustrations. Their closure because of the COVID-19 pandemic has caused a considerable amount of stress for youth as well as mounting levels of repressed anger, which has been the cause of the spread of several forms of violence amongst youth (hate speech on social media, numerous altercations with the police, widespread use of drugs, frequent cases of extreme violence including homicide towards teachers and other youth, etc.).

Although the governorate of Sousse is known for hosting many good educational institutions at all levels, the peri-urban areas such as Sidi Abdelhamid suffer from a prominent level of school dropouts. Some participants reported cases of violence against the educational staff in the local primary school of Sidi Abdelhamid. The participants reported also that the schools in poor areas lack clubs, unlike the well-off areas (lack of leisure opportunities). They also report that no civil society organizations address the needs of youth in those neighborhoods or work in those areas.

Participants indicated that many teachers from other regions in Tunisia who are sent to teach in Sidi Abdelhamid schools felt angry and perceived their assignment as unfair. According to participants, this causes great tension in the relationship between teachers and local students. Some of the participants mentioned that some teachers verbally abuse students to which some students respond with physical violence.

An important level of delinquency is reported by the participants. According to them, there are different degrees of delinquency and criminality between the different regions of Sousse and even between the different popular neighborhoods themselves. Some of them are perceived as harboring acute and more dangerous forms of criminality like the neighborhood of Taffela, Bir Echebbek and Hay El-Matar (parts of Sidi Abdelhamid). Children are socialized into violence and delinquent behavior such as drug use and stealing from an early age in those neighborhoods. Limited wages and long working hours do not allow parents to be there for teenagers, to support them or provide them with leisure opportunities.

The social experience of the inhabitants of the poor neighborhoods like Sidi Abdelhamid, especially of the poorest neighborhoods like Taffela and Bir Echebbek is strongly marked by social stigma against them. The young people who live in those areas suffer from being rejected by the more established communities of Sousse and they are denied a sense of belonging to the city, which seems to condem them to social isolation and marginalization. The participants highlighted that "as soon as the young people leave their neighborhoods, they are the object of discrimination from everyone and especially the police. The police chase them and restrict their movements".

Participants reported a stark class and cultural divide, with established families being "more conservative and critical of newcomers" who live in the areas left behind by the older working class and migrants to Sousse (the informal neighborhoods, which are not part of any formal urban planning). The popular neighborhoods are seen as "morally degenerate", with violence against women and children being common. Teenagers, especially, complain of a "dry relationship and the lack of warmth in relation to parents" as well as frequent conflict especially about money. Recent migrants were said to exhibit more liberal behavior, especially in terms of relationships, but face challenges in accessing healthcare. Although Sidi Abdelhamid has more than 55,000 inhabitants, there are no cultural centers or public theaters in the region. There is only one youth center located in an area that the participants said to be risky for children and teenagers. In contrast with the touristic coast of Sousse, areas like Sidi Abdelhamid lack recreational opportunities, forcing youth to spend their free time on the streets. In addition to this, access to leisure venues in the touristic areas is often restricted for youth from underprivileged neighborhoods, who face discrimination based on their appearance. According to the focus groups' participants, the main concern for young people in Sidi Abdelhamid is "not only to get a source of income that covers their necessities but also that gives them social recognition, acceptance by the upper class and access to the lifestyle enjoyed by the youth of this class". The social stigma and isolation they suffer from is unbearable to them and leads them to look for ways to earn quick and big money that will help them rise above those conditions. This is the channel that leads them to delinquency and criminality, readily available in their social context. This is also one of the reasons for a significant level of school dropout in Sidi Abdelhamid. The participants mentioned the "widespread drug trafficking amongst teenagers and youth" in the popular and disadvantaged neighborhoods of Sidi Abdelhamid. In the absence of real rehabilitation, these participants noted that "after having served their prison sentence, the young people resume the exercise of the same trade".

4.3 A Tense Relationship with the Police and the Punitive Justice System

In all three case studies, there is a notable tension in the relationship between the local populations and state institutions, particularly the police and security forces. This tension is exacerbated by feelings of exclusion, marginalization, and resentment towards the state.

In Feriana, research findings pointed to strong feelings of marginalization due to economic, social, and political grievances, along with perceived territorial inequalities, contribute to resentment towards the state. This leads to a complex and conflictual relationship with state symbols like the police and security forces, especially after 2011, following the tighter state security control of the border.

In response to the absence of economic opportunities and basic services, or of any development initiatives by the central government for more than six decades, participants expressed many times their deep feelings of resentment against the state. This had weakened and polarized the relationship between the Feriana communities and central government as it is perceived as failing to provide them with the most basic services for a decent life, while at the same time seeking to control a border that was for them historically a major source of subsistence.

Border smuggling is sometimes de facto accepted as harmless normal economic activity (in the case of small consumption goods), and sometimes considered illegal (in the case of drugs, arms, metals, etc.). Family and local networks have normalized work in the informal sector and push young people towards finding opportunities in this sector as their best option. These informal networks are supported by a strong social fabric with a "tribal" structure that defines the balance of power between local authorities and central government. Land ownership is still marked by the traditional tribal structure, and this has also determined the structure of the informal economy, as the routes of smuggling are dominated by specific tribes who occasionally get into conflict over the domination of these routes as well as the cooptation of local security members. The sway of these tribes, known as *arush*, over these routes is mostly stronger than the power of local authorities (Meddeb, 2016).

The police and security services do not seem to be interested in cracking down on smuggling activities in the case of daily consumption goods. It seems that there is a tacit historical deal struck between the state and these regions, where the absence of development is compensated by some tolerance towards the informal economy and informal activities. Young people in cafés hear and tell stories of several types of interactions between smuggler networks and border police which often glorify the former as heroes capable of defeating the unjust state or sometimes even gaining power over some of its representatives through "dirty money" and corruption (bribes).

The participants of Hamman Lif also described a complex and conflictual relationship with the police and the justice system. As feelings of exclusion and resentment are rising in the social and economic context of Hammam Lif, young people show prominent levels of frustration towards state institutions and symbols, especially towards the police. Some teenagers participating in one of the focus groups reported feeling euphoric and overjoyed when they defied the police who chased them on the playgrounds and the streets. The older youth (18–30 years old) negatively perceive the police as the hard fist of the state. They shared being frustrated with the police's "arrogant behavior" towards them inside and on the outskirts of their city. Several cases of police brutality towards young delinquents or even towards youth attending football matches were reported. A silent rage exists against the police as the youth of the region continue to feel unfairly treated.

Hammam Lif is also known for a prominent underground Rap music subculture (street art), whose themes and main narratives tell of an ongoing and continuing confrontation between the youth of the underprivileged neighborhoods of Hammam Lif with the police and the state, revealing underlying deep feelings of frustration. In addition to this theme, one of the most important themes of these rap songs is also illegal migration as a necessity for a decent life in response to "hogra" and social stigma.

As the popular neighborhoods of Hammam Lif also suffer from an important level of drug trade and use as well as delinquency, the case study additionally investigated the role of institutions and their relationship with delinquents, drug dealers, and addicts and the relationship with the radicalization of youth. Focus group participants as well as one of the practitioners in correction centers and prisons pointed out that the official institutions do not seem to be able to help the youth involved in such behaviour get out of the negative cycle where they are caught. The correctional institutions and prisons are not contributing to reforming young delinquents, but rather contribute to deepening the circumstances and causes of youth involvement in delinquency and criminality (theft, drugs dealing and drug addiction, violent extremism, etc.). Hence, correctional establishments and prisons do not play a role in reforming the behavior of these offenders but rather contribute to keeping them in the cycle of delinquency. This shows that the punitive justice system prevents the reform and rehabilitation of delinquents while reproducing and aggravating their delinquency.

Two interviewees working on local youth delinquency issues maintained that the young delinquents who go to prison are usually exposed to radical ideas. They explained that young delinquents are faced with the choice of either sinking deeper into the networks and cycles of crime and delinquency looking for solidarity with their delinquent friends, with whom they share a sense of common life experiences and a common sense of marginalization and rage, or, on the other hand, if they want to become "clean", they make their way towards what appears as a purer form of religious ideas. The second option leads them often to adopt new extremist forms of religious practice that offer them the promise of purification, redemption and alternative belonging. The focus group participants also confirmed what many previous studies (Raghavan, 2018) have highlighted: radicalization often occurs in prisons.

As to Sidi Abdelhamid, it is often the scene of confrontations between the police and locals. The participants reported several stories of such clashes. These altercations between the police and the locals frequently make local news headlines, which take the side of the police and the official institutions "without highlighting or analyzing the real causes of the conflicts and protests". The protesters' social demands remain unaddressed, and the policing and securitization of these social issues are the main official response to them.

4.4 Religion

While macro-level research findings have shown that institutional approaches tend to identify religion as one of the most important push factors for radicalization and VE, meso-level research through case studies provides a more nuanced and refined analysis of the role of religion. Social contexts play a key role in activating the role of religion as a push or pull factor. Moreover, young people and local communities tend to identify religion as a preventive factor more than a driver. In addition, more emphasis is given to the lack of religious education as an explanation for the acceptance of radical religious narratives. In Feriana, according to many participants, those who join or help violent extremist groups are not usually very religious. Some of them go from drugs to supporting VE and back to drug addiction and dealing. The role of religion, in this regard, does not seem significant, in their view, as religious engagement is supposed, for them, to help people avoid addiction and try to be more "righteous" rather than engage in criminal and deviant behavior.

This perception of the role of religion shared by many participants from Feriana may be explained by the strong religious traditions and institutions in their town and the attachment of the people of that region to their local historical religious heritage. Most of the participants, and even the youngest amongst them (from 15 to 18), expressed significant pride in one of the historical features of Feriana, which is the *zawiya* (religious shrine) of Sidi Ahmed al-Telili.[7] It is one of the heritage

[7] Our research revealed that this zawiya was founded in 1730 and is the oldest one established in the center-west of Tunisia. Feriana was historically an area of economic, cultural and religious convergence between many regions. It was the place of meeting between the production of cereals (wheat, barley, etc.) in the north on the one hand, and date production in the south on the other. Caravans travelling from the south to the north and vice versa used to choose it as their resting location and would use that time to benefit from a spiritual stop at the shrine. Culturally and reli-

landmarks of the region and they make all visitors to the city visit it as part of the local hospitality.

This suggests that there is a dissonance between local forms of religiosity and extremist narratives. Residents of Feriana expressed clear rejection and discomfort with extremist religious ideas. Extremist groups and the youth who join them from Feriana seem to be rather driven by a set of factors, including the geographical location of the city and the intense resentment against the central state, which leads to the acceptance of everything informal or outside the framework of the law and weakens the local population's feelings of national belonging. Locals, thus, do not actively embrace religious extremist ideas. The underlying rationale for why their region facilitates the passage of extremist networks may better be explained through the absence of a strong reason to refrain from engaging in lucrative informal activities facilitated by their geographical location. While these activities might indirectly constitute a form of support to the extremist groups, the state is not strongly perceived as worthy of their loyalty and defense because it has let them down for many decades and ignored their needs.

In Hammam Lif, despite the existence of strong local traditional religiosity,[8] Salafist jihadi narratives gained popularity amongst the most popular neighborhoods, where Salafi jihadi cells were active before 2011 (OFRPRA, 2021). The exchanges we had with youth from 12 to 30 years old in Hammam Lif, between 2021 and 2023, indicate that most young people were not attracted to VE narratives, although a few stories of young people being radicalied can still be heard. The state's counterterrorism efforts seem to have significantly reduced the influence of Salafists in Hammam Lif mosques. Their narratives seem to have moved to the digital sphere and social media networks as digital platforms facilitate interactions in closed online groups where the radical discourse is reported to be more direct and franker.

Hammam Lif, like other cities in Tunisia, experienced an extended period during which religion was banned from the public sphere, particularly under the Ben Ali regime before 2011. Salafist ideas found acceptance amongst youth in Hammam Lif in the early 2000s in their search for meaning (lacking in organized religion and education), and who experienced frustration with the political regime. One of the interviewees mentioned that many young people traveled from Hammam Lif to Iraq during the Gulf War, and others joined the Chechen/Russian war to fight with the

giously, Feriana was also the destination for students of religious knowledge from various neighboring regions and even from Algeria. In 1947, the zawiya turned into a branch of the Al-Zaytuna religious institution. The popular religiosity predominant in the city is a Sufi/Zeytuni traditional religiosity that has its origin in the presence of the zawiya in the city. During our conversations and data collection work with citizens and local leaders in Feriana, they stated that the zawiya maintained its presence and role in the city because it remained away from politics and was not targeted by the Ben Ali and Bourguiba regimes, who had a conflictual relationship with religious institutions and groups involved in politics and public affairs.

[8] Hammam Lif has had a historical presence of Christians (Saint Mary's Church) and Jews. The ancient Hammam Lif community was known for its tolerance towards religious diversity and its large spaces of coexistence, which freed it from ideas of religious extremism.

Chechens. These individuals were said not to be religious extremists, but "youth in search of what seems to them to be a lost Arab-Islamic identity". Most of them have not received a religious-traditional education in the family or at school. Rather, in search of meaning and cut off from religious education and concepts, they embrace the VE rhetoric and discourse as the truth.

The *Ansar al-Sharia* cell in Hammam Lif was one of the most powerful cells in the Greater Tunis area. Founded by the old Salafist movement, it included both the *Salafiyya 'ilmiyya* and *Salafiyya jihadiyya* currents. The first current, which can be translated as the "scientific" or "knowledge-based" Salafism, practices a very conservative form of Islam and does not engage in violence against power structures. The other current, the *Salafia jihadiyya*, is militant or Jihadi Salafism. Besides practicing a very conservative form of Islam, its followers also believe that violence is a legitimate means to fight perceived injustice and a *kafir* (non-believer) state (Haj Salem, 2014).

Extremist narratives reached their highest point in Hammam Lif when Salafist jihadism penetrated the area at the beginning of the 2000s after its leaders left prison. They spread in the new poor neighborhoods where young people suffered from few opportunities that fueled feelings of frustration, injustice, and despair. Salafist jihadi groups drew on the conditions of young people in these neighborhoods in Hammam Lif to propagate their narratives.

According to our interviewees in Hammam Lif, while *Ansar al-Sharia* included different types of Salafism, "Jihadi Salafism was the one that most tried to attract young people". They tried to adopt various subtle ways and methods for that purpose. The fact that *Ansar al-Sharia* was a horizontal organization, not a hierarchical one, was also said to be "attractive to young people looking for structures where they can quickly gain recognition and a sense of belonging and action".

Since 2014, with the legal ban on *Ansar al-Sharia* and the imprisonment of many leaders and followers, the group no longer has any activities in Hammam Lif. Many of its former Hammam Lif youth affiliates left the group, abandoning their former ideas and changing their perspectives, while many others continued to adhere to Salafi religious ideas without the jihadist narrative, sticking only to non-oppositional conservative forms of religious practice or notions.

In Sidi Abdelhamid, the discussion of the topic was marked by the post-2015 security crackdown on Salafi groups in Sousse. The atmosphere of suspicion and fear regarding discussing religion was palpable. According to our interviewees in Sidi Abdelhamid, those who join these extremist groups are more likely to be from the popular neighborhoods than from the affluent ones in Sousse. They spoke of "two profiles of people who follow Salafi ideas: those who used to be involved in crimes such as stealing/holdups, have or have not spent time in prison or escaped prison, and are familiar with violent behavior such as using arms (knives mainly)". On the other hand, "there are young people who become Salafi without having such a prior violent or criminal record". The first type tends to explain the existence of social discrimination and inequalities by the subservience of rulers to foreign powers and believe that fighting against the ruler is a duty through Jihad against foreign powers (outside of Tunisia) and they become the foreign fighters who travel abroad to join extremist violent groups. Such collective action is what they perceive as needed to improve the situation of subservience, inferiority and *hogra*. The second type of Salafists explains inequalities and social injustice by the "lack of faith" and of religious practice within the ruling class and in society at large. Believing that the social order is "not on the right path", they tend to isolate themselves from society. Their religiosity remains mainly apparent in individual behavior and does not include a political evaluation of the state and the social order nor any engagement in collective action to change them.

Focus Group participants said that the period of 2014–2015 witnessed the spread of extremist Salafist discourse in the region's mosques. Participants described those who were attracted by Salafism and radical ideas as having been suffering prior to that from "family pressures" and tensions as well as "intellectual and spiritual emptiness." Extremist groups have taken advantage of this "void," filling it by reaching out to them and making them feel like they belong to a group that cares about them and about improving their lives. Focus group participants considered that extremist groups exploit the lack of support structures to address family issues, and socioeconomic and political grievances.

Nonetheless, participants in Sidi Abdelhamid believe that Salafist religious ideas do not necessarily lead to extremist violence. One of the interviewees assessed that "Salafist ideas may or may not lead their followers to Jihadi Salafism," maintaining that "the Salafists who move from Salafist religiosity to Jihadi Salafism are more likely to be the youth who already have been involved in violence, delinquency, and criminality." The interviewee also highlighted the role of torture and harassment by the power structures (police, prison) in the transition to violence of young men targeted because of mosque attendance or holding preaching meetings.

One of the interviewees in Sidi Abdelhamid divided violent extremism and radicalization in Sousse and Tunisia into two waves: "One that existed before 2011 and was closer to Al-Qaeda and one that gained more followers after 2011 and was less close to Al-Qaeda". Accordingly, "the followers of Jihadi Salafism before 2011 had more solid belonging to the group and organizational affiliation to its global and regional networks. Their scholarly religious training was continuous through mosques, prisons, and online teaching. Whereas the followers of Jihadi Salafism after 2011, who were in larger numbers, are a new generation that has no sense of organizational belonging and broadly individually identify or sympathize with Daesh without direct affiliation".

In the same vein, participants reported that "some of the individuals who were arrested in (their) neighborhoods for suspicion of involvement in extremist groups did not show signs of religious ethics or behavior (in their business dealings, etc.)." This is particularly true of the second wave of radicalization and violent extremist affiliation after 2011, as confirmed by one of our interviewees.

Many focus group participants believe that belonging to VE groups has a similar function to joining a criminal gang in that it gives youth a sense of power. As one participant put it: "just as belonging to criminal gangs provides youth from marginalized communities feelings of strength and social power, belonging to networks of violent extremism helps fight the *hogra* and discrimination against them." Criminal gangs and extremist groups share the same *modus operandi* in terms of violent behavior. The same social profile is shared by those who tend to engage in criminality in Sidi Abdelhamid and those who tend to engage in extremist groups. Joining such groups thus allows those who are excluded from social recognition and belonging to the city to "buy their position back" through ostentatious appearances and behavior.

Strong social discrimination against the poorer neighborhoods of Sousse is thus one of the significant sources of many vulnerabilities exploited by extremist groups. To young people who feel deeply marginalized both locally and nationally, as well as suffering from a lack of recognition and integration in their local community, extremist groups offer the promise of power and belonging. Moreover, young people suffering from unstable and violent family environments find strong figures to follow and guidance from leaders replacing the role of absent parents. According to one of the focus group discussions: "young people who have more solid and stable family bonds can be more resilient to the attractions of VE narratives and recruitment."

Other participants emphasized the role of economic and material incentives as one of the most important drivers for youth joining some Salafi groups. The lack of financial resources is a strong motivation that is exploited to recruit followers. There are many ways money is gained: through philanthropic solidarity actions organized by the Salafi groups or through working for them like in transporting goods. This points out the role of economic and social grievances in combination with the role of ideology/religion in activating the attraction to VE narratives in the absence of balanced inclusive state policies.

4.5 Digital Socialization

Macro-level research highlighted social media as a key recruitment tool for youth in Tunisia. However, meso-level case studies provide deeper insights. Indeed, access to the internet in Feriana is limited and weak, which adds to the other indicators of discrimination from the point of view of the participants. This situation exacerbates the negative perceptions and feelings stemming from deep-seated territorial inequalities and sociopolitical grievances.

Although the internet is not always available due to the poor network in various locations of the city, teenage participants mostly reported spending long hours on their phones playing electronic games in the absence of entertainment spaces. In the case of Feriana, there was no perception of recruitment risks by extremist groups of young people via digital platforms. However, we have found that teens heavily use games known to contain violence (e.g., Free Fire), which strengthens the already existing socialization into violence at school and in the local social context, all of which increases the potential of further normalization with and acceptance of violence and violent narratives among young people.

In Sidi Abdelhamid, the religious extremist discourse mobilizes the social and economic grievances of the poor neighborhoods in Sousse to nurture their feelings of marginalization and class polarization through religious polarization that is made easier through digital networks and the recycling of old extremist networks, like Al-Qaeda, for new mobilizations. The recruited youth are gradually isolated from their families and society, psychologically, and an alternative community of belief is created virtually and maintained through an emotional integration that is careful to the needs of the recruited youth and their potential skills. They are also made to feel useful and given specific roles based on their potential for different tasks to be implemented: direct acts of violence, digital tasks, etc.

Influence of VE narratives through digital platforms was mentioned also within focus group discussions in Hammam Lif. However, digital platforms appear mostly as alternative socialization and participation spheres making up for the lack of leisure opportunities and recognition of youth alternative lifestyles. The online activities of adolescents and the young people we spoke to in Hammam Lif are structured through regular and purposeful participation in well-organized closed groups where they follow and pursue objectives and topics of their interest. These closed groups orient them in pursuing their interests and broadening their social networks as welll as their opportunities as they specialize in a specific interest (ultras, rap, gaming). However, these closed groups also close off their horizons in culture, tolerance, and openness as they cultivate monocultural thinking and closed group identity, which makes them more vulnerable to extremist narratives.

Digital platforms and social networks are thus perceived by youth as having a dual role. They are not considered a factor of radicalization in themselves but rather their communication potential facilitates recruitment and the spread of radical narratives. Vulnerable youth, lacking critical judgment and already marginalized socially and economically, may be susceptible to online radicalization. Additionally, those experiencing alienation and a need for social recognition may seek to fulfill them through these digital spheres, often in closed groups where they risk being recruited. However, these social vulnerabilities are the product of the intersection of other factors with specific social contexts and are not produced by the digital media themselves. Most of the young participants, on the contrary, insist on the advantages of digital media for them and support broadening access of youth to digital media. They oppose limitations on their access to the digital sphere through monitoring social media and favor open discussions online about these and other topics and widening the access of youth to the internet and social media.

4.6 Political Participation

In the governorate of Kasserine, where Feriana is situated, we find that the region has the lowest political participation levels in the country: in legislative elections nationwide (Mosaique, 2019b). Fieldwork indicated that the tribal structure of society influences election dynamics both at the local and national levels. This structure is intertwined with the informal economy structure. As for youth political participation, it takes the form of protests. Fieldwork revealed that youth of the region often take part in protests to express dissatisfaction with the government and bring attention to their social and economic grievances. The region has the highest participation rate in protests nationwide.

Regarding political participation in Hammam Lif, participants reported what seems like passive and utilitarian forms of participation. They also expressed their disappointment in political parties, and especially with elections' promises of finding solutions to their problems. One of our interviewees maintained that these promises raised the ceiling for people's expectations from democracy as people expected that democracy and their political representatives would quickly find solutions to the long-standing social and economic issues like unemployment, soaring prices and access to quality public services (health, education, transport, etc.). The slow pace of change in their social and economic conditions brought frustration and anger towards political parties and institutions. This disenchantment and frustration were palpable in the most disenfranchised neighborhoods. Moreover, some participants considered that political parties, as well as most civil society organizations, did not involve young people in decision-making, but rather confiscated their right to autonomy and participation.

Finally, violent protests in the form of "road blocking" and "tire burning" seem to be the main political forms of expression of the demands and grievances of the youth of Sidi Abdelhamid. Focus group participants mentioned that "the inhabitants of Sidi Abdelhamid do not take part in elections." They explained this by the fact that "the inhabitants of those neighborhoods do not find candidates that resemble them or express their needs and demands for whom they can vote." They added that "businessmen (who become candidates for legislative elections[9]) from Sousse do not represent (them) or take into consideration their demands and needs since they represent their interests and those of the higher and middle classes." Despite their demographic size, the communities of Taffela, Hay Ezouhour and other disenfranchised areas do not have electoral weight for the political parties as "they do not register in the electoral register." The vulnerable communities of Sidi Abdelhamid in Hay Ezouhour and Taffela are thus "cut off from" and indifferent to the political discourses of the political elites of the country. Also, one of our interviewees stated that "political participation needs a level of education that is mostly available to middle classes and above, rather than to the disenfranchised populations of Taffela for example."

[9] Several of them become candidates for legislative elections (see Mosaique, 2019a).

5 Conclusion

Since the late 1980s, the Tunisian regime claimed to adopt economic policies, characterized by liberalization and privatization with the objective of opening the economy to foreign investment. Nonetheless, the regime crafted and gradually implemented laws and procedures restricting competition and private initiative, and thus maintaining a monopolistic economic model (Hibou et al., 2011). This model extended into state institutions, where corruption and privileges served the ruling circle and its allies, exacerbating feelings of injustice among the population (Chirchi et al., 2021).

This growing sense of injustice, particularly among educated youth, and especially graduates unable to find decent employment, contributed to the 2010–2011 revolution against the regime. From a macro-level perspective, the governance model in Tunisia and its impact on the economy and society played a significant role in driving radicalization and violent extremism in Tunisia.

Seen from the citizens' perspective, the post-independence state model having caused deep multidimensional disparities between regions, has generated deep-seated perceptions of alienation and neglect of the population that are widely shared not only in the most marginalized and peripheral regions (like in northwest Tunisia), but also closer to the central cities like Tunis and Sousse. Even in those areas, inequalities are present as the peri-urban and urban neighborhoods also experience various degrees of marginalization with the presence of deep-rooted social and economic inequalities.

Discussions with the citizens throughout the various case studies, situated in different geographical and social contexts, reveal shared grievances that people have against the state policies, whose exacerbation led to the uprising of 2010 and 2011 and created multiple vulnerabilities. The post-independence state had established an economic system with complex authorization processes, giving state institutions exclusive control over economic activities (Chirchi et al., 2021). This system limited economic initiatives, leading to a growing informal economy, especially in marginalized areas and popular neighborhoods. The marginalized areas suffered from poor infrastructure, affecting access to education, culture, and entertainment, and exacerbating regional disparities. State policies and administrative procedures in Tunisia not only organized economic activities but also facilitated social control (Chirchi et al., 2021; Meddeb, 2016), as well as social and political alienation of large parts of society. This exclusion pushed various social groups into marginality, perpetuating a system of alienation and depriving individuals, territories, and regions of participation and development opportunities. At the basis of this marginalization and deprivation system, we find a set of factors and dynamics that could be schematically represented by a triangle, whose elements are: regional disparities, economic and political grievances, and the vertical and hierarchical governance/development model, which contributed to the construction of a rentier state, society and culture (Chirchi et al., 2021). Case studies examined at the meso level confirm the consequences of this triangle both at the local and community as well as the individual levels, enabling us to better understand how macro drivers work at the meso level.

The first dimension of this triangle is the intersection between transnational dynamics, local social contexts, and religion. Indeed, while transnational dynamics are active in the country, local grievances are much more important. The presence of transnational dynamics has been noted through case studies, either through geographic (border) dynamics in Feriana and Sidi Abdelhamid or through digital presence via online content. However, transnational dynamics are only operative when local contexts have several prior vulnerability factors and grievances, making the local social context play a major role in determining the potential for radicalization that the transnational dynamics have. Transnational dynamics are activated as push factors only in association with local grievances. The deep feelings of marginalization stemming from economic, social, and political grievances and the prevalent perceptions of deep territorial inequalities have nurtured a complex and conflictual relationship with the symbols of the state (the police, and the security forces). In Feriana, violent extremist networks benefit from the region's border location for their functioning, which is facilitated by these complex relations. These informal networks are supported by a strong social fabric that has a "tribal" structure. This structure defines the balance of power between local authorities and the central state (Meddeb, 2016). Furthermore, although it is one of the regions most affected by the drivers and dynamics of radicalization and VE, Feriana does not seem to produce, itself, any local religious narratives supporting violent extremism. The community's religious heritage constitutes a sort of resilience factor against a real embracing of extremist narratives. Strong local religious traditions still have sociocultural authority in the region, with strong social and tribal family structures that prevented ultraconservative religious narratives (Salafi, Wahhabi) from taking root in the local social fabric and discourses.

The second dynamic of the triangle that we have identified is highlighted by the urban and peri urban tensions raising multidimensional fractures and multi-level consequences that can be especially observed in the social contexts of two of the major urban centers in Tunisia: Tunis and Sousse. The asymmetrical and unequal development of the country in the past decades, created structural inequalities in terms of infrastructure and services, with the underprivileged neighborhoods of urban centers suffering from greater infrastructure deficiencies, and environmental neglect severely impairing the quality of life, all of which threaten social cohesion within the city. If not corrected, this may disrupt the future development of these urban centers.

In Sidi Abdelhamid, the underprivileged neighborhoods are mostly inhabited by families coming from 80% to 90% of internal migratory flows from the interior regions towards urban centers cities (Boubakri, 2020; General Office for Regional Development, 2020). The consequences and impacts of these flows manifest through spontaneous or informal housing, inadequate infrastructure, and marginalization and exclusion of the most vulnerable urban social groups: the working poor, the unemployed, women, disabled people, single-parent families, and others.

Perceptions of deep regional inequalities and multidimensional marginalization are thus not limited to the interior regions in Tunisia. They can also be found in peri-urban low-income neighborhoods of large urban centers, such as Tunis and Sousse. These extreme inequalities in infrastructure, economic opportunities, and services between neighboring districts contribute to fueling violence and weakening social cohesion, all of which provide a fertile ground for feelings of marginalization and injustice, exacerbated by acutely perceived exclusion despite geographical and social closeness to the centers of power and wealth. Moreover, the development of informal housing causes challenges in providing road services, sanitation, urban infrastructure, transport, health, education, and social services in the neighborhoods concerned.

As for Hammam Lif, it is made up of different poor neighborhoods, some of them are historically old and others have been recently established. Most of the inhabitants of the older neighborhoods come from the middle class (state employees and craftsmen) who consider themselves to be the first inhabitants of the area and constitute a more homogeneous social group. These neighborhoods lack basic services, which makes life and access to the city difficult. These new neighborhoods are stigmatized by the older inhabitants of the city as outsiders, dangerous and violent social outcasts. This social differentiation between the community groups of the old and new neighborhoods also comes from economic differentiation: the inhabitants of the new neighborhoods mostly practice precarious jobs that make them isolated from those of the old neighborhoods (middle class).

The feelings of exclusion and resentment (commonly expressed by the term *hogra*) are heightened in this urban context, where young people express high levels of frustration towards state institutions and symbols of power, especially towards security forces. This is expressed through acts of violence and delinquency in Sidi Abdelhamid, but also through slang, graffiti and several forms of subculture that could be found in Hammam Lif and Sidi Abdelhamid and many other popular neighborhoods in Tunisia.

Socioeconomic grievances also emerge from the combination of economic hardship with real or perceived relative deprivation when compared with other more well-off areas in the governorate at large. These heightened grievances tied to unemployment and deteriorating economic conditions are key sources of vulnerability in Hammam Lif and Sidi Abdelhamid, which are especially problematic when combined with an intense sense of marginalization and class-based discrimination.

Finally, the last axis of the triangle that emerges from the analysis of the case studies is the link between alienation and alternative belonging. Indeed, our data concludes that vulnerable groups to VE threat are mostly school dropouts, marginalized youth, and individuals not in a stable family environment. Through meso-level observations, these individuals seem to have been failed by existing mechanisms and spheres of mainstream socialization—the family, traditional religious institutions, education, employment, culture—which are replaced by alternative socialization spheres and mechanisms provided by violent extremist groups, their belief systems and their internal subcultures and dynamics.

In the same vein, our data showed that in Sousse (Sidi Abdelhamid), individuals often move from the criminal world to the terrorist register. One of the possible explanations highlighted through our interviews is that those individuals find in the practice of violent extremism what they find in the practice of gang criminality, namely the high adrenaline levels that violence in criminality used to provide them. With those frustrated with the state, it also provides "radical solutions" to the absence or slowness of the change that they would like to see to their condition.

Thus, the two types of belonging and activities (criminal/terrorist) are revealed to be interrelated in our data analysis. They are both pathological expressions of the results of failed or absent policies of social integration, labor protection, and poor urban planning.

In Hammam Lif, marginalization by the state's policies and economic model over decades has produced a sense of disappointment and frustration among young people in the region. Normalization with violence occurs in the family and at school, where there is a tense relationship with educational staff, especially in the poor neighborhoods of the area. Many young people in the region belong to closed online groups (ultras, rap, gaming...) in which they exercise their hobbies and create strong virtual relationships around a common passion (sub-affiliation). These closed groups, where the feeling of belonging to a subculture grows, contribute to the abandonment by young people of the values of acceptance of others and tolerance of difference. As a result, young people become intolerant of other views and adopt monocultural thinking. These risks make them more ready to accept extremist ideas.

These groups are nonetheless spaces of expression for these young people and adolescents, but they often lack the guidance and supervision to create constructive meaning. It needs to be noted that strong affiliation to subcultures like the football fan groups and the rap fan groups in impoverished areas in Hammam Lif can be a factor of prevention by strengthening self-expression and channeling frustration in a positive way through sports and art. However, the lack of civic space and civic and political participation within the disenfranchised communities under study makes violent protest and road blocking such as in Sidi Abdelhamid the main available forms of political expression. The lack of avenues for frustration and anger to be expressed in a peaceful way provides fertile soil for the radicalization of youth more clearly in the popular neighborhoods. These social, economic, and political grievances caused by structural and systemic inequalities, asymmetrical governance and development models necessitate comprehensive and situated responses and strategies.

References

Anzil, V., Monserrate, S., Olivé, E., & Rubio-Rico, L. (2022). *Policy paper on countering and preventing macro-level drivers of radicalisation and violent extremism in MENA and Balkans*. The European Institute of the Mediterranean (IEMED). Retrieved September 2024, from https://h2020connekt.eu/publications/policy-paper-on-countering-and-preventing-macro-level-drivers-of-radicalisation-and-violent-extremism-in-mena-and-balkans/

Ayari, M. (2017). Violent extremism and its motivating factors in Tunisia in the 2010s. *UNDP Analytical Review*. Retrieved September 2024, from http://opev.org/wp-content/uploads/2019/10/AYARI-Michae%CC%881-Revue-Framing-Violent-Extremism-in-the-MENA-region-and-the-Balkansanalytique-Les-facteurs-favorisant-l%E2%80%99extre%CC%81misme-violent-dans-la-Tunisie-des-anne%CC%81es-2010-ENG.pdf

Bieber, F., & Pollozhani, L. (2021). *Macro approaches the study of radicalisation and violent extremism in MENA and the Balkans*. The European Institute of the Mediterranean (IEMED). Retrieved September 2024, from https://h2020connekt.eu/wp-content/uploads/2021/12/D7.1-Macro-approaches-to-the-study-of-radicalisation-and-violent-extremism-in-MENA-and-the-Balkans.pdf

Boubakri, H. (2020). *Profil migratoire de la ville de Sousse*. International Center for Migration Policy/UN Habitat. Retrieved November 2024, from https://www.icmpd.org/file/download/59548/file/MC2CM_City_Migration_Profile_Sousse_FR.pdf

Boukhars, A. (2017). *The geographic trajectory of conflict and militancy in Tunisia*. Carnegie Institute. Retrieved September 2024, from https://www.researchgate.net/publication/318710831_THE_GEOGRAPHIC_TRAJECTORY_OF_CONFLICT_AND_MILITANCY_IN_TUNISIA

Braham, S. (2014). *Salafiya Jihadiya in Tunisia after the revolution and the failure of the experience of regularity*. Tunisian Institute for Strategic Studies.

Cavatorta, F. (2015). Salafism, liberalism, and democratic learning in Tunisia, September. *The Journal of North African Studies, 20*(5), 1–14.

Center of Strategic and International Studies (CSIS). (2016). Foreign fighter project. Domestic context after the revolution. Retrieved June 2024, from http://foreignfighters.csis.org/tunisia/domestic-context.html.

Chirchi, T., & Ghribi, K. (2023). *Meso approaches to the study of radicalisation and violent extremism: A view from the MENA region* in Bieber, Florian and Pollozhani, Lura (eds.). IEMED Publications. Available at: https://h2020connekt.eu/wp-content/uploads/2023/11/CONNEKT-MENA-MESO-Regional-Report.pdf

Chirchi, T., Ghribi, K., Aloui, R., & Kherigi, I. (2021). *CONNEKT, Tunisia—Macro-drivers of radicalization and violent extremism*. The European Institute of the Mediterranean (IEMED). Retrieved September 2024, from https://h2020connekt.eu/publications/tunisia-macro-drivers-of-radicalisation-and-violent-extremism/

General Commission for Regional Development (GCRD). (2020). *The Governorate of Ben Arous in figures for the year 2020*. The European Institute of the Mediterranean (IEMED). Retrieved September 2024, from http://cgdr.nat.tn/upload/files/gouvchiffres/gech%202020/BA_%20 2020.pdf

General Office for Regional Development. (2020). *Sousse in numbers*. Retrieved September 2024, from https://cgdr.nat.tn/upload/files/gouvchiffres/gech%202020/gech%202020%20(2)/Souss_2020.pdf

Haj Salem, M. (ed.) (2014). السلفيّة الجهادية في تونس: الواقع والآفا [Salafiya Jihadiya in Tunisia]. Tunisian Institute for Strategic Studies (ITES). Retrieved September 2024, from https://archive.org/details/AssalafiaAljihadiaFiTounes.

Herbert, M. (2018). *The insurgency in Tunisia's Western Borderlands*. Carnegie Endowment for International Peace. Retrieved September 2024, from https://carnegieendowment.org/research/2018/08/the-insurgency-in-tunisias-western-borderlands?lang=en

Hibou, B., Bayart, J.-F., & Meddeb, H. (2011). *La révolution tunisienne vue des régions. Néolibéralisme et trajectoire de la formation asymétrique de l'État en Tunisie*. Etudes du FASOPO.

Institut National de Statistiques. (2014). SOUSSE *A travers le Recensement Général de la Population et de l'Habitat 2014*. Retrieved September 2024, from https://www.ins.tn/sites/default/files-ftp3/files/publication/pdf/RGPH%202014-Sousse.pdf.

Institut National de Statistiques. (2016). *Ben Arous à Travers le Recensement Général de la Population et de l'Habitat*. Retrieved September 2024, from http://www.ins.tn/fr/publication/ben-arous-%C3%A0-travers-le-recensement-g%C3%A9n%C3%A9ral-de-la-population-et-de-l%E2%80%99habitat-2014

Institut National de Statistiques and World Bank. (2020). *Map of poverty in Tunisia*. Retrieved September 2024, from http://www.ins.tn/sites/default/files/publication/pdf/Carte%20de%20la%20pauvret%C3%A9%20en%20Tunisie_final_0.pdf

Institute for Security Study (ISS). (2008). Terrorism in the Maghreb. *The Transnationalisation of Domestic Terrorism, 144*, 121–122.

International Crisis Group (ICG). (2017, July 24). *How the Islamic State Rose, Fell and Could Rise Again in the Maghreb*. Retrieved September 2024, from https://www.crisisgroup.org/middle-east-north-africa/north-africa/178-how-islamic-state-rose-fell-and-could-rise-again-maghreb

Lamloum, O. (2016). *Politics on the margins in Tunisia: Vulnerable young people in Douar Hicher and Ettadhamen*. International Alert. Retrieved September 2024, from https://www.international-alert.org/app/uploads/2021/08/Tunisia-Politics-On-The-Margins-EN-2016.pdf

Marsad Tunisie. (2015, April 20). *Secretary of State to the Minister of the Interior in charge of security Rafik alShelly*. Retrieved September 2024, from https://www.observatoire-securite.tn/ar/2015/04/20/?doing_wp_cron=1588935438.0550880432128906250000

Meddeb, H. (2016). *Young people and smuggling in the Kasserine region of Tunisia. Stories of dispossession and the dynamics of exclusion*. International Alert. Retrieved September 2024, from https://www.international-alert.org/app/uploads/2021/08/Tunisia-Young-People-Smuggling-EN-2016.pdf

Mosaique, F. M. (2019a, October 19). انقابة الديوانة: أكبر مهرّب في القصرين أصبح نائب [Frontiers Police Union: Kasserine's biggest smuggler has become a deputy], Babnet. Retrieved September 2024, from https://www.babnet.net/rttdetail-190658.asp

Mosaique, F. M. (2019b, September 15). نسب المشاركة في الإنتخابات الرئاسية 2019 حسب الجهات [Participation rate in the 2019 presidential elections by region]. Mosaique FM. Retrieved September 2024, from https://www.mosaiquefm.net/ar/%D8%A7%D9%84%D8%B1%D8%A6%D8%A7%D8%B3%D9%8A%D8%A9/606784/%D9%86%D8%B3%D8%A8-%D8%A7%D9%84%D9%85%D8%B4%D8%A7%D8%B1%D9%83%D8%A9-%D9%81%D9%8A-%D8%A7%D9%84%D8%A5%D9%86%D8%AA%D8%AE%D8%A7%D8%A8%D8%A7%D8%AA-%D8%A7%D9%84%D8%B1%D8%A6%D8%A7%D8%B3%D9%8A%D8%A9-2019-%D8%AD%D8%B3%D8%A8-%D8%A7%D9%84%D8%AC%D9%87%D8%A7%D8%AA

Mouna, K., & Er-Rifaiy, A. (2021). *CONNEKT regional report on macro approaches to the study of radicalisation and violent extremism: A view from the MENA region*. The European Institute of the Mediterranean (IEMED). Retrieved September 2024, from https://h2020connekt.eu/publications/mena_macro_approaches_to_the_study_of_radicalisatio_and_violent_extremism/

Office de développement du Centre Ouest (ORD). (2020). *Gouvernorat de Kasserine en Chiffres*. Retrieved September 2024, from https://www.odco.nat.tn/wp-content/uploads/2023/02/KASSERINE-EN-CHIFFRE-2021.pdf

OFRPRA (Office Français de protection des réfugiés et des Apatrides). (2021, January 18). *Tunisie: L'opération antiterroriste de Soliman*. Retrieved September 2024, from https://www.ofpra.gouv.fr/sites/default/files/ofpra_flora/2101_tun_operation_soliman_151731_web.pdf.

Petré, C. (2015, December 8). *How Tunisia's moderate imams are seeking to reclaim Islam from extremists*. Al-Monitor. Retrieved September 2024, from https://www.al-monitor.com/pulse/originals/2015/12/tunisia-mosques-effortsreclaim-islam-jihadis-radicalism.html#ixzz6M7ULD3FS

Raghavan, S. (2018, September 8). Tunisia feared the return of foreign fighters from abroad. The threat now is those who never left. *The Washington Post*. Retrieved September 2024, from https://www.washingtonpost.com/world/tunisia-feared-the-return-of-militants-from-abroad-the-threat-now-is-those-who-never-left/2018/09/07/aafa6c84-aacf-11e8-9a7d-cd30504ff902_story.html

Sterman, D., & Rosenblatt, N. (2018). *All Jihad is local* (Vol. II). ISIS in North Africa and the Arabian Peninsula. Retrieved September 2024, from https://d1y8sb8igg2f8e.cloudfront.net/documents/All_Jihad_Local_Vol2.pdf

The Soufan Group. (2020). *Foreign fighters: An updated assessment of the flow of foreign fighters into Syria and Iraq*. Retrieved September 2024, from https://wb-iisg.com/wp-content/uploads/bp-attachments/4826/TSG_ForeignFightersUpflow.pdf

Tunisian Forum for Economics and Social Rights (TFESR). (2016). الإرهاب في تونس من خلال الملفات القضائية [Terrorism in Tunisia through Judicial Files]. Retrieved September 2024, from https://ftdes.net/ar/etude-terrorisme-en-tunisie/

United Nations Human Rights (UNHR). (2015). *Preliminary findings by the United Nations Working Group on the use of mercenaries on its official visit to Tunisia—1 to 8 July 2015*. Retrieved September 2024, from https://www.ohchr.org/EN/NewsEvents/Pages/DisplayNews.aspx?NewsID=16219&LangID=E

Wolf, A. (2013). An Islamist 'renaissance'? Religion and politics in post-revolutionary Tunisia. *The Journal of North African Studies, 18*(4), 560–573.

Zelin, A. Y. (2018). *Tunisian foreign fighters in Iraq and Syria*. The Washington Institute for Near East Policy. Retrieved September 2024, from https://www.washingtoninstitute.org/uploads/Documents/pubs/PolicyNote55-Zelin.pdf

Zoghlami, M., & Toumi, H. (2019). *Rethinking the concept of human security and its approaches to preventing and combating violent extremism in Tunisia*. WANA Institute. Retrieved September 2024, from http://wanainstitute.org/en/publication/rethinking-concept-human-security-and-its-approaches-preventing-and-combating-v

Community-Level Drivers of Violent Extremism in Jordan

Neven Bondokji, Barik Mhadeen, Aisha Bint Faisal, and Jadranka Štikovac Clark

1 Introduction

Jordan presents significant territorial inequalities, in particular in the situation which is marked by increasing unemployment rates and public debt that affects the majority of the population. They become a real concern when coupled with economic deprivation, as they produce effects that are noticed in at least two ways. The first effect is that certain areas are being more targeted with prevention or countering of violent extremism (C/PVE) programming than others, meaning that these territories were also the ones either experiencing more distress due to these inequalities and/or are being categorized as "radicalization hotspots". Second, the excessive targeting of territorial inequalities in certain areas has prompted the mushrooming of local actors directly linked to the abundance of funds that were channeled to C/PVE efforts in these locations. In turn, this has encouraged numerous community-based organizations (CBOs) that "neither had the previous C/PVE expertise nor the level of sensitivity" needed to deal with such an issue (Mhadeen et al., 2021).

One of the recommendations of the macro-level analysis in Jordan was to look beyond specific spaces or territories, and to identify relational frameworks between drivers, interventions, and shifting institutional patterns arising in response to violent extremism (Mhadeen et al., 2021) Specifically, the research highlighted that economic deprivation is the most prominent driver impacting dynamics of violent extremism (VE) in Jordan (Mhadeen et al., 2021). Still, the macro-level analysis revealed that a more in-depth investigation of the changing patterns in the understanding of causes and the way of addressing violent extremism in Jordan was

N. Bondokji (✉) · B. Mhadeen · A. Bint Faisal · J. Štikovac Clark
Generations for Peace Institute, Amman, Jordan
e-mail: nbondokji@gfp.ngo; abfaisal@gfp.ngo

C. Torrekens et al. (eds.), *Social Contexts of Radicalization and Violent Extremism in the MENA and Balkans*,
https://doi.org/10.1007/978-3-031-84521-5_3

needed, specifically in communities that are under-studied but highly relevant to the topic. The macro-level findings equally showed the state's strong focus on the dimension of religion/ideology in its conceptualization of and response to the prevention of violent extremism.

Also significant are the findings about radicalization among refugees, generally, and among Syrian refugees, more specifically. Available literature has different conclusions on this aspect. For example, a policy brief warns the EU actors about Daesh (ISIS) members infiltrating Syrian refugees in the EU (Funk & Parkes, 2016) whereas a different study argues that 46.7% of Syrian refugees in Jordan hold radical views (Al-Badayneh et al., 2017). However, fieldwork in Jordan negates any strong correlation between Syrian refugee youth and violent extremism (VE) (Bondokji et al., 2017).

Also, the acknowledgment as well as the understanding of the role of women and girls play in violent extremism in Jordan revealed to be a gap in the CONNEKT project's macro-level analysis of drivers of radicalization and violent extremism (Mhadeen et al., 2021). This lack of acknowledgment pointed to a limited understanding of the role of a particular segment of the female population, the one of female preachers (Grieve, 2016). This is why fieldwork was devoted to analyse the role of female preachers in the particular context of Ma'an. The region of Ma'an is marked by economic deprivation with the highest levels of poverty and unemployment in Jordan, and smuggling and illegal activities on the border with Saudi Arabia. The illiteracy rate among women is nearly 5% higher than the national average, and unemployment for women in Ma'an is also nearly 3% higher than the Kingdom's average (Perrin, 2021), pointing to pronounced gender divisions.

The south of Jordan has historically seen active social movements, opposition, and anti-government protests. In particular, Ma'an is known across Jordan as a city with a strong historical presence of an active Salafi-Jihadi movement (Osborne, 2017). Home of the leader of the movement in Jordan, Mohammad Al-Shalabi (Abu Sayyaf), and a base for his activities, (Katulis et al., 2024) the city is one of five major Jordanian cities where the Salafi-Jihadi movement has "the greatest concentration and expansion" (Combaz, 2015). In 2014, its citizens actively rallied in support of Daesh (Ghboun, 2014), raising its flag (Sude, 2021) and encouraging tens of individuals to join the violent extremist groups in Iraq and Syria. Unsurprisingly, within the governorate, the city of Ma'an is considered a key radicalization hotspot in Jordan. Factors such as boredom, drug abuse, negative impression of authorities, inequality, social injustice, etc., impacting on the propensity toward violent extremism in Jordan had alarmingly shown high quantitative scores in Ma'an (Madison Springfield Inc., 2017).

Considering this, three different case studies in Jordan were made in order to address the interplay between drivers and social contexts in three different contexts: vulnerable youth in Karak; Syrian refugees in Northern Jordan; and female preachers in Ma'an.

The selection of Karak as a case study was not based on the geographic or territorial setting, but rather on the breadth of relational frameworks in this governorate.

To do so, this case study opted for understanding what affects vulnerable young people at risk of radicalization, both male and female. Overall, the case study tries to explain why this specific community of Karak, with its prominent tribal context, has not been affected more significantly by radicalization and violent extremism despite the evident presence of key macro drivers such as economic deprivation and territorial inequalities.

The case study regarding the refugees in Northern Jordan examines radicalization drivers among urban and camp-based Syrian refugees in the two northern cities of Irbid and Mafraq. Most studies that generalize radicalization among Syrian refugees measure radicalization based on respondents' agreement to vague sentences about religious practices and value systems that cannot be specifically associated with radicalization.[1] As these generalizations stigmatize the refugee population, this case study examines the radicalization drivers that may affect Syrian refugees in Jordan within the general framework of the seven drivers of radicalization identified by CONNEKT's project.[2] VE in Jordan needs to be reconceptualized based on the reality of contextual grievances, rather than ideology to understand the dynamics of VE at the meso level (Mhadeen et al., 2021). Selecting Syrian refugees for this case study highlights how contextual grievances of Syrian refugees shape drivers of VE, and the work on the case study has identified the most prominent drivers and social contexts of VE in Jordan.

The case study about female preachers in the governorate of Ma'an in south Jordan has examined their role within a meso-level investigation of radicalization drivers affecting youth between 12–30 years. Female preachers access female family members and youth formally through schools, mosques, and other state institutions, or informally in CSOs and houses. Two groups of preachers operate in Jordan and in Ma'an: formal preachers affiliated with the Ministry of Endowments *(Awqaf)* and Religious Affairs and informal preachers who voluntarily preach and are affiliated with various religious groups. The marginalization of informal preachers by state institutions has placed them in a unique position where although alienated by the state they volunteer in various charity and preaching roles, thus allowing them to build direct and trusting relations with audiences.

[1] For example, one survey with 840 residents in three cities in Jordan in 2017 measured radicalization against indicators such as wearing a headscarf (in a conservative city in south Jordan), and the frequency of praying at a mosque. Both indicators are common practices among Muslims and are practiced due to various social and religious beliefs or convictions, they do not necessarily signify radicalization. In this specific example, the pollsters were advised against publishing it.

[2] The seven drivers studied by the CONNEKT project are: religion, economic deprivation, political issues, territorial inequalities, transnational dynamics, digital socialization and education, culture and leisure opportunities.

2 Case Studies

All three case studies in Jordan focused on the socioeconomic aspects and territorial dynamics that could reinforce radicalization of youth towards VE. The Karak case study examines drivers of violent extremism that have affected or are affecting young people in a southern hub of Jordan known for its political activism, multireligious identity, and since recently, more radicalized views of some of its inhabitants. It specifically looks at youth of a certain age and "at-risk", to gain insights into the drivers that have either pushed them or could be pushing them, towards violent extremism. The study allowed for an analysis of VE drivers that affect young people in a community deemed as a "hotspot", as well as primary data collection with a young demographic, children and youth 12–18 years old and beyond, who have been on a brink or had crossed the invisible and often hidden boundaries that led them to violence. Discussions on drivers of violent extremism with young people constitute a contribution to the field in which the majority of learning comes from "recycled" secondary data as opposed to very little direct contact with communities, youth included.

In Karak, violent extremism literature and research in Jordan did not show as a flashpoint or a location whose population expressed support for violent extremism until 2016. The available, even if albeit scarce existing data (Abu Rumman & Shteiwi, 2018), has shown Karak on the list of "radicalization hotspots", along with the "traditional" locations, such as Ma'an, Zarqa, and parts of Amman (Al Assaf, 2018). The December 2015 incident in which Daesh (ISIS) took Royal Jordanian Air Force Pilot Lt. Muath Al-Kassasbeh as a hostage, and later brutally murdered him, resounded throughout his hometown of Karak. The 2016 deadly terrorist attack on the city's famous Castle, for which ISIS claimed responsibility (Monte Carlo Doualiya, 2016), revealed that four of the perpetrators were residents of the city, raising concerns about the extent to which radical ideology and extremism implanted itself among the younger population.

In Jordan, Karak has long been known for its history of political activism, with politics exercised through the tribes, the most important and powerful sociopolitical structure in the governorate (Gubser, 1986). Although Karak witnessed its tribal powers decline in recent years (Alterman, 2019), their pull is still important in the country. Furthermore, Karak has a relatively significant Christian population, with a solid, historical record of Christian-Muslim's peaceful coexistence and interdependence (Luck, 2017). The choice of Karak as a case study on the meso level allows for examining the role of religious reference as a factor that can enhance or dismantle the processes of polarization regarding "other" groups or religious communities.

Likewise, macro-level analysis findings disclosed the state's strong focus on the dimension of security. In this area, too, Karak provides a compelling case to explore, particularly in relation to the traditional state-centered security in opposition to the provisions of human security (economic, political, social, etc.) (Bondokji & AlHaj, 2019). The city was central to the 1989 events in Jordan, as it was the second city to rise and join the protests that originated in Ma'an, following the price increase of fuel, other commodities, and food products (Andoni, 1989). Similarly, the city was occupied by the army in light of the 1996 so-called "bread riots" and was put under a strict curfew for 11 days, with hundreds of people arrested in connection with the protests (Andoni & Schwedler, 1996). Finally, during the Arab Spring, Jordan has witnessed an active tribal *Hirak* (social movement) (Ramadan, 2021). The *Hirak* in Karak provided an additional venue for investigating the meso-level dynamics relating to political and social participation, with the increasingly difficult socioeconomic situation including unemployment and poverty offering a leeway for examining the employment and labor relations. The challenging socioeconomic context has left a mark on the city which is manifested through the limited opportunities (Milton-Edwards, 2018) for young people, a prevailing inequality (Ramadan, 2021), and a difficult relationship (Yom & Al-Khatib, 2018) between the state and the citizens.

The case study concerning the refugees in Northern Jordan examines drivers of VE that can affect or are affecting Syrian refugees in the two northern cities of Irbid and Mafraq. The case study also examines discrepancies between urban refugees and those living in Za'atari Camp, to analyze the impact of life in a refugee camp on drivers of VE. The research sought to solicit insights and knowledge on several dimensions: the accessibility of services available to them, how they compensate for lacking leisure and cultural activities, the discrepancies in access to these activities between urban refugees and those in the camp, the extent of technological use and digital socialization they experience, refugees' relation with the host community, as well as the life prospects they identify for themselves.

There are 1.3 million Syrian refugees living in Jordan, nearly 20% of the country's population (UNHCR, 2022). Of these, 130.000 live in Za'atari, Emirates Jordanian Camp, and Azraq Camp. The rest live in urban areas, so-called host communities. In addition, not all Syrian refugees register with UNHCR, hence the discrepancy between figures for registered refugees and their total number in Jordan. As the Syrian conflict enters its eleventh year, the situation of Syrian refugees in Jordan is still a source of concern for the international community and the Jordanian government. Despite significant efforts of the international humanitarian sector, some service provision is in shortage. There is no data on the number of refugees who have joined Violent Extremist Organisations (VEOs), and no concrete evidence of radicalization among Syrian refugees in Jordan. However, Jordanian authorities captured members of a Daesh cell that attacked a Jordanian army post near Rukban camp in 2016 (Al Khitan, 2017) located inside Syria on the Syrian-Jordanian border.

The analytical focus for the Syrian refugees in Northern Jordan case study relies on available educational, cultural, and leisure opportunities for them. The shortage of these opportunities impacts on educational and employment prospects for Syrian refugees in the future, despite the eagerness of refugee children to have access to these opportunities (Abu Hamad et al., 2017). By unpacking this driver (education, culture, and leisure opportunities) this case study contributes to examining the threats of VE.

Education, culture, and leisure opportunities are in shortage, particularly for Syrian refugees in the Za'atari camp in particular. In contrast, urban refugees have better access to these opportunities, even if they are not always affordable, either due to the fees required to be paid to access the activities or the high transportation costs. The limited access to these opportunities makes the family the key provider of informal educational opportunities and sometimes leisure activities. Moreover, digital socialization attains prominence among refugees as a potential driver of VE due to the lack of educational, cultural and leisure activities, and due to difficulties of accessing work opportunities. Having nothing else to do, many refugee youths spend considerable hours every day using their mobile phones. This makes them vulnerable to the influence of narratives circulating online, including extremist ones. Although there is no evidence of radicalization among Syrian refugees in Jordan, the finding on this driver points to an important prevention of violent extremism entry point to protect against radicalization among refugee youth. Digital socialization increases the potential impact of transnational dynamics because of widely spread narratives of victimization, the views of injustice regarding fellow Syrians and Muslims, and the news about atrocities in Syria that are communicated online. In addition, Syrian refugees are proud of their Syrian identity and culture, identify with relatives and friends who are still in Syria and are empathetic to their plight, in addition to their sense of frustration with their status as refugees.

In the case study regarding the female preachers in Ma'an, the focus is on how drivers of VE affect women preachers in the governorate of Ma'an, as a unique segment of female actors in the radicalization process. However, it should be noted from the outset that this case study does not assume that preachers contribute to radicalization. In fact, the findings shed more light on their role in C/PVE efforts. There are two different types of female preachers operating in two parallel structures in Jordan. There is a "formal" type that is part of the official state structures through its affiliation to the Ministry of *Awqaf*, Islamic Affairs and Holy Places. They are the ones appointed by security and military agencies, within the military and security ranks, who are typically part of the Women Police Unit (Jordan Times, 2017). They have greater access to the existing state structures, such as schools, youth centers, hospitals, etc. They are paid by the Ministry and have to report their activities monthly. While the "informal" type exercises preaching and Islamic missionary roles voluntarily, often affiliated with Islamic groups such as the Salafi stream or the Muslim Brotherhood. This also includes Sufis and other groups active in Jordan, most notably the all-women preaching group of Al-Qubaysiat (Al-Qubaysiat, 2017). This group is neither appointed nor acknowledged by formal structures—civil or military—and is pushed to operate outside said structures and take on a more personalized, communal role based on their own relations and networks. They operate in a decentralized model with unreported/unknown channels of funding, with their numbers not being captured in any official statistics, and their qualifications, geographic distribution, or any other characteristic being scarce, if at all, documented.

The women's role related to VE in Jordan is underestimated, underinvestigated and scarcely acknowledged. In interviews for the macro-level research within the

CONNEKT project, policymakers, including female ones, did not acknowledge how the radicalization process affects women. They simply dismissed the subject of women in general (Mhadeen et al., 2021). Among the factors that deepen the impact of drivers of VE on women in Jordan, the male guardianship system is particularly important in the socioeconomic sense. This system implies that a woman must have a male guardian, normally a father or husband (but in some cases a brother or even a son) who will make all critical decisions on her behalf. Women are subject to ill-treatment if they disobey their male guardians or transgress gender norms, with measures ranging from imprisonment and detention, to separation of the women from their children (Amnesty International, 2019).

Women in Jordan have low economic participation and face imbalanced gender dynamics (Abu Shamma, 2019), and as a consequence, they have unequal access to power and opportunities compared to men. In fact, Jordan has one of the world's lowest rates of women's economic participation, with only 14% of women being engaged in the formal economy, and an additional 15% engaged in the informal economy, according to recent estimates (Jacobs Anderson, 2020). While the evidence on the relation between unemployment and radicalization is inconclusive at best, dissatisfaction about one's income compared to their employment and education is found to contribute to radicalization in Jordan. However, very few studies have examined radicalization specifically among Jordanian women, but two studies have cautioned against women being more vulnerable to extremism and recruitment via social media (Bagenal, 2016). Local evidence points to the influence of partners and despair as factors behind Jordanian young women joining or attempting to join Daesh (ISIS). The male guardianship system mentioned above contributes to both factors. Some Jordanian women left to join Daesh with their husbands who were extremists and their wives simply joined. However, there is also evidence of women who refused to join their husbands. Thus, different levels of women's empowerment have led to the decisions women took in this regard even when the wives were ideologically radical. Like other women in the region, Jordanian women who joined extremist groups have been influenced by the empowerment agenda of Daesh. Although it seems contradictory to the overall ideology of Daesh, it has provided women agency and leadership roles compared to extremist groups like Al-Qaeda that limited the role of women in caring for households. Extremist women across the region were attracted by this unique place for women in an extremist group (Abu Rumman & Abu Hanieh, 2017).

3 Research Methods and Challenges

In all three case studies, primary data was collected based on the findings of CONNEKT's macro-level research phase through Focus Group Discussions (FGDs), where discussions were conducted in a semi-structured manner, giving the respondents the opportunity to freely shape the conversation. The age of the participants varied between 12 and 30 years old, except for the female preacher group which focused on the 22 y/o—60 y/o variation for its specification, and the number of participants varied between 18 and 22 for each case.

In Karak, a sensitive framing of the research was applied, which included looking at the groups of youth who were at risk of joining VEOs. The FGDs were conducted with two groups of, in total, 18 participants, out of which five were female. The first FGD was conducted with eight "at-risk" male youth participants, while the second FGD was conducted with 10 "at-risk" youth with five male and five female participants. The key criteria for their selection were defined as:

1. Having attempted to cross the Jordanian or other borders (towards Syria) to join VEOs,
2. Having been detained in Jordan for expressing support for and/or desire to join VEOs,
3. Having expressed support for and/or desire to join VEOs but faced no detention, and
4. Having gone through informal processes of adopting more moderate religious ideologies.

For the refugees' case study, the key criterion for the selection of participants was defined as being a Syrian refugee in the age bracket of 12–30 y/o living in the two northern cities of Irbid and Mafraq, where the majority of urban Syrian refugees live in Jordan today (UNHCR, 2022). Additionally, the research team sought to engage Syrian refugees of the same age living in a refugee camp, for the purpose of this research in the Za'atari Camp. As a result, the research engaged a group of Syrian refugees, females and males, living in host communities and in the Za'atari refugee camp, of the combined age groups ranging from age 10–23. The common threads among the groups that were interviewed were their long residency in the cities of Irbid and Mafraq, as well as their perspectives as young people living inside the Za'atari Camp.

Primary data was obtained by consulting with two groups: a group of Syrian refugees living in urban settings, aged 13–18 y/o, and a group of young Syrian males living inside the Za'atari camp aged 10–23 y/o. For the urban group, four FGDs with 18 young Syrians (nine males and nine females ensuring a perfect gender balance) were conducted and data collection took place in February 2022. For the group living inside the camp, one FGD was conducted with six males, aged 10–23 y/o. The total number of participants engaged from inside and outside the camps was 24: 9 females and 15 males. The research team was unable to engage females from within the Za'atari camp due to logistical reasons and local gender sensitivities. Data collection for the in-camp group was carried out in April 2022 (during the month of Ramadan).

For the female preachers' case study, the age interval had to surpass the CONNEKT project focus on youth of 12–30 years old, as female preachers attain this role after completing a level of higher education in Islamic law (*Sharia*). Therefore, the youngest possible age in this research sample was 22 years old. Likewise, many female preachers, especially the more experienced and trusted by the community, are older than 30 years. Therefore, the age group for this case study was 22–30+ years old. Primary data was obtained by conducting two FGDs with 23 female preachers who live and operate in the governorate of Ma'an. The first FGD engaged 12 formal preachers and the second FGD engaged with 11 informal preachers. The age group for FGD 1 ranged from 27 to 42 y/o, whilst in FGD 2 participants ranged from 22 to 60 y/o. However, female preachers usually work with families and children that include those between 12–18 years, thus, this case study indirectly examines the influence of female preachers on the radicalization of this age group.

The discussion addressed informal education in Ma'an and the role of female preachers in this informal education. It also explored issues related to digital literacy, the skills of female preachers in using online platforms, and their usage patterns. In the process, references were made to narratives and type of content female preachers engage with. In investigating the preachers' role and access with family members, the discussion sought the self-assessment of preachers on their role and influence on individuals on family patterns and dynamics in Ma'an. Direct questions on the radicalization of female preachers were avoided to maintain a trusting and open discussion with respondents, but the discussion generally referred to VE in Jordan and Ma'an.

The challenges faced while conducting these different case studies referred to recruiting participants in the pre-established age groups, the access to research respondents, and their willingness to participate due to the sensitivity of the approached subjects. In the Karak case study, the access to research respondents, as well as the respondents' willingness to take part in this research in view of its sensibility, limited the representation, resulting in the age range for the first FGD being between 20 and 46 y/o, whilst the age of respondents in the second FGD ranged between 20 and 29 y/o. Nonetheless, the main challenge was first identifying then getting access to and acceptance of youth that are deemed to be "at-risk". This was due to the sensitivity of discussions with youth who were involved with VEOs, and the security access and clearance to conduct FGDs with them.

In conducting the research with Syrian refugees, the first challenge concerned gathering the parental/guardian assents for research respondents under 18 y/o, which required time, in addition to requiring additional information sessions to explain the purpose of the project, why the assent was needed, provide reassurances about the data being anonymized. In both cases, the research team faced the challenge of presenting the research and its objectives in a simple, neutral, and context-sensitive manner that had to ensure that young respondents would not be stigmatized, would not be exposed to the appeal of VE, and to explain that the added value of their participation would not offer something tangible in return. Whilst in the female preachers' case, the project faced challenges with securing official clearances due to the high sensitivity regarding both the group being selected to take part in the research, and the topics being discussed. By liaising with local partners and the Ministry of *Awqaf*, the research was conducted in a familiar-for-respondents setting provided by one of the local partners, with locally trusted female facilitators engaging respondents in the discussions. As a result, the selection of participants was influenced by the knowledge and relations of the local partners with some of the respondents. This did not affect the quality of the discussion or findings, but an element of bias in the selection of respondents is probable although not objectively established.

4 Results

4.1 Shrinking Civil Space and Unemployment in Karak

In Karak, two contexts of social interaction are directly linked to radicalization processes. In terms of cultural and leisure activities, respondents mentioned the shrinking civil space across Jordan, due mostly to freedom of speech restrictions and COVID-19, which narrowed civic interactions and diminished space for civic activism. While in terms of employment and labor relations, unemployment is seen as a factor that limits access to a decent level of social welfare. In 2020, Jordan's economic growth is at 2%, projected to either stagnate or go below that percentage, and the unemployment of young people is at 52% (Challenge Fund for Youth Employment, 2021). Consequently, young, educated males and females are faced with a frustrating situation in which there are very few jobs that could employ them. In addition to that, participants mentioned "security procedures" as a factor that contributes to individuals being denied security clearances for jobs, hence remaining unemployed, due to "their history or their family history". Here, "history" refers to the individual's record, or that of his/her relative, in being linked to VE or VEOs, or generally being "critical" against the government or its policies.

When it comes to the meso-level results, the findings show that the VE drivers such as economic deprivation and territorial inequalities are the most significant. Economic deprivation "carved" a space for itself in the PVE strategies and national action plans discussed in macro-level analysis, through economic empowerment actions. However, participants cited the inability of the government and its policies to address the question of economic deprivation and unemployment, as they did not take into consideration the youth's expectations. Such an approach in fact further reinforces the issue of economic deprivation as opposed to addressing it, according to the participants. With respect to territorial inequalities, it was noticeably cited as a factor of distance from the capital, Amman, which turned out to be an impediment to economic growth and development. Overall, the way the two macro-level drivers of territorial inequalities and economic deprivation seem to work at the meso level is by fuelling the youth's sense of alienation, as they feel discriminated against and outcasted. Whilst territorial inequalities present in Karak do negatively impact cultural and leisure activities as well as employment and labour relations, there seems to be a positive development in recent times. The notable move towards digital space, caused by the COVID-19 pandemic has made more jobs available online. This was seen as a potential shift by research respondents as online opportunities could contribute to overcoming the barrier of distance to/from the capital.

When questioned about the most relevant prevention indicators, respondents listed family as the first and foremost preventative factor deterring young people from turning to violent extremism. The state was noted as the second layer of prevention due to its capacity to account for the consequences of one's actions not only in terms of potential imprisonment or individual suffering but also, interestingly, in the context of collective consequences. The state has the power to deny access to employment opportunities due to a "red flag on your security record" but is equally able to do the same for one's relatives who do not necessarily have anything to do with the choice of one of their family members to join VEOs or harboring support for VE/VEOs. The third prevention indicator listed by respondents was religion, as the pillar of Islamic teachings and philosophy of religion asks to pursue and persist, and not to steal, kill, or do harm to others. Respondents stated that narrow socioeconomic prospects, the lack of a better alternative, or the marginalization they felt as individuals were the factors that could push them toward VE.

When asked about the specific options that might result from the prevention indicators mentioned above, participants noted that these should be derived from the positive shifts they see in their local community. The first positive shift the participants noted was the changing, more positive attitude towards community-based organizations (CBOs) and their work in the local community, cementing the culture of volunteering and active citizenship. The second positive reaction relates to the role of females in society. Whilst indeed females are still facing social restrictions, there is on the other side, increased presence, and activism of females in the local community of Karak. Families are slowly becoming more accepting of females joining the armed forces or police, despite the highly patriarchal nature of the community in Karak. The third micro path relates to young people's greater embracing and use of digital spaces to generate income by selling homemade and other products and services. This is a way of supporting individual initiatives that seek positive alternatives to the negative socioeconomic situation, which is deemed responsible for pushing young people towards VE and VEOs pathways.

4.2 The Role of Education, Culture, and Leisure Opportunities, and Digital Socialization for Refugees in Northern Jordan

The data collected through the refugees in Northern Jordan case study shows intersections between three drivers: education, culture, and leisure opportunities, transnational dynamics and digital socialization. As discussed earlier, Syrian refugees have limited access to educational, leisure, and cultural opportunities. A few available opportunities are also not largely accessible to Syrian refugees due to their geographical distance (in the case of urban settings) or limited freedom of movement (in the case of living inside the camps). In addition, the transportation costs and financial fees that need to be paid to access these opportunities make them de facto inaccessible. Overall, educational, leisure, and cultural opportunities seem to be available in principle, yet hard to access in practice due to different factors. Some of these factors are institutional, such as the opportunities not being widely offered in schools or being offered via formal channels of education, while other factors point to logistics, such as living in remote urban areas distant from the city center where these opportunities are concentrated or residing in refugee camps. Not to mention the financial hardships as young refugees (or their families) are simply not able to afford these opportunities (the price of a course and/or price of transportation fees, for example).

Refugees consider these opportunities as a key element to their social mobility. To compensate for this shortage, they spend more time online. This in return makes digital socialization the most prominent factor when examining the potential impact of VE drivers on radicalization of youth in two ways. First, respondents seem to have a positive view of technology when it comes to accessing education, culture, and leisure opportunities. Of the females engaged in the study, 44% mentioned that they take free English lessons online to improve their language skills, 22% of males mentioned taking online courses on coding programs such as C++, and learning about bitcoins and digital currency investment, while 27% of the respondents from a mixed group of males and females cited YouTube channels and online courses as source of their non-academic learning. However, the findings point to a notable discrepancy in the role of digital socialization based on the place of refugees' residence, as Za'atari camp respondents reported making little to no usage of technology for the same purposes. Second, the internet is "there" to fill the free time of refugees—and free time is abundant, particularly for refugees in Za'atari camp. Using mobile phones as the only option during idle time makes refugees vulnerable to radicalization, if they are specifically targeted. As militants generally tend to recruit youth in refugee camps (Sude, 2021), PVE efforts must focus on this. For this reason, PVE efforts should provide recreational and cultural activities to protect young refugees based in the camps against recruitment; to enhance refugees' self-esteem and hope; and to offer avenues for self-development and skills development and attainment.

Heavy reliance on the internet (digital socialization) as a medium used to fill idle time increases the influence of transnational dynamics as a potential driver for VE among Syrian refugee youth. Participants in this case study were all proud to be Syrians. Their identification with the (in)group, when combined with a heavy sense of victimization, might lead to radicalization, if other radicalization factors are at play (Falkowski & Lang, 2015). The transnational dynamics, therefore, when influenced by digital socialization, might potentially lead to radicalization among Syrian refugees. However, the findings show positive perceptions about Jordan and Jordanians among Syrian refugees. This protects to a certain extent from radicalization, particularly. For example, the refugees who participated in the research acknowledged a much better situation compared to Syrian refugees in other countries in the region or to Syrians still in Syria. The meso-level analysis also shows that the family plays a primary role in shaping informal education amongst the young refugee respondents. Families, therefore, can help instill and develop views and values that could protect youth against radicalization, but there is no evidence that they encourage or harbor radical views.

The first prevention indicator listed was the notable positive relationship with, and perception of, Jordanians amongst young Syrian refugees. As noted by the respondents, most of the young Syrians today are now speaking with the Jordanian dialect, and it reflects how integrated the young Syrians feel in Jordanian society. This social capital should be tapped into when discussing PVE efforts amongst urban Syrian refugees. Second, as families play an integral role in shaping the formal and informal education of refugee youth, effective C/PVE efforts should engage with parents, male and female figures alike, to instill transformation skills, critical thinking, and empowerment of refugee youth and children. Third, the positive view of the police and the expressed desire by some female participants to join the force, and the positive outlook and wide acceptance of the local police among some participants, could be used to improve C/PVE efforts. They could focus on the institutional participation of Syrian refugees inside and outside the camps. This should not be limited to C/PVE goals but could also enhance social cohesion, respect for law and order, and local ownership of local security efforts. Fourth, the enhancement of basic services inside the camp(s) should be a C/PVE priority. Participants living in the Za'atari camp were referring to the "frequent electricity cuts", installing "air conditioning units inside the caravans", building a public "swimming pool for youngsters", extending "the duration of the exit permit[3]", and "forgoing the fees for issuing a work permit". All seem possible intervention measures that would enhance their quality of life and keep them busy, avoiding spending an entire day on their mobile phones and not contributing positively to society.

Given that this case study focused on two distinct groups, one of urban refugees in Irbid and Mafraq, and another settled in the Za'atari camp the options envisioned were not identical. Urban refugees have a sharper understanding of their individualized paths ahead when compared to those living inside the camp. Urban refugees in Mafraq and Irbid named specific professional pathways they wish to undertake, such as "becoming a petroleum engineer in the UAE", a "lawyer", a "doctor", a "fashion designer", an "economist", a "policewoman [although not possible in Jordan for Syrian refugees]", or an "English teacher". Their options were outward looking using the "I" single pronoun. In contrast, those living inside the camp displayed a genuine struggle to name one specific professional career goal. In fact, the question seemed to have taken them by surprise as something they had not thought about or considered before. After a short silence, they timidly shared thoughts about what "they"—in the plural pronoun—wish to have, not to be, to enhance their life prospects. Options included a swimming pool, air conditioning units, having electricity at school or extended duration of the exit permit when they go outside the camp for leisure or family visits. At best, the most personal articulation of all was "lowered fees for issuing my work permit". The options of camp refugees were

[3]Currently, an exit permit to go out for visits or for seeking leisure opportunities outside the camp is granted for 7 days only, while the refugees are asking for it to be valid 15 days or more.

defined by their group identification as refugees in Za'atari, using the "we" plural pronoun. It is unclear whether these insights on individual pathways are driven by the greater possibility of realizing one's ambitions outside camps in the case of urban refugees, or by the stark contrast of limited opportunities and social mobility for those living inside the camps. However, it was clear that options amongst young Syrian refugees are determined by the role of the individual's relationship with their immediate social environment and the individual internalization of the conditions, drivers, and messages which are of relevance to one's life prospects.

4.3 The Discrepancy Between Formal and Informal Female Preachers in Ma'an

The analysis of meso-level drivers has revealed the prominence of three drivers: digital socialization, transnational dynamics, and territorial inequality in relation to the work of female preachers in Ma'an. In addition, religion as a driver of VE directly intersects with these drivers because of the informal religious educational role the preachers play. These drivers interact with three social contexts in the governorate: socialization/education, employment and labor relations, and urban and peri-urban areas.

The focus on female preachers in this case study goes against the state's presumption of religion as the main driver of VE in relation to preachers. It highlights how structural and even regional dynamics can affect the radicalization of female preachers, who might then influence the radicalization of their audiences, whether these are youth between 12–30 years or family members of the youth. Radicalization is a family phenomenon in Jordan (Abu Rumman & Shteiwi, 2018). Therefore, the relations that female preachers have with female family members are crucial to radicalization dynamics, and equally to PVE efforts.

There are six main findings in this study. The first is the discrepancy between the formal and informal structures in which female preachers operate in Ma'an. The informal preachers' limited access to services and capacity building and educational opportunities, as well as the security scrutiny they are subjected to, are deeply frustrating informal preachers who feel unappreciated and neglected. The second relates to the discrepancy when it comes to the digital socialization spectrum. For the informal group, using/integrating technology into their preaching and missionary work is part of their routine, as they have been denied access to official state structures. In contrast, the formal group has a more recent engagement with communication technologies. There has been a notable improvement as a result of the COVID-19 pandemic, but that does extend to engaging with social media and internet narratives relevant to the radicalization process. Third, as a result of the marginalization of informal preachers and their digital literacy, they reached educational online opportunities offered by entities and/or Islamic groups in the region and built networks of peers in the region. This digital space can lead to the radicalization of female preachers, who can radicalize their audiences. The same applies to formal preachers who expanded their online activities during and after COVID-19. Fourth, the online access and reach of female preachers make them susceptible to the influence of transnational dynamics in identifying with religious groups, building peer networks, and finding empowerment and appreciation denied to them by state structures. Extremist narratives that build on religious interpretations or political Muslim grievances can attract female preachers and indoctrinate them. Fifth, perceptions of territorial inequalities are evident among preachers, but more pronounced among informal preachers who feel alienated by state structures as preachers in addition to the general marginalization perceived in Ma'an. This contributes to their frustration and anger towards the state. Sixth, preachers encourage women to be housewives. In their estimate, unemployment is more dangerous to male members. Women should focus on traditional roles and the religious education of family members. These views contribute to the economic deprivation of households, which overall contributes to radicalization. It also indirectly reinforces Daesh's empowering narrative for women, whereby Daesh offers unique active agency for women.

Potential entries for prevention indicators are mainly centered around the use of technology and digital communication amongst both formal and informal female preachers as it provides a relevant entry for prevention and combatting radical thought/ideology. In addition, any form of regulating/institutionalizing or recognizing informal preachers will help assess and understand the nature of how digitalization is affecting female preachers and to offer alternate avenues for capacity building, empowerment, and developing trusted peer networks. Given the sensitivities regarding the respondents and the subject matter, respondents were not asked to directly comment on drivers of radicalization. However, four drivers can be identified: digital socialization, transnational dynamics through online peer groups, and territorial inequalities felt by citizens of Ma'an, as well as informal religious education that can promote interpretations justifying violence against the religious "other."

5 Conclusion

The case studies in Jordan reveal a complex interplay of drivers in their impact on three segments of the population in local communities: vulnerable youth, Syrian refugees, and female preachers. The Karak case study opted for understanding the resilience factors affecting a group of vulnerable youth (at risk of radicalization), some of which have a proven past record of an explicit appeal to radical thought or behavior. The meso-level analysis has revealed that no single driver is present in Karak, rather it is the combination of several drivers that explains the meso-level situation. Namely, the most prominent drivers in Karak are the ones of territorial inequalities and economic deprivation. In turn, such drivers interact within diverse contexts of social interaction, such as cultural and leisure activities as well as employment and labor relations and, as a result, seem to produce greater frustration, lack of hope, and a strong sense of social injustice amongst youth. Youth's idle time remains a strong driver limiting the constructive life prospects for young adults in Karak, as it feeds off the drug use and the VE drivers. The COVID-19 pandemic has equally been mentioned as a prominent factor, as it limited movement and activities bringing as a result a "miserable" economic situation, further exacerbating the impact of economic deprivation. Nepotism in Karak also seems to play a key role in driving economic deprivation as it negatively impacts employment prospects and labor relations and seems to further cement the already-existing lack of development. The research participants noted the following three key prevention actors: family, state, and religion. The family was seen as the first and foremost preventive factor deterring young people from pursuing the appeal of violent extremism. The respondents are/were deterred by the thought that their actions might bring shame and discomfort to their immediate relatives, or potentially taint the reputation of their tribe at large. The state was noted as the second layer of prevention, as it has the potential of imprisoning individuals, and thus causing individual suffering. Religion was the third noted prevention actor, as participants explained that the strong religious motif serves(ed) as a key prevention indicator to pursuing the VE pathway. Religious ideology was barely associated with violent extremism. Rather, it was the narrow socioeconomic prospects, the lack of hope, or the marginalization they felt as individuals that would be more appealing. Finally, participants noted that preventive interventions should look for and support individual initiatives that seek positive alternatives to the negative socioeconomic situation, which is deemed responsible for pushing young people towards violent extremism and VEOs pathways.

The refugees in Northern Jordan case study sought to examine the case of young Syrian refugees in Jordan, inside and outside the refugee camps. This subnational group provides a fitting case for understanding a community-level context that allows for testing the social factors that could potentially feed patterns of violent extremism amongst this group, and determine relations between the national, community, and individual dimensions of the CONNEKT research project. With Syrian refugees constituting nearly 20% of Jordan's population, it was simply impossible to overlook the C/PVE and VE dynamics amongst this group. Yet, the case study considered the notable sensitivities that are typically associated with this topic and sought to carefully avoid stigmatizing the refugee population or feeding the prejudices and stereotypes around refugees in Jordan, particularly Syrian refugees. The analysis of meso-level VE drivers revealed that three drivers are at play amongst young Syrian refugees: educational, leisure, and cultural opportunities; transnational dynamics; and digital socialization. The third driver of digital socialization offers a new window for understanding this subnational group as it seems to have gained increased prominence that has not been captured in the macro-level analysis.

The insights solicited from the respondents clarify that the family is the first and most prominent "shaper" of their identities and growth opportunities. Captured across the three macro-level drivers examined in this case study (education, culture, and leisure opportunities; transnational dynamics; and digital socialization), the family supports formal and informal education of youth refugees. Notable gender variations were also revealed. Family support in formal education is gender segregated, whereas female family members take full responsibility for the informal education of children and youth. Additionally, a clear variation was noted in the availability, quality, and nature of educational, cultural, and leisure activities provided to young Syrian refugees, inside and outside refugee camps. Opportunities are more abundant for urban refugees. Inside the camps, cultural, leisure and informal educational opportunities are very limited or not widely available, therefore, the respondents indirectly alluded to their feeling of entrapment. However, the refugees inside the camp exhibited a level of self-awareness and reconciliation—or unspoken despair—with the situation they were in, which would require further research. Generally, though, Syrian refugees voiced positive views about Jordan, and this positive outlook should be a key area to capitalize on in C/PVE efforts to strengthen social cohesion. Finally, as drivers of violent extremism, both digital socialization and transnational dynamics offer a clear channel for shaping the identities, motivation, and solidarity amongst young Syrians in Jordan. Transnational dynamics are evident from the sense of victimization of Syrians, feelings of sympathy and identification with the plight of Syrians still living in the conditions of war, and the pride in their own shared Syrian identity. This case study provides no evidence of radicalization due to transnational dynamics, but these might be at play if and when a Syrian individual develops radical ideas. Likewise, digital socialization is a determinant factor in examining drivers of VE among Syrian refugees, not because of concrete evidence on this, but rather due to the high level of consumption of digital media. This is apparent from testimonials of young refugees spending long hours using their mobile phones as they cannot pursue other educational and leisure activities, or due to the lack of and difficult access to work opportunities—the abundance of free time increases the risk of radicalization through digital socialization.

Regarding the state approach to radicalization, while the state response focuses on religion as a driver, the female preachers' case study placed more importance on territorial inequalities, digital socialization, and transnational dynamics. Interestingly, and contrary to findings on macro-level drivers of VE, digital socialization stands out as the most crucial driver that can radicalize female preachers, compared to all others. It was hardly addressed or identified by respondents on macro-level drivers as a concern. If female preachers are radicalised, through the identified drivers, combined with their frustrations due to state marginalization of their role and contributions, the preachers can radicalize female youth and their families. The findings do not establish a direct causality but point out plausible causalities in this regard. Research findings also point to several pathways and contributions of female preachers to C/PVE that have to be addressed in future research.

References

Abu Hamad, B., Jones, N., Samuels, F., Gercama, I., Presler-Marshall, E., & Plank, G. (2017). *A promise of tomorrow: The effects of UNHCR and UNICEF cash assistance on Syrian refugees in Jordan*. Oversees Development Institute (ODI).

Abu Rumman, M., & Abu Hanieh, H. (2017). *Infatuated with martyrdom female Jihadism from Al Qaeda to the "Islamic State"*. Friedrich Ebert Stiftung. Retrieved May 7, 2024, from https://library.fes.de/pdf-files/bueros/amman/13303.pdf

Abu Rumman, M., & Shteiwi, M. (2018, December 20). *Sociology of extremism and terrorism in Jordan*. مركز الدراسات الإستراتيجية. Retrieved May 7, 2024, from https://jcss.org/3016/sociology-of-extremism-and-terrorism-in-jordan/

Abu Shamma, F. (2019, August 9). *Women's economic participation in Jordan*. Center for International Private Enterprise. Retrieved May 7, 2024, from https://www.cipe.org/blog/2019/08/09/womens-economic-participation-in-jordan/#:~:text=Despite%20these%20high%20numbers%2C%20women

Al Assaf, R. (2018). *Where are the jihadists in Jordan?* الأنباط. Retrieved May 7, 2024, from https://alanbatnews.net/article/202010

Al Khitan, F. (2017, March 15). *The Rukban Cell and the Perils of the Camp*. جريدة الغد | مصدرك الأول لأخبار الأردن والعالم. Retrieved May 7, 2024, from https://alghad.com/Section-208/uncategorized/The-Rukban-Cell-and-the-Perils-of-the-Camp-96323.

Al Qubaysiat. (2017). *Al Qubaysiat Organization Its Emergence and Formation*. جسور للدراسات. Retrieved May 7, 2024, from https://rb.gy/vyrvn9

Al-Badayneh, A., Alshawi, A. A., & Alhasan, K. (2017). Strains and radicalization among syrians youth refugees in Jordan. *International Journal of Scientific Research, 6*(7), 523.

Alterman, J. (2019). *Ties that bind family, tribe, nation, and the rise of Arab individualism*. Retrieved May 7, 2024, from https://csis-website-prod.s3.amazonaws.com/s3fs-public/publication/Alterman_Loyalty_interior_v8_WEB_FULL.pdf

Amnesty International. (2019, October 23). Jordan: End arbitrary detention of women who disobey male guardians or have unsanctioned relationships. Retrieved May 7, 2024, from https://www.amnesty.org/en/latest/news/2019/10/jordan-end-arbitrary-detention-of-women-who-disobey-male-guardians-or-have-unsanctioned-relationships

Andoni, L. (1989, April 21). 10 Reported Dead in Riots in Jordan. *The Washington Post*. Retrieved May 7, 2024, from https://www.washingtonpost.com/archive/politics/1989/04/21/10-reported-dead-in-riots-in-jordan/e2a7415d-acf9-468d-be6a-328522ad6b03/

Andoni, L., & Schwedler, J. (1996, December 21). *Bread riots in Jordan*. MERIP. Retrieved May 7, 2024, from https://merip.org/1996/12/bread-riots-in-jordan/.

Bagenal, F. (2016, September 20). *In Jordan, women more vulnerable to effects of extremism, says report*. Women and Girls. Retrieved May 7, 2024, from https://deeply.thenewhumanitarian.org/womenandgirls/articles/2016/09/20/in-jordan-women-more-vulnerable-to-effects-of-extremism-says-report

Bondokji, D. N., & AlHaj Ahmad L. (2019). *Determinants of human security and state-centric security in Karak*. Retrieved May 7, 2024, from https://wanainstitute.org/sites/default/files/publications/Publication_HSKarak_English.pdf

Bondokji, D. N., Wilkinson, K., & Aghabi, L. (2017). *Trapped between destructive choices: Radicalisation drivers affecting youth in Jordan*. WANA Institute - West Asia, North Africa Forum. Retrieved May 7, 2024, from https://wanainstitute.org/en/publication/trapped-between-destructive-choices-radicalisation-drivers-affecting-youth-jordan

Challenge Fund for Youth Employment. (2021). *Jordan Scoping Report*. Retrieved May 7, 2024, from https://fundforyouthemployment.nl/wp-content/uploads/2021/02/Scoping-Report-Jordan-2021-Challenge-Fund-for-Youth-Employment.pdf

Combaz, E. (2015). *Helpdesk Research Report Extremist radicalisation towards non-state political violence in Jordan*. Retrieved May 7, 2024, from https://www.academia.edu/28888156/Helpdesk_Report_Extremist_Radicalisation_towards_Non_State_Political_Violence_in_Jordan?hb-sb-sw=28887224

Falkowski, M., & Lang, J. (2015, September 21). *Homo Jihadicus*. OSW Centre for Eastern Studies. Retrieved May 7, 2024, from https://www.osw.waw.pl/en/publikacje/osw-report/2015-09-21/homo-jihadicus

Funk, M., & Parkes, R. (2016). *Syrian refugee flows—And ebbs*. European Union Institute for Security Studies (EUISS). Retrieved May 7, 2024, from https://www.files.ethz.ch/isn/195868/Alert_5_Refugee_flows.pdf

Ghboun, H. (2014, June 22). *A March in Ma'an "to Support ISIS" confuses Jordan's Jihadists, and the Authorities Sound the Alarm*. CNN Arabic. Retrieved May 7, 2024, from https://arabic.cnn.com/middleeast/2014/06/22/jordan-rally-pro-isis.

Grieve, C. (2016, December 2). *Meet the Female Sheikhas Tackling Islamic Extremism in Jordan*. SBS. Retrieved May 7, 2024, from https://www.sbs.com.au/topics/voices/culture/article/2016/11/28/meet-female-sheikhas-tackling-islamic-extremism-jordan.

Gubser, P. (1986). *Politics and change in Alkarak, Jordan. A study of a small Arab town and its district*. Routledge.

Jacobs Anderson, A. (2020). Promoting women's economic activity in Jordan. *The Washington Institute*. Retrieved May 7, 2024, from https://www.washingtoninstitute.org/policy-analysis/promoting-womens-economic-activity-jordan

Jordan Times. (2017, November 5). *Awqaf minister opens workshop for female preachers*. Retrieved May 7, 2024, from https://www.jordantimes.com/news/local/awqaf-minister-opens-workshop-female-preachers

Katulis, B., Lang, H., & Awad, M. (2024, April 18). Gatekeeper of the Jihad. *Foreign Policy*. Retrieved May 7, 2024, from https://foreignpolicy.com/2014/04/18/gatekeeper-of-the-jihad

Luck, T. (2017, May 23). In Jordanian city hit by ISIS, old lessons on Christian-Muslim coexistence. *Christian Science Monitor*. Retrieved May 7, 2024, from https://www.csmonitor.com/World/Middle-East/2017/0523/In-Jordanian-city-hit-by-ISIS-old-lessons-on-Christian-Muslim-coexistence

Madison Springfield Inc. (2017). Factors impacting propensity and influence pathways toward violent extremism in Jordan. Retrieved May 7, 2024, from https://jordankmportal.com/resources/factors-impacting-propensity-and-influence-pathways-toward-violent-extremism-in-jordan.

Mhadeen, B., Feisal, A., & Štikovac Clark, J. (2021). CONNEKT country paper on macro-level drivers: Jordan. Retrieved May 7, 2024, from https://h2020connekt.eu/wp-content/uploads/2021/09/Jordan_CONNEKT_Macro_Drivers.pdf.

Milton-Edwards, B. (2018, June 6). *Marginalized youth: Toward an inclusive Jordan*. Brookings. Retrieved May 7, 2024, from https://www.brookings.edu/research/marginalized-youth-toward-an-inclusive-jordan/.

Monte Carlo Doualiya. (2016, December 20). تنظيم "الدولة الإسلامية" يتبنى هجوم الكرك في الأردن. مونت كارلو الدولية. [ISIL adopts the Karak attack in Jordan]. Monte Carlo Doualiya. https://tinyurl.com/bdck7d3h

Osborne, A. (2017). *Ma'an: Dangerous or just desperate?* WANA Institute - West Asia, North Africa Forum. Retrieved May 7, 2024, from https://wanainstitute.org/en/blog/maan-dangerous-or-just-desperate

Perrin, J.-P. (2021). *Why we care: An overview of the distribution of unpaid care work in Ma'an, Southern Jordan*. Oxfam Policy & Practice. Retrieved May 7, 2024, from https://policy-practice.oxfam.org/resources/why-we-care-an-overview-of-the-distribution-of-unpaid-care-work-in-maan-souther-621199/

Ramadan, R. (2021). *Determinants of income inequality in Jordan*. Economic Research Forum. Retrieved May 7, 2024, from https://erf.org.eg/publications/determinants-of-income-inequality-in-jordan/

Sude, B. H. (2021). Prevention of radicalization to terrorism in refugee camps and asylum centers. In A. P. Schmid (Ed.), *Handbook of prevention and preparedness*. The International Centre for Counter-Terrorism (ICCT).

UNHCR. (2022). *Operational data portal*. Retrieved May 7, 2024, from https://data.unhcr.org/ar/situations/syria/location/36

Yom, S., & Al-Khatib, W. (2018, August 2). *The politics of youth policymaking in Jordan*. Project on Middle East Political Science. Retrieved May 7, 2024, from https://pomeps.org/the-politics-of-youth-policymaking-in-jordan

Meso-Level Dynamics and the Drivers of Violent Extremism in Egypt

Maye Kassem

1 Introduction

Radicalization and Violent Extremism (VE) are not new phenomena in Egypt. The roots of VE stem back from the creation of the Society of Muslim Brothers (Munson, 2001; Salem, 2018), more commonly known as the Muslim Brotherhood (MB). The Society was established and licensed as a charitable organisation in Egypt in 1928 by Hassan El Bana. The objective of the founder was to "guide Muslims back to the true religion [of Islam], and away from the corrupt aspirations and conduct created by European dominance" (Zubaida, 1989: 35). This organization was the cornerstone of what would become future Islamist organizations within and outside Egypt (Mitchell, 1963). For the first time since its establishment, the MB acquired legal status as a political party immediately following the fall of the Mubarak presidency in 2011. The party, titled the Freedom and Justice Party, participated in the presidential elections of 2012 with its chairman, Mohamed Morsi becoming the new president of the Republic (Al-Anani, 2015). The new presidency did not last long as Morsi was overthrown in 2013, following a vast movement of popular protests supported by the military, led by the then newly appointed Defense Minister. The Freedom and Justice Party was legally disbanded and, in 2014, the Egyptian State went on to officially declare the entire MB a terrorist organization (Jaraba, 2014).

Since the overthrow and disbanding of the MB and the rise of Defense Minister Abdel Fattah al-Sisi to the Presidency in 2014, Egypt witnessed a prominent increase in VE. Most of the terrorist attacks were predominantly concentrated in the Northern part of the Sinai Peninsula (Torelli, 2015). The Matrouh Coast (which incorporates the Egyptian-Libyan borders) also became, albeit to a lesser degree

M. Kassem (✉)
AUC, Cairo, Egypt
e-mail: mayekasm@aucegypt.edu

C. Torrekens et al. (eds.), *Social Contexts of Radicalization and Violent Extremism in the MENA and Balkans*,
https://doi.org/10.1007/978-3-031-84521-5_4

than north Sinai, a significant area of VE operations. While those operations in these areas share similar characteristics to the VE attacks in south Sinai in the late 1990–2000s, following the split of *Tanzim al-Jihad* and *al-Jama'a al-Islamiyah* (Drevon, 2015), the context scale, and motives behind these attacks were more intense and complicated than what Egypt previously witnessed. In response, the Egyptian state-initiated efforts for combating radicalisation and VE through various pillars, which can be summarized as follows: security, legal, religious and socioeconomic development interlinked with state-civil society partnerships. The security, legal and religious pillars became the state's direct means of curbing extremist violence. In other words, through direct combative actions, legal provisions defining extremist violence and restructuring religious education, the state adjusted its approach to incorporate a more comprehensive line of action to counter this new escalation of VE. It must be stressed that all major state policies and initiatives emanate from the Executive Office of the President with the personal approval and support of the President. It is the role of state institutions to follow these directions and implement, expand, and refine them according to their respective capacity and resources.

In regard to state security institutions, the Egyptian Ministry of Defense, is the institution responsible for managing the affairs of the Egyptian Armed Forces. It also handles the affairs of military colleges, the recruitment and mobilization of veterans, and the management of military production in Egypt. The Egyptian Ministry of Interior, supervises law enforcement and internal security, including the Public Security Sector Police, the Central Security Force, the National Security Sector and the Passports, Immigration, and Nationality Administration. It should be noted that the National Security Sector of the Ministry is also responsible for internal security threats and counterterrorism along with other security services.

According to a report from the Ministry of Interior (State Information Service, 2020), the security apparatus managed to eliminate 1500 terrorist outposts and arrested 22,000 terrorists in possession of large quantities of weapons, ammunition, explosive materials, and explosive devices between 2014–2017. According to the same report, Egypt has witnessed a sharp decrease in terrorist attacks from 481 attacks in 2014 to 22 attacks reported in 2017 (State Information Service, 2020). It appears that since 2021, the counterterrorism operations have succeeded in maintaining a solid grip on VE attacks rendering them inconsequential to the stability of Egypt (U.S. Department of State, 2021).

In regard to the non-combative pillars, the legislative framework constitutes the most significant aspect that has enabled the state to directly intervene in combating radicalization and VE. Article 237 of the 2014 Constitution, for example, stipulates that "the state commits to fighting all types and forms of terrorism and tracking its sources of funding within a specific time frame in light of the threat it represents to the nation and citizens" (The Tahrir Institute for Middle East Policy, 2019). Moreover, the establishment of Law 8/2015 in February defined terrorist entities as "any association, organization, group, gang, cell or other grouping that, through any means, inside or outside the country, calls for the harming of individuals; the spreading of terror; or the endangering of the lives, freedoms, rights, or security of the people" (Buchanan, 2015). According to article 2 of the same law, a terrorist is "an individual who calls for or involves themselves in harming the environment; natural resources; antiquities; the communication infrastructure; and land; air; or sea transportation or harming or seizure of public or private funds, buildings, or properties" (Buchanan, 2015). The subsequent introduction of Law 94/2015 in August of the same year elaborates further. Consisting of 54 articles, it set a sweeping legal and procedural framework to cover this phenomenon, including the creation of special courts to adjudicate cases specifically linked to this matter (Ministry of Foreign Affairs, 2021).

Equally important, the legal aspect was utilised to regulate religious activities in Egypt. Regarding the traditional religious institutions, Al-Azhar (est. 970 AD), is the oldest leading Islamic institution in the world and one of the main reference bodies in Sunni Islamic affairs along with *Dar al-Ifta* (est. 1895), which is Egypt's formal governmental Islamic advisory and regulating body. Prior to becoming an independent state institution, *Dar al-Ifta* was the Islamic branch of the Ministry of Justice. The Ministry of Endowments and Islamic Affairs (*Awqaf*, est. 1835), constitutes the third main religious institution in Egypt. The role of the Ministry of Endowments is twofold. First, it is responsible for the creation and investment of Islamic assets that comprise endowments intended to provide socioeconomic assistance to the underprivileged. Second, the Ministry of Endowments is responsible for the overall supervision and regulation of mosques in Egypt (El Beheery, 2017; Shorouk News, 2017). The post-2013 religious-based reforms include but are not limited to the implementation of Law 52/2014 (to prohibit preaching in mosques without a state license) allowing the Ministry of Endowments and Islamic Affairs (*Awqaf*) the legal authority to supervise and regulate those who preach in mosques. This, in turn, led in 2015 to revoke the license of 55.000 preachers whose sermons were believed to entice radicalism and VE (Radwan, 2015). Religious organizations were also created, such as the inauguration in 2015 of the Al-Azhar Observatory for Combating Extremism, and in 2017 the establishment *Dar al-Ifta al Misriyyah*, an institution directed to ensure the correct translation of religious texts and advocate moderation in religious sermons. These state initiatives were implemented to ratify unmediated state involvement in the practice of religion and its interpretation. Indeed, it is not religion, but rather, the misinterpretation of religion due to the lack of religious knowledge, that is deemed by the Egyptian state as a fundamental driver behind the rise of VE globally. It is worth noting that before such direct intervention, local disadvantaged communities had, for decades, depended upon the religious teachings of informal schools and mosques. These informal entities were largely subsidized by local Islamic charities due to insufficient state funding and lax state monitoring.

In addition, the development of socioeconomic initiatives interlinked with state-civil society partnerships began to be utilized as a soft power tactic by the Egyptian state as a supplementary measure to further target the root causes of VE. Economic deprivation and unemployment are examples of such root causes that potentially make youth susceptible to extremist narratives (Adelaja & George, 2020). Employment statistics suggest that the informal sector is the first, and often only, choice for youth with poor education attainment levels. It can be argued that youth unemployment can potentially increase crime in society and is likely to be a driver of radicalization and VE (Suleiman, 2022). In a context where there are more than 21.9 million youth between the ages of 18 and 29 years old (constituting 21% of the total population) (State Information Service, 2023), it appears evident through the adoption of these soft power measures that the state acknowledged the need to expand its policies towards VE beyond its dependence on the security pillar.

Indicative of this soft approach, the Egyptian government sought to invest in concrete actions that target socioeconomic factors in marginalized communities including borderland communities and informal settlements. The increase in VE activities within the Northern part of the Sinai Peninsula in 2013, made the area not only a combative zone but also a priority for socioeconomic assistance. This aspect is reflected for example in the establishment of its "Constructing the Bedouin Developmental Communities" that started in 2017 (Daily News Egypt, 2020). In parallel, the Ministry of Defense, the Ministry of Social Solidarity, the Ministry of Transportation, and the Ministry of Health, the Ministry of Housing have all been highly active on national mega projects for the construction of social housing and public transportation infrastructure predominantly targeting the development of marginalized and informal communities nationwide (Nassar, 2021).

On the meso level, international organizations and non-governmental organizations (NGOs) played a pivotal role in confronting the underlying drivers of extremism and actively contributing to its prevention. Egypt post-2013 saw the launching of various cooperation initiatives with UN bodies such as the United Nations Office on Drugs and Crime (UNODC) and the United Nations Development Program (UNDP) to support the state's social welfare and development initiatives. Furthermore, the UNDP, in conjunction with Egypt's public sector, private enterprises, and civil society, not only targeted economic growth but also centered its efforts on empowering women, children, and individuals with disabilities (UNODC Strategy 2021–2025). It is worth noting that the involvement of civil society organizations appears to have shifted towards working in support of, and in coordination with, state institutions rather than as independent entities. This shift cannot be viewed as coincidental. Rather, the government's move to involve NGOs in aiding the state's developmental objectives can be perceived as a pragmatic strategy, given that civil initiatives accounted for a large portion of Egypt's social capital.

It is clear that the Egyptian state post-2013 initiated a combination of soft and hard strategies simultaneously to combat VE and radicalization. In the process, severe limitations on non-violent forms of political protests and independent activities of civil society actors were also implemented. The gaps left by the independent charities, most of which were supported by religious organizations including the MB, have now been dismantled (Pollard, 2014). Although the Egyptian government initiated and implemented vast development programs, the purpose of the case studies below is to investigate on the grassroots level, the impact of such initiatives. In addition to acquiring direct interaction with meso-level institutions within communities that are deemed most susceptible to VE tendencies, these case studies also examine the factors that potentially affect youth vulnerability to radicalization and violent extremism post-2014. Equally important, the impact of closing informal charities and its effects on these communities will be addressed. In this context, meso-level institutions can be defined as: "smaller scale, lower-level social arrangements or units with a different set of guidelines for societal organization" (Richter & Dragano, 2018, p. 163).

The three meso-level case studies investigated here are: Al-Warraq Coptic Christian community, located in Giza Governorate, the informal community of Bahtim, within Qalyubia Governorate, and the case of Alexandria University students. The following section will start with a framework of the background and context of each case study and thereafter provide a sample description of each case study to outline the challenges encountered throughout the process. Subsequently, an analysis of the findings derived from the fieldwork, which is based on the seven CONNEKT drivers (religion, economic deprivation, political issues, territorial inequalities, digital socialization, transnational dynamics, and education, culture and leisure opportunities), will be presented. The conclusion is intended to consolidate the shared characteristics observed across these case studies.

2 Case Studies and Methodologies

2.1 Alexandria University: Challenges and Concessions of its Contemporary Youth

The governorate of Alexandria is located 70 Km northwest of the Nile Delta. Its capital, the city of Alexandria, is the second-largest city area in the country. It is home to Egypt's oldest and largest port, situated in the Mediterranean Sea, which made the city a trade and industry hub. Its population stood at 5367 million in 2020, with a slightly higher male-to-female population ratio. As of January 2021, 98.2% of the population resided in urban areas, with only 98.325 living on the outskirts. The population density now is 4800/m2 (World Population Review, 2023).

Alexandria is characterized by the Muslim Brotherhood strongholds in certain parts of the city over the decades pre-2013. In the period from 2011 following Mubarak's resignation until the fall of the MB presidency of Mohamed Morsi in July 2013 Alexandria witnessed a further increase in political activism predominantly stemming from Alexandria University. Indeed, some of the most violent confrontations between the youth and the security services took place in Alexandria in 2011 (Ahram Online, 2011). In the months following the removal of President Morsi, demonstrations in Alexandria University remained a regular occurrence. It is not erroneous to regard Alexandria University pre-2013 as one of the most politically active spaces in the country.[1]

In this context, one of the aims of this case study is to examine the degree to which the youth currently enrolled in Alexandria University address grievances in comparison to their pre-2013 predecessors. In order to do so, it is necessary to first identify the socioeconomic factors that contribute to VE trends at the youth community level and the manner in which these factors interact with other drivers. Moreover, the aim is also to analyze the perspective of youth in identifying socioeconomic and political factors that potentially foster VE and the degree to which macro-level policies post-2014 contribute or hinder these factors. As such, this case study explores and attempts to identify how the context of social interaction among youth within the university and their larger society impacts their perspectives and grievances.

In terms of empirical data, the criteria used for sample selection is based on coverage focus groups between the ages of (19–21) to assess the degree to which such drivers affect their perception as a community in context of VE and radical religious thought. In addition, the three interviews conducted comprised two senior university students and an influential community leader who holds an in-depth knowledge of the evolving social context of the last three decades in the city of Alexandria. This provided a better understanding and more comprehensive picture of enrolled youth in a major university and their views regarding VE and its drivers as it stood during the time of this research (2023). All participants involved in this case study are Alexandrian and have lived their entire lives in the city. The 13 participants (including the three in-depth interviewees) comprised six males and seven females. Excluding one Christian Copt, all participants are Muslims. The focus group selected here consisted of ten enrolled university students from various academic disciplines, five of whom were males and five females. The socioeconomic background of the students ranges from lower middle to middle class. The first two in-depth interviews were conducted with two female students. The first was Muslim while the second was Christian. The third interview was conducted with a middle-aged teacher who, at the time of the interview, had been promoted to supervising multiple schools and was certified as an official imam affiliated with the Egyptian Ministry of Endowments.

2.2 *Informal Communities in Greater Cairo: The Case of Bahtim*

Marginalized communities, whether in urban informal settings or impoverished villages, witness various forms of illegal activities including drug trafficking, theft, and other forms of violence (Krivo & Peterson, 1996). As such, Bahtim stands as a

[1] According to official statistics, student enrolment at Alexandria University is 158.701 individuals. Alexandria University (2015, December 06). Important statistics. Retrieved June 2024, from https://www.alexu.edu.eg/index.php/en/statistics-data

compelling case study due to the presence of factors that are potentially conducive to the rise of VE. Bahtim is located 30 kilometers north of Cairo, in the larger district of Shubra el-Kheima. This area was historically a prominent textile industry hub. The population of Bahtim is 557.857 individuals of which 291.470 are males and 266.387 are females (Central Agency for Public Mobilization and Statistics, 2018). As an informal settlement, Bahtim exhibits common traits inherent in such areas, such as economic deprivation, lack of education and cultural and leisurely opportunities rendering its youth vulnerable to multiple drivers. Additionally, due to the unregulated nature of these informal neighborhoods, which have adopted, a well-consolidated system built on corruption and clientalism (Kipper & Fischer, 2009), could potentially serve as a breeding ground of extremism in communities such as Bahtim. In addition, the lack of state support and the absence of basic services further reinforce marginalization (Diab et al., 2020) and encourage an environment conducive to unlawful activities.

Bathim constitutes a prime case study for researching the significance of Islamic charitable organizations in deprived areas. Thousands of informal Islamic NGOs—some of whom possessed political agendas and at times radical Islamic ideologies—have, over many decades, entered these marginalized communities and subsequently occupied the welfare support gap that was neglected by the state. Some of these NGOs provided informal mosques with their own preachers and sometimes provided free informal schools and daycare centers in the neighborhoods. In addition, these disparate organizations provided free healthcare assistance, food banks, and other forms of material and financial support to those in need, thus turning them into an integral substitute welfare system for residents in socioeconomically deprived areas (Sieverding et al., 2019).

The informal area of Bahtim is one such case study in which Islamist organizations (peaceful or violent) had a strong presence in pre-2014. Since then, informal areas including Bahtim have minimal, if any, visible Islamist activities due to state initiatives that severely limited the role of local civil society organizations. This, in turn, has created a major socioeconomic void within these communities that has yet to be substituted by public initiatives and other welfare programs. Indeed, some of the only support residents of these communities receive is through small-scale NGOs that are funded by individuals residing in more affluent areas of Cairo. One such case is a local NGO in an area that serves some of the most socioeconomically deprived residents within Bahtim. This NGO was selected to investigate the social context of interaction between members of the community and meso-level institutions. The methodology in this research is intended to examine the perspective of the local youth in order to identify socioeconomic and political characteristics that potentially foster VE and the degree to which post-2014 macro-level policies contribute or hinder these characteristics. The NGO selected for the purpose of this case study is one of the only two legally registered establishments that still exist in Bahtim in post-2014 Egypt. Its limited finances depend solely on the contributions of charitable donors, most of whom are upper-middle-class professionals from the more affluent areas of Greater Cairo. Donations by these individuals, whether in the form of finances, goods, or charitable services have been maintained largely through personal networks and word of mouth. According to the Secretary General of this NGO, the nearly 600.000 residents of Bahtim had access to five legally registered socioeconomically oriented NGOs in the pre-2014 period. However, during that time, this small number of formal NGOs was compensated by the informal Islamist/ MB-supported NGOs which were referred to as "families". It is estimated that around 100–150 organizations or "families" existed in the Bahtim area. These informal NGOs and "families" were immediately raided and shut down along with the socioeconomic support centres that were established post-2011 following the fall of the Mohammed Morsi Presidency. In addition, three of the five legally registered NGOs were also shut down during the crackdown. As such, it was not too difficult during the research process to identify one of the two remaining meso-level institutions that still function in the community.

The selected sample for the focus group was youth (between the ages of 15–30) who benefited from disparate forms of assistance from the local NGO selected for this case study. Assistance included but was not limited to financial support, attending religious classes offered free of charge, and receiving food and/or clothes from the NGO subject to availability. The criteria for selecting the three individuals to partake in the one-on-one in-depth interviews were as follows: First, all participants were local residents with an in-depth knowledge of the community. Second, their in-depth knowledge stemmed from their professional interaction with the community and educational attributes which, subsequently, positioned them as recognized leaders by the community, possessing the ability to influence certain sectors of society. One community leader was a senior teacher at one of the local public schools, the second was the head of the local NGO and the third was an elder imam at a local mosque. Regarding the focus groups, one group comprised four female participants from the ages of 18–30. The second group comprised four male participants between the ages of 18–30. The third group was conducted for minors consisting of two females and two males between the ages of 15–17. The focus groups in this particular case study were segregated according to gender and ages at the request of the participants.

The main challenge faced with the three focus groups was the sheer lack of knowledge by the youth participants regarding topics linked to politics, religious radicalism and VE. The 18–30 male group mentioned the regular use of drugs. This may explain another reason that they were unable to understand and respond to questions leading to questions having to be repeated or rephrased. As mentioned above, it was already difficult to engage the focus groups to discuss issues that they did not seem to be familiar with, and the lack of sobriety in a few instances reinforced the difficulties faced during research. The female 18–30 focus group generally wanted to focus solely on their personal family problems and therefore at times it was necessary to redirect them to the research questions. It is interesting to note that the youngest of the three groups appeared to be the most knowledgeable of the topics addressed compared to the older two groups.

2.3 Al-Warraq: Drivers of Violent Extremism within an Informal Coptic Community-Greater Cairo

Al-Warraq is an informal settlement in the governorate of Giza, part of Greater Cairo. Al-Warraq was formerly an agricultural area, but over the last three decades, it quickly became more urbanized as residents from across Egypt moved there and constructed informal housing. According to the Central Agency for Public Mobilization and Statistics (2021), the population of Al-Warraq is 774.581. Overall, the area has a high unemployment rate and the majority of inhabitants are not educated further than the basic public-school level (Participatory Development Program in Urban Areas, 2017; Shaheen, 2012). The main sources of income in Al-Warraq are predominantly within the informal sector such as day laboring, transportation drivers (car drivers, truck drivers or minibus drivers), or working informally in small shops, workshops, and as domestic help in the more affluent areas. A minority of employment is in the formal sector such as public-school teachers and lower-level civil servants. Consequently, most of Al-Warraq's residents earn a living on a day-to-day basis, due to their low income levels and the high unemployment rate, especially among youth (Participatory Development Program in Urban Areas, 2017).

Another major characteristic of Al-Warraq is that it hosts a large Coptic Christian population. In this context, the Coptic Christian youth in Al-Warraq present themselves as a notably distinct group of interest for this research. Their active engagement with the local church serves as a distinct area of focus that illustrates how specific social environments and contexts can potentially perform important roles in reshaping youth perspectives on radicalization and VE. Moreover, it appears that the local church within the community functions as a pivotal meso-level institution, offering youth various opportunities that appear to counterweight the socioeconomic difficulties faced by the youth. The church provides not only religious guidance and education, but also financial and socioeconomic assistance to its members. Furthermore, the church offers a wide range of services within the realms of cultural and leisure opportunities, especially for its youth. Moreover, it also appears that the family unit is an integral part of the Al-Warraq Church community. Most of the youth who took part in the focus groups conducted, emphasized the positive role and influence of their families in their lives. The role of the family, according to the majority of youth participants, was perceived to be their most important source of stability, protection, and support.

The presence of cultural and leisurely activities and services for the youth plays a potential role in deterring radicalization and VE, since its absence leaves the youth with little alternative but to congregate on the streets thus exposing them to potential forms of crime including violence and radicalization. In addition, it emerged during the macro-level research (Kassem, 2022) conducted for this project that the lack of independent and critical thinking due to the poor quality of education, the marginalization of independent creativity, and a lack of cultural awareness allows radical (religious) beliefs to be more easily and unquestionably accepted as the truth (Kassem, 2022). As a result, the type and quality of education and cultural opportunities available to the youth directly affect the youth's ability to pursue their employment aspirations and steer clear of radicalization. The essence of this case study is to examine the ties linking youth living in informal communities to their local church, and the extent to which the church shapes the nature of its community. In general Coptic Christians are Egypt's largest and most significant religious community after Sunni Muslims, comprising approximately 10–15% of Egypt's population. The local churches in Egypt have historically tended to play a significant role as meso-level institutions for their local communities.

The selected sample of participants were youths ranging between the ages of 12–30 years who regularly attend church services and, in some cases, also conduct charitable work within the church. Gender was also taken into consideration while selecting the focus group sample to better understand to what degree perspectives differ according to age and gender. Two focus groups were conducted: one group consisted of two females and one male participant between the ages of 12–17 and the other focus group comprised 9 participants (6 male and 3 female participants between the ages of 20–30 years). Both focus groups and in-depth interviews were conducted in a local church at Al-Warraq.

The main two challenges were to find a church that would grant permission to conduct fieldwork and to find participants willing to participate in the focus group discussions and in-depth interviews. The Coptic Church in Egypt tends to avoid political participation in whatever form and encourages its congregation to abide by such advice. In part, the topic of this research is highly sensitive when approaching a Christian minority group to give their opinions on radicalization and VE. In addition, the Coptic community generally obeys their local churches and hence it would have been extremely difficult to gather Coptic youth to discuss their opinions without the approval of their local Church leaders.

3 Results

3.1 Political Issues

The youth who participated in the Alexandria University focus group and two of its three in-depth interviewees appeared to possess political apathy. However, it was clear that they were more knowledgeable regarding the political environment in which they live compared to the youth participating in the two other case studies. However, it is worth noting that their knowledge of vital political events such as the January 25th protests of 2011, and the removal of the senior MB representative, President Mohamed Morsi, is limited. As one female participant remarked: "We know nothing about politics. Why are we talking about this? I swear to God. I am not joking here. We are all here talking about social issues". This comment, which appeared to be supported by the entire focus group provides us with an indication that one of the most previously politically active youth (Alexandria University student body) currently appears to be as apathetic towards the political arena as the less educated and less privileged youth from informal areas of the two other cases examined in Egypt. Such apathy is potentially the result of stringent control on political activity and the lack of integration within the larger political arena that would encourage youth affiliation.

The Bahtim focus groups yielded similar results albeit participants seemed to lack even the most basic knowledge of politics. None of the participants could name any president before Mubarak. Only two were able to name the first elected president following the fall of Mubarak, President Mohammed Morsi, or the circumstances that led to President Sisi acquiring power. It seems that the lack of strong family units, the weakness of formal education, lack of extracurricular activities, depleted access to spaces such as NGOs, leisure and cultural attractions, and inaccessibility to even formal mosques except during prayer time have placed the youth in an intellectual and political vacuum. The lack of opportunities in this respect and dependence on obtaining information from movies and TV shows limited to Egyptian TV (state-driven content) constitutes the dominant influence of political understanding. Additionally, youth participating in the focus groups did not necessarily recall nor understand the events of the 2011 uprisings. Indeed, all youth members of the Bahtim focus groups claim no memory of the role of the informal NGOs that MB and Islamists financed in their communities. As such, the participants had no knowledge of the significance of these NGOs as major socioeconomic educational and leisure providers within their community. On the other hand, community leaders during the individual in-depth interviews seemed to express strong political grievances. In fact, one of the three in-depth interviewees identified himself as a member of the MB and the other two expressed private support and sympathy for the organization. According to one participant "during the last nine years, people have witnessed repression and violence, and the standard of living has decreased because the state did not replace the void when they closed the informal Islamist NGOs and mosques. This, in turn, has made the youth unwilling to participate in civil society and politics". When asked about the role of youth in politics, he said: "they are not into politics, religion, being productive or their work… they feel that they have no role in society, and this is because there is no participation and youth do not perceive their value… they feel they are the problem, not the solution". Moreover, according to him, after the revolution young people became lost and hopeless as they had little to no employment opportunities which, in his view, was a problem directly linked to political strategies.

Political grievances for the youth of Al-Warraq appeared to be predominantly linked to religion. One major concern is the belief that, as a minority, they are not perceived as equal citizens and consequently do not have access to equal opportunities. One participant, for example, stated that "until now, we have not come across a Christian who has joined a football national team". The older focus group participants claimed that they have no interest in keeping up with current political issues on television or social media nor do they feel the need to do so. When asked the reason for this, many of the respondents believed that such apathy stemmed from their belief that they could not change anything.

As discussions regarding the political grievances of the youth progressed, the topic of the Morsi/MB presidency in 2013 was raised by several participants. Many of them stated that their community was negatively affected in terms of the sense that their freedoms were becoming increasingly restricted. Indicative of this feeling was that females started dressing in a more conservative manner to avoid hassle in public spaces such as work, school, or simply the street. Additionally, they felt increasingly alienated in their country, during this period. In this regard, the rise of one important aspect of political grievances within the Coptic community appeared to be linked to the significance of political Islam within the formal governmental structures (macro institutions).

3.2 Economic Deprivation

Economic deprivation appears to be one of the most prominent concerns for the youth focus group participants. The economic factor remains largely intertwined with other VE drivers. According to the views of one of the Alexandria community leaders, for example, the main drivers for VE amongst Egyptian youth can be interpreted via a combination of three main drivers: "poverty, ignorance and [mental] illness". This view highlights the importance of economic security as of utmost essence and stability for youth and, in its absence, radical ideologies potentially provide an alternative sense of purpose in which martyrdom is an ultimate achievement. Against this background, economic instability and lack of secure employment continue to be the most concerning aspects for the youth as well as for their parents. On another level, the costs associated with education seem to also add to the economic hardships of families. Economic grievances for the parents are also a consequence of the fact that most participants have multiple siblings in various stages of education which necessitates the need for private tutoring to supplement the substandard government education further adding to the basic costs of traditional school supplies. Three participants indicated that their fathers supplemented their income by pursuing additional employment such as driving private cars. This form of self-employment is widely practiced in Egypt as it allows people to earn extra income, but it is by no means secure. As it is an informal sector, health care, pensions and other forms of security, benefits are not applicable.

According to one of the respondents of the interview in the Bahtim case study, the state-led initiative *Takaful and Karama* (Solidarity and Dignity)[2] is not perceived as particularly beneficial for the eligible members of the community because the financial assistance it provides is a very small amount that ranges from from 350 EGP to 450 EGP per month (approx. 16 US dollars), per household. Moreover, the

[2] This is a social security programme designed to provide social welfare and direct financial assistance targeting the underprivileged population that for diverse reasons are unable to work (disabled, elderly, orphaned children, etc.). For more information see: https://www.sis.gov.eg/Story/173372/Takaful-%26-Karama-Program?lang=en-us

program benefits only a small portion of those eligible to apply. According to a community leader: "less than 1 out of 10 people benefit from the program because there are no clear guidelines on the eligibility of recipients and poorly trained civil servants are left to personally decide the eligibility of an applicant". It also seemed that many people were not aware of such programs and those who do, face difficulties when applying. A common occurrence is that for example, elderly people who are eligible and can benefit from this program would find it hard to apply if they reside in an area that is distant from the governorate in which their ID is registered. Therefore, it appears that the success of these state-led programs is not necessarily effective on the implementation level. As a consequence, it would appear that the state has yet to fill the socioeconomic welfare vacuum that was left by the banned Islamic NGOs. In this regard, all three interviewees expressed that in 2013, many Islamic-affiliated NGOs that used to work and offer support in the area were forced to shut down and this had a major effect on residents of Bahtim. According to one community leader, not only did these organisations financially support residents of the area but they provided a space for the youth to discuss their problems and offer spiritual and religious guidance.

While the area of Al-Warraq is also considered one of the poorest informal areas of Cairo, the shutdown of informal Islamic NGOs did not result in the meso-institutional void experienced in Bahtim. This seems to be due to the presence of a large Coptic Christian community and the fact that the important role of the church within that community was unaffected by the state policies as was the case for Islamic meso-level institutions. The Church has traditionally focused on addressing drivers that would potentially lead their youth toward the direction of radicalization and VE. More importantly, all church members are expected to pay their local church in accordance with their capabilities the *oshour* (annual religious taxes), and those who are more economically fortunate are expected to donate extra on a regular basis to help the less fortunate. These funds financially support the economically deprived sectors of the community as they can turn to the church for financial assistance. Such assistance includes but is not limited to regular monthly payments of medications for those who cannot afford them, and financial assistance to other socioeconomically deprived members, including orphans, the handicapped, and the unemployed.

This is not to imply that the welfare provided by the church is sufficient to satisfy the needs of its congregation. In fact, it is worth noting that the deteriorating economic situation has led to financial cutbacks of religiously-based donations (*oshour*) which in turn, have affected the church and hence the underprivileged people who are dependent on this assistance. In the words of one church community leader: "people are becoming more in need because the financial situation is becoming more difficult… This is something we all feel. The number of poor families is starting to increase and so are their needs. Instead of helping one family, now you are helping two or three… it is even difficult for us as service providers… We are trying to help as many families as possible but I won't lie, some families may not get what they need". In analyzing the three case studies, it is important to note that economic grievances intertwine and significantly influence other drivers, notably affecting the accessibility of education and cultural and leisure opportunities. Moreover, these economic challenges are intricately linked to territorial inequalities prevalent within these communities. It is therefore essential to recognize this interplay between the different drivers and acknowledge their interdependence in order to gain a deeper understanding of the reality of the dynamics within these communities.

3.3 Territorial Inequalities

Territorial disparities can be seen as an indicator of the unequal distribution of public resources as a result of decades of ineffective governmental policies. Due to such distribution disparities, and lack of services such as healthcare and basic utilities to certain neighborhoods and territories, Islamist groups—predominantly the Muslim Brotherhood—played a pivotal role in substituting the welfare gap. The provision of social services to compensate the impoverished and marginalized communities led, in turn, to the increased popularity of these organisations. The profound sense of injustice that the youth expressed in both Bahtim and Al-Warraq regarding the uneven distribution of state resources was very evident. The youth of Bahtim for example, criticized the lack of police responses toward the increasing prevalence of local drug dealers, drug users, and acts of violence. One focus group participant, for example, mentioned that there had been over 50 complaints against local drug dealers over the last few months to little or no avail. The fact that the authorities rarely responded to such situations, the community was left with little option other than resorting to community leaders to assist in settling conflicts. In general, conflict arises from issues such as families requiring intervention regarding the drug use of individual family members, violent street arguments, whereby one individual is physically harmed, and general domestic and criminal violence. As a community leader, the Sheikh is regarded as the first route of approach and, in general, tends to ensure that the wronged individual is compensated. In crime and drug-related cases, the Sheikh utilizes his knowledge to extend religious and personal advice to the involved parties. In other words, the community leader acts as an important meso-level institution that is considered an alternative to the police, judge, and jury. It also seemed that community members also rallied together to address other issues within the community. As one participant explained: "we are self-sufficient. We got the sewage system into the area. It was all personal efforts. The streets, we are the ones that drew them. The government has nothing to do with the area". In this regard, participants expressed a desire for better higher-quality services that were fair and on par with those offered in more affluent areas. It is also worth pointing out that all participants claimed to dislike their local area and would not hesitate to leave if their financial circumstances allowed. As one participant stated: "if God granted us just one room outside of Bahtim we would be very happy".

While it is clear from the participants' response that the area seemed to face a lot of neglect in terms of state-directed resources, preliminary investigations indicated a few governmental initiatives that have been recently introduced. The most prominent of these initiatives seems to be the construction of subsidized formal housing for Bahtim's informal community (Mohamed Adel, 2017). Unfortunately, when participants were asked about their views on these settlements and their potential benefits to the community, participants responded that such housing was beyond their financial means.

In the case of Al-Warraq, the focus group and the Coptic community leaders interviewed, all acknowledged that the area lacked a substantial level of state services and attention in comparison to the more prosperous neighborhoods in Egypt. According to one community leader, the biggest setback that she perceived as a female was the lack of safety in the neighborhood due to street violence and excessive male drug abuse on the street. It was also noted by the same respondent that excluding the church-provided amenities, the few public culture and leisure resources are either unaffordable or unsafe. It is worth mentioning that Al-Warraq was clearly the only area where state security personnel were very prominent and visible at the time of fieldwork. According to one of the community leaders, the reason behind this is linked to the fact that during the months of December and January, which are the highlight of Christian celebrations, previous terrorist attacks took place in the area leading the security apparatus to focus heavily on the community especially during these religious celebratory periods.

As a minority group, it would appear that the nature of territorial inequalities is more prominent. In other words, the Coptic community in Al-Warraq indicated during interviews that while they may suffer from the same territorial inequalities as their Muslim counterparts in the community, they felt that additional inequalities due to their minority religious status exist on several levels. The political violence that they regard as specifically aimed at them (such as attacks on churches) is one such example.

3.4 Religion

Macro-level analysis indicated that religious misconceptions played an integral part in directing youth towards extremism (Kassem, 2022). While this may be the situation in certain cases, it would appear that religion plays a minor role in the lives of post-2014 youth. The Alexandria University students' case study indicated some degree of distrust and caution towards religious ideologies and leadership existed. When asked about the meaning of radicalization in terms of religion one participant stated: "religious extremism is when someone misconstrues the real meaning of religion and places it within a political framework... but cannot provide genuine Islamic proof or evidence when challenged about their opinion". A male participant added that he does not have trust or faith in Sheikhs generally. His justification (that was supported by other participants) was: "I do not listen to Sheikhs. There is something called the Islamic Holy Book". All participants in both focus groups denounced the use of violence under the pretext of religion. Indeed, all participants acknowledged that religion condemns the use of violence. As one female participant elaborated: "the use of religion to justify violence used to happen in the past but not nowadays, people used to think if they went and bombed a church or a Jewish Temple then that would guarantee them a place in heaven as it would be regarded as a defense of Islam".

While Alexandria University students possess a certain degree of educational background to form an opinion on the subject matter (whether justified or not), in the case of Bahtim, this was not the case. The focus group participants in Bahtim were unable to form any opinion at all due to their extremely limited knowledge of religion. Indeed, none of the Bahtim youth knew more than two *Surahs* (Verses) in the Quran. The sparse knowledge that they did possess of religion was mainly acquired from day-to-day socialization due to the limited access to religious education avenues. The local NGO and one of the local mosques in the Bahtim area comprise the sole sources for those seeking religious knowledge within the community. However, according to the local Sheikh, the mosque where he prays offers clandestine religious lessons since such lessons are against state policies that limit mosque activities to only prayer. According to him, the mosque remains open because it is hidden and, therefore, they can conduct their religious lessons. However, when asked about the type of teachings offered at the mosque, he stated that they only taught the Quran and general religious teachings (nothing related to extremism).

All participants in the Al-Warraq case study believed that Coptic religious teachings, to which they are exposed in the Church, were generally very moderate. It is worth pointing out that it was also acknowledged that in some cases, Christian religious leaders were also prone to incorrect and manipulated religious interpretations. One participant in the focus group, for example, while identifying as a Coptic, notes that in the Church people sometimes "get misled by the information presented to them… [which can] have a big impact on the people's perception of religion". Perception of religion and VE within the Coptic youth community should not be underestimated. Research in this case study indicates that Coptic youth have a strong and sophisticated understanding of radicalization and VE. As one youth noted: "violence is an instinct in humans. It is originally in each single one of us. But there are those who can control it, and this is something we get taught at church and at our homes... We have Pope Shenouda, he stated that when you go through some hardships, it is all for the good, it shall pass, and God exists. God knows that He has made me go through this experience and I do not have to face these hardships through violence, because if I do it means that I am escaping the hardships. And, whoever escapes the hardships escapes God".

It is interesting to note that the Coptic youth are aware that extremists use religion as a form of credibility for their own political cause and that it is not very difficult to convince socioeconomically deprived and uneducated people to adopt their ideology. All participants believed that those who adopt VE, do so because of their inability to analyze or rationalize a judgement in the absence of moderate religious education. The respondents' consensus indicated that all strongly believe that religion is not a driver of VE but rather the misinterpretation of religion is utilized as a tool to manipulate people into participating in VE.

3.5 Digital Socialization

Social media constitutes a core aspect of the daily lives of Alexandrian youth (all of whom have daily access to the internet). As one female student at Alexandria University remarked: "the internet is regarded as the main forum for youth entertainment, leisure and socialization". Indeed, in addition to leisure and entertainment, social media, according to the focus group, also functions as a platform where they engage with others to discuss their opinions as well as to research information. While social media and other internet platforms function as a source of exchanging ideas, it is vital to note that they were aware that it cannot be used as a platform to openly criticise the government without repercussions. The youth also use the internet for more practical matters such as economic and educational opportunities. Indicative of this is that some youth preferred to utilize the internet for educational lectures rather than resorting to expensive private lessons. Others used the internet to start small businesses such as selling local merchandise. Thus, many participants indicated a knowledge of the decimation of radical thought on the internet and its relationship to the process of radicalization. Accordingly, all participants believed that the internet was the main source of spreading radical ideas since it was the least supervised form of communication available.

In the case of Bathim, only three of the twelve youth focus group participants had regular access to social media. Therefore, content on social media was not considered a main driver shaping their views on VE. Even the few participants who accessed the internet mentioned that they did not watch politically-related content. Instead, it seems that Egyptian television had a bigger role in influencing the youths' limited understanding of politics and VE. In this regard, when asked about the meaning of words such as "extremism", "radicalization" and "terrorism", participants generally showed a lack of knowledge since their limited understanding of such terms was derived from state television channels. One participant stated that "terrorism is equivalent to destruction, and from what we see on TV it is not acceptable". Another participant stated that "terrorists are those who misinterpret religion, and those who convince people of religious ideas that are untrue… for example, stating that the voice of a woman is illicit". Regarding the male focus group, one participant linked the term "radicalization" to the Muslim Brotherhood, and when asked about where he got this idea from, he stated that it was from television. The younger participants also seemed to lack any understanding of terms such as "radicalization" and "extremism". However when asked about the MB, one participant stated that television discourse is that "we should not listen to them".

Internet and social media platforms played a more prominent role for the youth of Al-Warraq compared to their socioeconomically deprived counterparts in Bahtim. It would appear that a possible reason for this is that the Coptic church provides economic assistance to its youth, therefore allowing them the opportunity to pursue leisurely activities including access to the internet. It should be noted that the Coptic youth of Al-Warraq perceived social media and internet access to be a form of leisure as well as education. Additionally, it was also considered an alternative platform for obtaining political, religious and general knowledge. The Al-Warraq focus groups participants raised an issue that was not mentioned by either the Bahtim or the Alexandrian case study: posts directed at them that were religiously discriminating. It is interesting to note that the youth did not feel the inclination to reply or retaliate towards such offensive posts. Therefore, while digital socialization may be a useful tool of information to youth, it may not necessarily be regarded as a major driver for radicalization and VE in these specific contexts.

3.6 Education, Culture and Leisure Opportunities

One major observation regarding the findings of the focus group in Alexandria was the fact that these university students predominantly had close-knit ties to their respective families. Almost all the parents of the participants had completed at least the most basic formal education and, in many instances, at least one parent possessed a college degree. Regardless of their socioeconomic status, the Alexandrian youth were highly aware of the efforts exerted by their families in order to be able to continue their education. It was also very clear that most participants perceived education as the main avenue to enhance their socioeconomic situation. The focus group participants studied different disciplines including medicine, engineering, law, commerce, art, and agriculture. Regarding the cultural and leisure opportunities made available, several male participants expressed how actively engaged they were in sports and physical activities. Most participants noted that sports activities were considered an important part of their lives since childhood and that facilities offered by their university were a significant factor in allowing them to continue leisure and sports pursuits.

In contrast to the Alexandria University student youth, the focus groups conducted with the Bahtim youth, strongly indicated that the overwhelming majority of participants did not see any benefits to education. Indeed, none of the eight individuals that comprised the 18–30 age group acquired a university degree. Of the four participants in the female focus group, two did not pursue any education whatsoever, whilst the other two withdrew from school at the age of 11 (which is the end of the primary stage of education in Egypt). As a consequence of such limited formal education, or indeed no formal education, employment opportunities for the four female participants were extremely limited. One major observation regarding all three focus groups in Bahtim was the fact that 10 out of the 12 focus group youth participants came from broken homes with an average of four siblings. This information can be analyzed on two levels. On one level, the parents, most of whom were not educated, perceived reproduction as an economic advantage in terms of having more children working, thus contributing extra income to the household. On another level, the fact that broken homes were a very common phenomenon within the Bahtim youth community indicated the volatile nature of family ties and the unstable nature of socioeconomic resources.

In the Al-Warraq Coptic community case study, with the exception of one participant, those who took part in the two focus groups and in-depth interviews were students in school, university, or had already achieved a higher-level degree. Overall, this community appeared to give significant priority towards education. Research indicated that participants perceived education as a tool for social mobility and subsequently raising their socioeconomic standards. The Church, according to the research findings, can be perceived as a major meso-level institution that performed a pivotal role for the Christian youth, not only as a religious institution but also as a major cultural and educational forum. The Church offered leisure opportunities as previously mentioned such as social clubs, sports and subsidized vacations as well as financial assistance. It should be noted that the youth participants were aware that the opportunities, offered by the Church, provided them with sufficient activities to constructively occupy their free time. It is important to note that outside the realms of the church, the Al-Warraq youth have very limited access to cultural and leisurely avenues. As such, their situation does not differ from their Muslim youth counterparts within the socioeconomically deprived areas such as Bahtim.

4 Conclusion

The conclusions drawn from the three case studies present a multifaceted understanding of the drivers influencing radicalization and VE within the different communities in Egypt. Moreover, the findings from this level of analysis solidified the fact that no single driver can explain youth susceptibility to radicalization and VE. Rather, it is the complex interactions between different drivers and within a specific political and socioeconomic context that potentially shape youth susceptibility to radicalization and VE. The three case studies demonstrated the interaction of drivers rooted in economic deprivation, territorial inequalities, and limited access to education, culture and leisure opportunities. However, research findings on the meso level did not indicate the prevalence of religious radicalization or VE ideologies within the youth case studies. The intertwined drivers, however, appear to have contributed to an overall pattern of youth disenfranchisement and socioeconomic isolation.

The case of Bahtim for example, highlighted the state of apathy amongst youth which is further emphasized by the evident lack of political awareness, limited education, and almost non-existent access to cultural and socioeconomic opportunities. The political apathy and fragmentation of youth in this community, however, did not prevent the rise of violence. Rather, the rise of violence is more linked to socioeconomic frustrations and appears to be completely detached from the unifying powers of religious and political ideologies.

Similar to the case of Bahtim, the Coptic youth of Al-Warraq expressed the most concern about economic grievances and the lack of employment opportunities. Moreover, it appears that political grievances are directly linked to their religious identity as a minority and the inequalities this status entails. The Al-Warraq case study also demonstrated the pivotal role of meso-level institutions like the Church in cultivating moderate and stable youth perspectives.

It would seem that socioeconomic concerns relating to fears of unemployment and blocked social mobility after graduation are also the main source of anxiety and resentment for the Alexandria University case study. Arguably, due to the higher socioeconomic and educational status of the youth participants in Alexandria, their grievances suggest a more politically-inclined perception as the majority viewed the root cause of their problems is due to governmental incompetence. Arguably, this sector of the youth is potentially more prone to the influence of VE and extremist narratives because while socioeconomic issues are also their main cause of concern, such issues were interpreted by them within the larger ideological framework of political issues.

On a final note, the three case studies appear to indicate economic deprivation to be one of the most pressing concerns for Egyptian youth. Within the Bahtim community, it was clear that socioeconomic grievances were exacerbated following the closure of all the Islamic-based NGOs that had pre-2014 performed a vital role in responding to the socioeconomic and religious needs of the community. The void left by the closures has yet to be filled by alternative governmental or secular civil society organizations. As a result, the Bahtim community in general, and its youth in particular, appear to be in an increasingly vulnerable predicament, that has fostered a significant increase in youth delinquency, violence, and participation in illegal activities. In contrast, the significant role of the local church within the Coptic community of Al-Warraq, demonstrated in this study the vital role of meso-level institutions in shaping and moderating Egyptian youth, particularly those living in informal and socioeconomically-deprived communities. The significance of meso-level institutions in these communities—whether a local church or a local NGO—cannot be underestimated and overlooked. Such organizations serve as intermediaries between the state and the local community, vastly contributing to overall stability and security.

References

Adelaja, A., & George, J. (2020). Is youth unemployment related to domestic terrorism? *Perspectives on Terrorism, 14*(5), 41–62.

Ahram Online. (2011, November 26). Alexandria's security directorate building sees constant confrontations. Retrieved June 2024, from https://english.ahram.org.eg/NewsContent/1/64/27657/Egypt/Politics-/Alexandria%E2%80%99s-security-directorate-building-sees-co.aspx

Al-Anani, K. (2015). Upended path: The rise and fall of Egypt's Muslim brotherhood. *The Middle East Journal, 69*(4), 527–543.

Buchanan, K. (2015). FALQS: Egypt's new antiterrorism law. *Custodia legis. The Library of Congress*. Retrieved June 2024, from https://blogs.loc.gov/law/2015/09/falqs-egypts-new-antiterrorism-law/

Central Agency for Public Mobilization and Statistics. (2018). Estimating the number of Egyptians in the districts according to gender and place of residence in 1/7/2018. Retrieved June 2024, from https://www.capmas.gov.eg/Admin/Pages%20Files/20181017124714shika1-2018.pdf

Central Agency for Public Mobilization and Statistics. (2021). The estimated population of the districts and centers in 1/7/2021. Retrieved June 2024, from https://www.capmas.gov.eg/Admin/Pages%20Files/2021111115156%D8%A7%D9%82%D8%B3%D8%A7%D9%85%20%D9%88%D9%85%D8%B1%D8%A7%D9%83%D8%B2%201%D9%80%D9%80%D9%80%207%20%D9%80%D9%80%D9%80%D9%80%202021.pdf

Daily News Egypt. (2020, September 13). Egypt Invests in Bedouin Communities Development: Al-Mashat. Retrieved June 2024, from https://www.dailynewsegypt.com/2020/09/13/egypt-invests-in-bedouin-communities-development-al-mashat/

Diab, Y., El Shaarawy, B., & Yousry, S. (2020). *Informal settlements in the Arab region: Towards Arab cities without informal areas*. UN-Habitat.

Drevon, J. (2015). The emergence of ex-Jihadi political parties in post-Mubarak Egypt. *The Middle East Journal, 69*(4), 511–526.

Jaraba, M. (2014). Why did the Egyptian Muslim Brotherhood's year-long rule fall? *Zeitschrift Für Politik, 61*(1), 61–80.

Kassem, M. (2022). *Egypt - Macro-drivers of radicalisation and violent extremism*. The European Institute of the Mediterranean (IEMed). Retrieved June 2024, from https://h2020connekt.eu/publications/egypt-macro-drivers-of-radicalisation-and-violent-extremism/

Kipper, R., & Fischer, M. (Eds.). (2009). *Cairo's informal areas: Between urban challenges and hidden potentials*. Cities Alliance. Retrieved June 2024 from https://www.citiesalliance.org/sites/default/files/2019-07/CairosInformalAreas_fulltext.pdf

Krivo, L. J., & Peterson, R. D. (1996). Extremely disadvantaged neighborhoods and urban crime. *Social Forces, 75*(2), 619.

Ministry of Foreign Affairs. (2021, August 2). *National Report on Countering Terrorism 2021*. Counter Terrorism Unit-Ministry of Foreign Affairs. Retrieved June 2024, from https://mfaegypt.org/2021/08/02/national-report-on-countering-terrorism-2021/

Mitchell, R. (1963). *The society of Muslim Brothers*. Oxford University Press.

Munson, Z. (2001). Islamic mobilization: Social movement theory and the Egyptian Muslim Brotherhood. *Sociological Quarterly, 42*(4), 487–510.

Nassar, M. (2021). From Asmarat & Bashayer Al Khair to Ahalina 2 as Sisi Pursues Decent Housing. *Csr Egypt*. Retrieved June 2024, from https://www.csregypt.com/en/from-asmarat-bashayer-al-khair-to-ahalina-2-as-sisi-pursues-decent-housing/

Participatory Development Program in Urban Areas. (2017). Markaz El Abhath/El Warraq. Retrieved June 2024, from https://www.egypt-urban.net/markaz-el-abhathel-warraq/

Pollard, L. (2014). Egyptian by association: Charitable states and service societies, circa 1850–1945. *International Journal of Middle East Studies, 46*(2), 239–257.

Radwan, T. (2015). Egypt's Ministry of Endowments and the Fight Against Extremism. *Atlantic Council*. Retrieved June 2024, from https://www.atlanticcouncil.org/blogs/menasource/egypt-s-ministry-of-endowments-and-the-fight-against-extremism/

Richter, M., & Dragano, N. (2018). Micro, macro, but what about meso? The institutional context of health inequalities. *International Journal of Public Health, 63*(2), 163–164.

Salem, P. (2018). The rise of violent transnational movements in the Middle East. *Counterterrorism Series, 1*.

Shaheen, H. (2012). *Civil society engagement and education for sustainable development (ESD) in Egypt: A case study of El-Warraq are*. AUC Knowledge Fountain. Retrieved June 2024, from https://fount.aucegypt.edu/etds/1409/

Shorouk News. (2017). الأكثر قراءة. "الإفتاء" تعلن استراتيجيتها لمواجهة التطرف والعنف والأفكار التكفيرية - بوابة الشروق. [Al-Ifta Announces a Strategy to Combat Extremism, Violence and Excommunication Ideology]. Retrieved June 2024, from https://www.shorouknews.com/news/view.aspx?cdate=10072017&id=dcfbfc51-5412-4ad8-8025-897813b776d8

Sieverding, M., Roushdy, R., Hassan, R., & Ali, A. (2019). Perceptions of service access in a context of marginalization: The case of young people in Informal Greater Cairo. *Economic Research Forum (ERF)*. Retrieved June 2024, from https://erf.org.eg/publications/perceptions-of-service-access-in-a-context-of-marginalization-the-case-of-young-people-in-informal-greater-cairo/

State Information Service. (2020, June 17). 6 years of achievements, a security strategy to confront challenges and extremism.

State Information Service. (2023). *CAPMAS: 89% of youths use internet in Egypt*. Retrieved June 2024, from https://www.sis.gov.eg/Story/185162/CAPMAS-89%25-of-youths-use-internet-in-Egypt?lang=en-us

Suleiman, H. (2022). Youth Unemployment in The South of the Mediterranean: A chronic challenge to development and stability. *EUROMESCO*. Retrieved June 2024, from https://www.euromesco.net/wp-content/uploads/2022/01/Paper-N%C2%BA48.pdf

The Tahrir Institute for Middle East Policy. (2019, April 4). TIMEP Brief: Terrorist Entities Law. Retrieved June 2024, from https://timep.org/2019/04/04/timep-brief-terrorist-entities-law/

Torelli, S. M. (2015). *The return of Egypt: Internal challenges and regional game*. Edizioni Epoké.

U.S. Department of State. (2021). Country Reports on Terrorism 2021: Egypt. Retrieved June 2024, from https://www.state.gov/reports/country-reports-on-terrorism-2021/egypt

World Population Review. (2023). Alexandria Population 2023. Retrieved June 2024, from world-populationreview.com

Zubaida, S. (1989). *Islam, the people and the state: Essays on political ideas and movements in the Middle East*. Routledge.

أحمد البحيري [Ahmed El Beheery] (2017). "مرصد الإفتاء" يطلق استراتيجية لمواجهة التطرف تتضمن رسومًا متحركة. المصري اليوم. [Al-Ifta Monitor Lunches Strategy to Combat Extremism Which Includes Animated Cartoons] Retrieved June 2024, from https://www.almasryalyoum.com/news/details/1160807

محمد عادل [Mohamed Adel] (2017). "14 مكتب بريد لطرح كراسات الإسكان الاجتماعي بالقليوبية" [14 Postal Offices to Issue Pamphlets About Social Housing in Qalubeya] https://gate.ahram.org.eg/News/1564841.aspx

Analysis of the Phenomenon of Violent Extremism: The Social Experiences of Moroccan Youth

Sara Azim, Amina Er-rifaiy, and Khalid Mouna

1 Introduction

Like many investigations into the process of radicalization at the macro level, understanding the phenomenon also requires a meso approach that sheds light on the role of communities in the construction of this phenomenon. It is also a question of opening up the scientific debate on the nature of these communities and their interpretations of violent extremism in their own environment. We would like to mention in this respect that meso studies on the Moroccan context are rare, which gives this contribution an added value in the sociological field.

Despite the fact that the phenomenon of radicalization has come to occupy a place in scientific studies in various fields since the 2001 attacks, particularly in the political and sociological sciences, the definition of the concept remains complex. Therefore, in order to grasp and understand this phenomenon, several approaches have been attempted. Some studies have explained the phenomenon in terms of the factors that motivate and incite individuals to violent extremism. In fact, this sort of extremism, the kind expressed through violence, seems to find a common definition in the academic field, a definition that emphasizes above all the attitude of rupture of groups and individuals from society, the political regime and the religious framework. But this rupture is not perceived in the same way by states and institutions, even if states share the same standard of definition of violent extremism. Thus, in Morocco, a country where Islam is both the reference of the state as the religion of the King's subjects, but also a political framework through which the Commander of the Faithful exercises his monarchical power, violent extremism even attacks the legitimacy of this royal institution.

S. Azim · A. Er-rifaiy · K. Mouna (✉)
Moulay Ismail University, Meknes, Morocco
e-mail: s.azim@edu.umi.ac.ma; a.errifaiy@edu.umi.ac.ma; k.mouna@umi.ac.ma

C. Torrekens et al. (eds.), *Social Contexts of Radicalization and Violent Extremism in the MENA and Balkans*,
https://doi.org/10.1007/978-3-031-84521-5_5

In this respect, studies carried out in the Moroccan context have focused on the different factors of violent extremism. Masbah (2019) in his work on Moroccan jihadists, considers that the motivations for the phenomenon are linked mainly to four factors, which are political, logistical, sociological or ideological. And it is these factors that mark the paths of Moroccan jihadists who leave for conflict zones.

The work carried out by Samouni (2017) focused on the religious factor that encourages young Moroccans to develop an idea of jihadism. He also described some specific characteristics of the spaces and participants, as well as some of the life paths of ex-jihadists after their return from war zones. The researcher reveals the relationship between violent extremism and religion and shows how the social situation of Moroccan jihadists changes from one state to another. The cases cited in the book show that young people's perception of religion plays an important role in their decision to commit violent acts, and the examples of young Salafists' refusal of the cultural rituals of their Amazigh region reveal their relationship with their social life and its impact on their social environment. With regard to the gender approach, Bassou (2019) considers that the life trajectories of young girls involved in radicalization processes are characterized by three projects: firstly, radicalization is perceived as a means of constructing their identity for those seeking a social position; secondly, radicalization is perceived as a form of education; and thirdly, radicalization is seen as an experience through which girls seek marriage.

As we see, these studies have shed light on the various aspects that explain violent extremism in the Moroccan context. However, they also highlight the importance of exploring the phenomenon from multiple angles and fields of research, in order to better understand and analyze the new forms of radicalization emerging among young people.

In this respect, and following the Casablanca bombings in 2003, Morocco has seen a dynamic mobilization in the fight against violent extremism, both within the state and civil society. This mobilization has been gradually reflected in a two-faceted institutional approach. Firstly, the involvement of a number of public or civil society bodies, which already existed in this field, by investing part of their resources and areas of activity in this respect (scientific councils, councils of *ulemas* (scholars), human rights, intellectual and artistic associations, etc.). Secondly, the creation of organizations dedicated exclusively to the objective of combating VE. The institutionalization of Moroccan mobilization on this issue will thus give rise to a whole landscape of organizations whose components and players differ according to their institutional forms (administrations, associations, centers, observatories, groupings, etc.), their areas of intervention (religion, economy, education, human rights, etc.), their relationship with the state (public authorities, civil society representatives), and the target of their intervention (the whole population, only a specific part of young people, children, people already involved in VE, etc.). This landscape can be categorized in two ways: one is official state policy, while the other is the initiative of civil society.

To combat VE at all levels, the Moroccan government has mobilized five pillars as part of its overall strategy: religion, security and legal aspects, socioeconomics dynamics, human rights and rule of law, and international cooperation. In general, the Moroccan government has devised an action plan that aims to offer better living conditions to improve economic factors and reduce territorial inequalities, which have been singled out as factors in violent extremism.

It is worth saying that the Moroccan government is one of the most important players in the fight against VE, as the multiplication of state bodies in Morocco to combat radical violence is an exception in the context of the Middle East and North Africa (MENA) region. Furthermore, Morocco wishes to stand out in the African continent within the counter-radicalization field. Indeed, Morocco has positioned itself as a peace mediator in Libya and Mali to increase its value as a regional security provider at the international level (Abouzzohour, 2020). Also, in this regard, Morocco recently inaugurated the Office of the United Nations Counter-Terrorism and Training Program in Africa (Kingdom of Morocco, 2021). More precisely, Morocco engaged in many efforts to curb radicalization in the religious sphere, but many gaps remain in the fight against VE. The socioeconomic pillar of the National Initiative for Human Development (INDH), launched in 2005 by King Mohammed VI, addressed to combat poverty and precariousness, particularly in fragile areas, is an example of such a gap. The work of the CONNEKT project in Morocco highlights the distance between the philosophy of the INDH and the reality of the programs' implementation, particularly in rural areas (Mouna et al., 2021).

To fulfill this challenge of fighting radicalization drivers in the religious field, the Moroccan kingdom can rely on two main state institutions: the Ministry of *Habous*/ Religious Affairs (*Ministère des Habous et des Affaires Islamiques*), which is a ministerial portfolio dedicated since 1955 to the management of everything that relates to Islam, the official religion of the state and the one practiced almost by the entire population, and the Higher Council of Ulemas (*Conseil supérieur des Oulémas*), which is a religious body created in 1981 to support the official religious policy of the state but which remained almost inactive until it was remobilized in 2000, when the new monarch launched the restructuring of the religious field. Moreover, a new dynamic was established directly linked with the attacks of Casablanca and the conception of the role that such religious authorities must play in the fight against VE. The Rabita Mohammadia of Ulemas (*Rabita Mohammadia des ulémas*) was created in 2006 at the initiative of King Mohammed VI in the context of the restructuring of the religious field and religious policy post-2003.

Thus, to address the religious driver of radicalization, the Moroccan government is looking to be omnipresent in the religious field, which leads to security and scholarly foundations and is aimed at an informed and adult population. Several measures have been taken, such as creating local authorities and regional offices of the Council of the Ulemas in control of imams and the Friday prayer, which need to be neutral and state-oriented politically. Another measure is the creation of the *qyimin diniyin*, religious leaders whose role is to provide literacy courses within the mosques and meet the needs of the faithful on religious issues. Finally, measures have been taken to ensure that the Moroccan Quranic schools would not become places of radicalization through the establishment of methods of memorizing the Quran. For example, the Quran Tablet—one of the methods of memorizing the Quran in Moroccan Quranic schools—is in force particularly in the regions of

Sousse-Massa and Tangier-Tétouan-Al Hoceima. These two regions account for 47.91% of religious schools nationwide. Of these, 50.35% are in rural areas and 71.68% are managed by associations controlled by the Ministry of *Habous*/Religious Affairs (Mouna and Mouna, 2021).

Other state institutions are taking care of other aspects of the five-pillar action plan, such as the National Human Rights Council (CNDH), the Social Development Agency (ADS), and the National Initiative for Human Development (INDH). These institutions are mostly taking care of improving the economic situation and reducing territorial inequalities.

On the other hand, since 2003, civil society has been fully involved in the fight against VE through civil society organizations. Associations working in the field of human rights, such as the Association de Défense des Droits de l'Homme au Maroc (ASDHOM), the Ligue Marocaine pour la Citoyenneté et les Droits de l'Homme (LMCDH) and the Forum marocain des droits de l'Homme, have made it a priority. Their margin of intervention is distributed on several levels, namely the control of security and judicial procedures, the legal accompaniment of victims, in addition to awareness and activism in favor of ideas that are supposed to help confront the socioeconomic sources of this extremism through the establishment of a democratic political system, the reform of justice, and the reduction of social inequalities. Moreover, scientific, artistic, cultural, sports and other associations were also created in this frame. Finally, political organizations not linked to the state, in particular political parties, have also demonstrated their willingness to get involved in this field. Centers for reflection and awareness have, in fact, been created within some political parties. We cite as an example the center *Al-Mizane* (the balance) created within the Istiqlal party and directed by Mohamed Abdelouhab Rafiqui, a former Salafist and detainee on the sidelines of the 2003 attacks, who is involved at all levels in the fight against religious extremism in Morocco.

The nature of their activities varies according to the diversity of the spaces where they are active and the sectors that they target such as working-class neighborhoods, school spaces, youth spaces or universities. However, all these activities are generally based on the same mission: raising awareness of the risk of youth involvement in extremist organizations and promoting the values of tolerance and openness. Despite the multiplication of these bodies, one observes an omnipresence of the state and the lack of coordination among them. Therefore, these two types of institutions (state and civil society) do not work closely together because of their different way of working and the strong grip of religious institutions over the counter-radicalization field. Indeed, the religious institution monopoly leads to a lack of resources for CSOs, even if they show a great capacity to mobilize young people with their human rights approach.

This lack of cooperation could be illustrated through the case of the Moroccan Observatory for the Fight against Terrorism and Extremism, developing a strategy to combat extremism and an action plan to prevent VE. Its strategy is transnational in scope and aims at depriving extremist groups of the tacit support of their sympathizers by broadening the participation of associative entities in the process of sensitizing groups against the regressive ideas of terrorism. However, this strategy is hampered by the lack of trust between civil society and the state. Restoring trust between official and associative institutions is thus a necessity to fight against VE, especially since civil associations are the first interface close to the population, direct interlocutors with it, and a safety valve against all forms of extremism (Azim et al., 2024).

But all these action plans are made from a top-down perspective and question us on the reliability and efficiency of these counteractions. In the short term, are they really effective, and especially, do they match citizens' needs and demands across the kingdom?

To answer these questions, we have conducted three meso-scale case studies within three different organizations in the Moroccan kingdom to witness field reality in terms of radicalization drivers among different local contexts: the *Amal* organization, the Ultras "Siempre Paloma" football supporters and the *Adl wal Ihsane* association. These associations are different in every aspect, which is profitable for the quality of broad-spectrum answers.

Each case will be presented regarding its specificity in terms of socioeconomic aspects and territorial dynamics. Methods used for each case study included focus groups and in-depth interviews. Details will be given for each field of research in terms of ethical problems and challenges we have faced. Finally, the main result will be displayed, leading to recommendations and new avenues of research.

2 Case Studies and Methodological Challenges

The study of communities takes an important place in the understanding of social phenomena. This is why this study is based on the analysis of the discourses of three different communities. The selected regions are marked by political movements and have different socioeconomic characteristics that have determined social change in these local contexts, particularly after 2011.

We chose three groups in different territories of Morocco that are active in various sportive, associative and politico-religious fields. Those groups are the *Amal* organization, Ultras "Siempre Paloma" football supporters, and the *Adl wal Ihsane* movement. We conducted one focus group and three interviews for each case. We kept gender as one of our selection criteria. The participants in these three groups come from different neighborhoods and represent various fields of activity.

2.1 The *Amal* Organization

Our aim with the *Amal* organization was to understand the collective interpretation of violent extremism by an associative group and the impact of the local space on their perception of the phenomenon, adding their strategy of fight and/or prevention.

The association *Amal* operates in the field of the fight against violence, especially against women, through the cooperation of other organizations. The organization members use the discourse of tolerance and acceptance of different social categories to spread its message. This association does not only work at the local level but has created synergies beyond. The members of the association frequently organize activities in the Fès-Meknès region, and also at the national level by creating a network of cooperation with other organizations in the Maghreb. The omnipresence of *Amal* in events at the international level is part of its work related to human rights and security. It is an association based on an approach and orientation for women victims of violence, which allows us to see how communities organize themselves to manage situations of violence and their reactions to the Moroccan laws that protect victims of violence. The active members of this association are young people from the Meknès-Fès region who have a different level of education and who develop their creativity in the process of social action.

Other institutions are involved in the organization's regional setting: the University where some participants continue their studies, the professional training centers, and the international associations with which *Amal* coordinates to organize activities at the Maghreb level.

Amal operates in the city of El-Hajeb, a small town in the region of Fès-Meknès, a region characterized by the sociocultural diversity and the presence of the Amazigh people of the Middle Atlas who speak Amazigh language and the *Darija* (Moroccan dialect). The youth of the region live in a situation of socioeconomic inequality and lack of opportunities to integrate into the labor market. This is reflected in the unemployment rise in 2021 being 13.4% (HCP, 2020a). The region presents an absence of investment projects for young people compared to larger regions such as the region of Casablanca, and economic activities are limited in the two areas of agriculture and trade. This situation is considered a territorial gap that increases the risk of young people becoming radicalized and producing violent acts or joining the path of delinquency. Therefore, associative work occupies an important place for young people, and it has an impact on their insertion into sociocultural activities in the absence of cultural and artistic centers in the city.

The selection criteria we used to organize our Focus Group Discussions (FGD) are based on gender and age, the nature of the role that each member plays within the association, as well as the level of education and professional training of each of them. These varied criteria give us a broad vision of the understanding this group holds of the facts related to violent extremism, through the collective experience lived in the field of fight and prevention against violence.

After the selection of the case study, we contacted the president of the association directly and explained the general framework of the project, the interest of the research and the ethical considerations of the research, as well as the criteria of the participants we needed for the focus groups and the individual interviews. During the focus groups, we took note of the participants' reactions through observation. This tool allowed us to select the relevant profiles for individual interviews. Then, we contacted the targeted participants directly to conduct in-depth interviews and completed them after their due consent. The meeting places were decided in common agreement with our interlocutors.

The members selected to participate in the research on the Amal association in the city of El-Hajeb were aged between 19 and 26 and had different education levels. The participants were active in the association and attended several activities such as listening sessions, artistic activities, and cultural events organized in the region or at the national level. In this case, it was not possible to include minors under 18 years old because the association does not integrate this population segment of under 18 in its activities. The focus group was composed of five members of the association: two young females and three young males aged between 19 and 26. Some of them were in higher education and others in professional activities. The interviewed participants are one young woman aged 23 and two young males aged 26 and 24.

Regarding the challenges encountered, participants had difficulties in expressing themselves, which prompted us to develop a suitable linguistic approach (use of easy notions in *Darija*) and to use examples to properly guide the interview according to the context of the group, especially in the case of the participants who had a low level of education. Their descriptions of social facts were oriented by daily observation and their own interactions in the family environment and social life. We adapted to the difficulties encountered by the flexibility in conducting the interviews, and the use of interactive communication. Furthermore, conducting the focus group within the premises of the organization was an asset for the participants to be comfortable.

2.2 Ultras "Siempre Paloma" Football Supporters

The second case study fieldwork was developed in the north of Morocco, among the Ultras "Siempre Paloma" football supporters. It is a group of active young people in the city of Tétouan. The specificity of this group lies in the departure of a significant number of its members to join Daesh. Indeed, this group of Ultras was impacted by a significant number of young people who joined Daesh in the period between 2011 and 2019 (according to confidential information provided by a state official). This group gathers more than 1000 members from different neighborhoods of Tétouan, especially neighborhoods characterized by socioeconomic fragility. Most of the members of the group have a low level of education. The group was selected because of the possibility it offered to better understand the factors that led some of its members to join violent extremism. This cased allowed for an interesting comparison with other regions regarding territorial inequalities and the impact of public development policies.

The objectives of the research aimed at exploring how sports play a role in the activism of Moroccan youth to claim rights, as well as grasping the elements that constitute violence, the nature of the conflicts produced within this community, and its relationship with violent extremism. The perceptions of the Ultras towards violence and the interaction between the community and the political structures of the region will be stressed.

The Tangier-Tétouan-Al Hoceima region ranks third in terms of participation in the national GDP (10.8%) in 2018 (HCP, 2020b). It is the second region in terms of economic activity, especially since the creation of Tangier-Med port in the 2000s. However, this region has experienced a significant departure of young people to war zones, particularly since the 1980s, with the rise of Salafism-Wahabism. It has also experienced several forms of violence practiced by the state, notably the repression of the revolt of 1958–59, then that of 1984, and more recently the *Hirak* of the Rif in 2016–17. The migration network in Belgium and Holland has also played an important role in the arrival of Wahabism but also Shi'ism, especially in Tangier. In this sense, the positive indicator of economic development has not slowed the development of radicalism, which is explained by some of our interlocutors with the historical burden of this region marked by strong state violence.

We first contacted one of the leaders of the group to explain the context of our research. We conducted a non-directive interview with him to establish a relationship of trust, and then we asked for an appointment to conduct a focus group. The participants of the focus group were selected based on their age and participation in the activities organized by the group throughout the year. We conducted two focus groups, one with participants aged between 18 and 30 years old, and another one with participants aged between 14 and 17 years old. This last focus group was organized inside the school with the permission of the school director. When it comes to gender, it needs to be emphasized that all the participants are young men, as no girls were identified as members of the Ultras. Since its creation, the majority of the group's members are men. Regarding individual interviews, three young males of 29, 23, and 26 years old were interviewed.

The work with the group of supporters was particularly delicate. Firstly, because this group has experienced a significant number of departures to war zones and, secondly, because we needed a trusted intermediary to be able to access them. The second obstacle was including minors under the age of 18 linked to the sports group and finding a suitable place for the discussion.

2.3 Adl Wal Ihsane Movement

The third research field is the *Adl wal Ihsane* association, a religious-political group that has been present in the Moroccan political scene for decades. Since the creation of this Islamist movement, the adherents have tried to found *Dawlat khilafa* (a caliphate state) and do not recognize the legitimacy of *Imarat al-Muminin* (the position of Commander of the Faithful exercised by the King) in Morocco. The nature of the conflict between the Islam of the state and the Islam exercised by this group is at the core of the issue. Since its inception, it has remained outside the Moroccan political scene, but it has always tried to exercise its strategy through the diversity of its activities: the organization of associative and religious activities, particularly within the University (Yafout, 2017). It has been considered an illegal group by the state since its creation and thus the number of its adherents is not provided officially, but its presence is strong at the level of the clandestine activities within the associations of a religious character. Through its representatives in Moroccan universities, they convey their ideas regarding freedoms, the relationship between the Muslim world and the West, and the position of women in the public space.

The politico-religious movement has a history of conflict with the Moroccan state and its exclusion from participation in political activities at the national level. However, it has structured an "authentic Islamic society" (Daoudi and Alami-Fischer, 2020). The purpose of the research is understanding the role of this politico-religious group in the socialization of young people regarding ideology and to what extent it has an impact on the trajectories of young Moroccans. This association is characterized by its religious-political ideology approach and by the fact that its members are among the most highly educated, holding PhD degrees for example.

The territorial coverage of this organization is threefold: local, regional, and national. The members of the group are active at the local level by organizing activities in the different cities, but the major decisions are made by the national leadership. The main selection criteria of the research participants were the diversity of the activities carried out within different organizations such as universities, the professional status of the participants, the presence of women, and the age span. We expressed our wish to have a meeting with the 14 to 17-year-olds belonging to this group, but our request was denied. The selection of the members who participated in the focus group was made by the group's regional management of Fès-Meknès.

The group members who were present in our focus group had a high level of education, holding a master's degree and above. The focus group was composed of five members of the movement, aged between 26 and 30, two women and three men, all with the same high level of education (PhD level in law and Islamic studies). The focus group was held in the presence of the group leader in a public space. Regarding the individual interviews, three were made with a young male student of 18, a 30-year-old woman, and a young female high school teacher.

We encountered several obstacles in the implementation of this phase of research. First, the resistance of the political-religious group to organize the initial focus group because of their conflictive relation with the state and the political nature of the topic. Our research was perceived as suspicious by participants, and we were confronted with the cancellation of several appointments for reasons that were not understood. It is thanks to our contacts with members of the group's central office, that we were finally able to set a date for the focus group in a public café, after they refused to enter the university, but also because of the university's refusal at the last minute for the group to access the premises of the institution. The second obstacle was the rejection of our request to conduct a focus group with the minors belonging to the group. Regarding the individual interviews, we used the Google Meet application for the three interviews as the interviewees refused several times to meet physically.

3 Results

In all three case studies, albeit differences, we questioned participants on the definition of violent extremism regarding CONNEKT's drivers: religion, economic deprivation, political issues, territorial inequalities, education, culture and leisure opportunities, transnational dynamics, and digital socialization. A large emphasis was put on the religious driver since it was the one that received the most dissenting opinions.

3.1 Religion

Religion is the driver with the most divergent opinions. Members of *Amal* described violent extremism using specific terms such as *tashadud* in Arabic (fundamentalism). According to them, religious extremism could be associated with clothing or appearance styles such as the beard for men and the veil for women. Furthermore, the obligation to respect some religious practices such as wearing the hijab represents a form of violence exercised by the family and by society. Religious practice should remain a personal aspect as well. In their view, socialization through religion is a key factor. While for a woman wearing the veil can be seen as a constraint, men perceive it as a religious value.

Regarding the location of the Ultras "Siempre Paloma" football group, one might think that the religious factor has a clear impact in the Northern region, especially since a set of youth who chose to join VEOs were impacted by the religious discourse. However, religion was not a driving force behind radicalization, as participants did not notice their religious practices as a primary element in their daily lives. For them, religious principles must be based on freedom and peace, and they justified their violent discourse and anger by the nature of their conflicts with state officials. This is why they think that the members who have been radicalized by Daesh had personal reasons and not collective ones. Participants also underlined the fact that religious parties like the PJD (Party of Justice and Development) have a weak predicament among the members since they consider that they do not take seriously the needs of the citizens and that have no concrete achievements at the political level in the region. Although members may perceive changes in other members' behavior, particularly religious changes, they attribute these changes to external rather than internal factors. For example, people who were once members of the association and who have become radicalized declare that playing soccer goes against the values of Islam, even though they were themselves members of the association. As the *Amal* members, they consider that the religious practice should remain personal. Being an ultra for them is a mechanism to fight against marginality and corruption in the region.

Finally, regarding *Adl wal Ihsane*, religion is a main element in the group's discourse. The participants link the transformation of the religious field in Morocco with the political transformations that Morocco has experienced. In this sense, they see that religion is a necessity for the whole society and it should not be limited to the private life of individuals. They consider that religion does not participate in the production of radicalism and violence, but in their opinion, the problem is the lack of the role of religious institutions, especially the mosque, in the socialization of young people on the principles of the Islamic religion. According to one participant: "the individual becomes like a blank page, an open book in front of everyone and easy to seduce. He becomes blind, he can't distinguish between what is wrong and what is right. And the media has played an extremely important role in the failure of socialization processes".

The interlocutors put forward an interpretation of religion as an absent and disappeared element in the educational system which they call the system of norms and values, whereas religion must be present at all levels to minimize physical violence. Their opinion is justified by the nature of Islam which depicts a tolerant religion. According to them, true Muslims refuse any type of violence either in the private or public sphere and radicalism is not a result of the religious factor.

From another point of view, religion is interpreted as a resilience mechanism in front of violence and radicalism. The participants added that Islam is a source of justice, peace and modernity, values that contribute to the fight against violent extremism, rather than being drivers of radicalization. The participants presented the example of moderate Islam from the behavior of group leaders as figures that express the principles of religion. In their opinion, human relations must be based on three main elements: rejection of violence, transparency, and the adoption of good behavior with strangers.

Violent extremism is perceived as being rooted in the decline and weak role that institutions occupy in changing the normative structure and its impact on the global religious culture, and, on the other hand, the state's monopoly on violence. The participants therefore consider that the official political practices are contradictory to the values of Islam. The speakers believe that religion became a secondary element in the educational system because the curriculum of Islamic education is devalued. They believe that the absence of this content in school programs pushes young people to practice and exercise several forms of violence. In their view, the source of this negative perception regarding religion lies in globalization and international policies that work to delegitimize Islam and Muslims.

3.2 *Political Issues*

The political driver for the *Amal* organization participants is represented in the lack of security. They referred to the attacks that Morocco has experienced as due to the lack of security in public spaces. On the other hand, the participants considered security a problem in large cities that are out of state control, specifically large cities like Casablanca and Tangier. However, a city like El-Hajeb was considered safe because it is easier to be under control. Participants expressed that citizens are responsible for the disadvantaged situation of the city, as they choose the elected officials of the local authorities through their vote. Our interlocutors defined violent acts as a form of claiming social rights, a way of expressing the sociopolitical situation of their territory.

According to the Ultras "Siempre Paloma" football participants, political issues are one of the main factors in their discourse. They mentioned the conflict between the group members, the elected local officials, the central government, and the regional sports representatives. This triangle indicates that the group takes sports as one of the instruments to reclaim power. They describe the disadvantaged situation of the city and the young people by using the slogans prepared and disseminated on social networks. The participants expressed that violence is not only a product of youth but also a phenomenon exercised by the state, as our interlocutors considered that their social exclusion is a form of violence exercised by the state. To them, violence is rooted in the social and economic inequalities in the Northern region, the violent prohibition to organize protests to claim social and political rights, as well as the lack of communication between elected politicians and citizens. They declared that their sports activity is a means of expression and revindication as our interlocutor underlined: "the foundation of the team was for several reasons: to defend the city, to defend the individuals". Therefore, the political in this context takes its place in the creation of a space of conflict between the state and the youth of the city, for this reason the actors of this group use different tools as a mechanism to protest against local public policies and express their situation of precariousness and poverty.

Political grievances are also very present in the speech of the *Adl wal Ihsane* members. They argued that "the State eliminated the young people from political participation as in the case of trade unions and political parties". The exclusion of participation of the members of this politico-religious group in the elections is a form of injustice and hindrance to the freedom of expression, opinion, and listening. More precisely, one of the participants declared that "the Moroccan state cannot be considered a democratic state because it treats the protests of the youth in the public space with violence (…) the state does not have the mechanisms of communication and dialogue". The political driver for this group is related to the situation of injustice and marginality, explained by the exclusion from political participation and expression of the people. For them, it is a kind of symbolic violence exercised by the state. In this sense, the interlocutors recall the elimination of the Union of Moroccan Students in 1985 within Moroccan universities. Finally, we can conclude that the interlocutors referred to two forms of violence: the violence exercised from the description of the conflicts between the group and the state, and the violence exercised by individuals as a reaction to the situation of political exclusion and marginalization.

3.3 *Economic Deprivation*

Territorial inequalities are also estimated as a major factor in the path to violence according to *Amal* participants. They expressed such an idea through a comparison between large cities and small towns. In their opinion, small cities like El-Hajeb do not represent a space of investment for young people. For them, it is a form of territorial marginalization translated by the centralization of power and economy in large monopolies like the city of Casablanca.

Unemployment and poverty are components declared by the Ultras "Siempre Paloma" football supporters. They explained violent extremism by the social and economic problems of the city's youth. The lack of means and economic resources marginalizes young people who want to change their future, according to one participant: "young people do not have the means to take a cab and pay to play". During the conversations, they questioned the reasons for the marginalization of young people while the state needs human resources to keep its peace and security. The interlocutors associated the adherence to violent groups with poverty: "they exploit the youth and take advantage of their poverty and marginality". The participants stated that in the absence of the main necessities young people look for alternatives to improve their life and satisfy their needs. All the participants expressed that poverty and precariousness are the driving forces behind violent extremism.

The low economic level is also considered by the participants of the *Adl wal Ihsane* association as a direct driver of radicalization. In their opinion, poverty builds in individuals a feeling of injustice in relation to others. For our interlocutors, terrorist groups take the poverty of the youth as one of the main elements to attract them to join conflict zones. The participants mentioned that the economic factor is a complementary element in the pattern of radicalization. In their opinion, poverty is a form of social injustice and exclusion. Thus, individuals who have suffered violence in their childhood and live in a situation of poverty and precariousness are more likely to be radicalized and are the target of terrorist groups, who offer economic incentives to young people to join terrorist groups and improve their economic situation.

3.4 *Territorial Inequalities*

As mentioned earlier, *Amal* participants pointed out that the path to violent extremism is thought to be significantly influenced by territorial disparities. In addition to the poor distribution of economic and political resources between big and small cities, the absence of the construction of social and cultural spaces for young people in the city also plays a role in the emergence of violence and the risk of radicalization. The interlocutors interpreted the passage to VE as a reaction to the absence of a space of expression and the absence of social rights, which provides the radical groups with the possibility to present tools for propaganda and to recruit an important number of marginalized young people who feel excluded from society. However, they considered that the violent answer to a situation of social inequality is limited to the individual attitude and does not take a collective form.

On the other hand, the participants confirmed that spatial inequalities do not represent a driving force of radicalization. They justified it with the example of the social success of several young people who come from working-class neighborhoods. Thus, violence is not a fact linked to social status or a specific standard of living, but it is a product of multiple personal reasons. Our interlocutors added that the association is a way to face violence, as their activities have helped young people, and women especially, to become aware of their social rights and to protect themselves from violence in the public and private spheres.

The Ultras "Siempre Paloma" football supporters perceived territorial inequalities as the lack of cultural and leisure infrastructure for young people, which pushes them into delinquency or violence. According to them, the state is now beginning to create recreational areas, such as soccer fields, after young people left to go to conflict areas. But before that, they could not find anywhere to play, either they had to pay to play or had no team. As a result, they lost hope and began using drugs and spending their days in coffee shops. For them, this situation indicates the total marginalization of young people from social life. They used the term *hogra* (contempt) in *Darija* to describe the feeling of isolation from other territories. This case study represents an example of the daily conflicts that young people from marginal spaces live. On the one hand, the feeling of social isolation, and the lack of social and economic integration strengthen the low position of young people from marginal spaces compared to those from more accommodated spaces. On the other hand, the young people interviewed see the activities of Ultras as a form of demonstration to convey a discourse that expresses social and economic dissatisfaction.

The *Adl wal Ihsane* association participants consider that violent extremism is not limited to a specific space. They believe that spatial characteristics do not produce radicalism. For them, it is the lack of socialization and/or personal and individual reasons that lead individuals to become radicalized or put forward violent acts. One of the participants expressed, though, that marginalized geographic spaces can be a field where terrorist organizations appear. Young people who suffer from social exclusion can be ready to learn radical ideas, and then, social and psychological problems are direct drivers of radicalization. However, the territorial characteristics do not represent a driver that leads to violent extremism for them. On the other hand, socialization is represented as a process that protects young people who live in fragile neighborhoods from becoming violent.

3.5 Education, Culture and Leisure Opportunities

The *Amal* organization participants witnessed that sociocultural extracurricular activities are absent in the schools of the city of El-Hajeb. Still, young people seek to attend local places such as youth centers to participate in cultural workshops, namely theater and music. In this sense, the participants have chosen to join the association to defend women's rights and become aware of social changes, in order to deal with the different situations of violence they may encounter in society. However, within the university, cultural activities replaced the role of public spaces in the listening and sharing of ideas: "in the University for example, there are several activities such as the theater, to which young people must be adhered to receive the information, because we do not have a communication with the administration, we need the activities to give us the opportunity of exchanging and sharing".

In response to the lack of youth centers in some neighborhoods, participants have sought a cultural alternative to participate in social and cultural life by joining the association. Yet, young people are not sufficiently integrated into social and cultural life, due to the failure to implement integral public policies in the small cities compared to the larger ones. The lack of interaction between the citizens and the representatives of the territorial communities can reinforce the risk of radicalization for young people who do not have access to sociocultural activities.

The Ultras "Siempre Paloma" football participants considered that being an active member of Ultras can enhance the cultural orientations of young people, especially since the principles of the group are openness to other cultures and the acceptance of the other, whether it is because of ideological or religious differences. They confirmed that young people are excluded from sociocultural programs, with the absence of youth centers, notably in the popular districts. They added that this absence plays an important role in the process of youth radicalization: "The lack of leisure spaces is a factor of radicalism, and the absences of these places are also the factors of the production of other social phenomena such as delinquency".

Group members have found that the way out of this isolation is to join the Ultras, where they can improve their relational network and find alternatives for young people in their city and region. Being part of the Ultras for our interlocutors is a mechanism to express their claims and grievances, particularly economic deprivation. The organized activities are run by the leaders of the group who manage the stages and the symbols used during their presence in the playgrounds. We have observed that one member among them uses the style of graffiti on the walls of the neighborhood depicting political, cultural, and sports symbols. Sport is therefore not the only cause targeted by the group, but it has become an integrated method in a process of conflict and confrontation with the state.

All the members of the *Adl wal Ihsane* association confirmed the lack of public spaces for youth recreation, which poses a problem of communication among young people who need mechanisms for dialogue to avoid violent expression. Another participant added that the existence of leisure places in the neighborhoods does not mean an ideal protection for young people. She believed that within these places, individuals produce attitudes rejected by society. So, what makes the issue more complex for her is the exclusion of group members from participating in the sociocultural dynamic, so they can raise awareness among young people and give them the means to protect themselves from violence and radicalism.

Moreover, the sports and cultural clubs created within the association and the University represent a mechanism for strengthening social ties among young people, enabling them to reinforce their desire to take action in the public sphere. One of the participants expressed that belonging to this group allowed him to create his own universe of expression despite his exclusion from the public sphere. He highlighted that from the cultural program of the movement, he can transfer messages to the young people to direct them to the right path. The participants show that the activities of the group are a space of expression for young people that fills the absence of spaces of social and political representation provided by the state.

3.6 Digital Socialization

Amal interviewees showed that they frequently visit virtual spaces and that they are knowledgeable of the different digital platforms. From the individual interviews, the participants gave examples of the violent content they found on social networks. They explained that digital space has an important impact on young people and teenagers especially. From the participants' point of view, the role of technology is to facilitate communication, but they observed that the content published on social networks is violent, even containing torture, and the young people's comments on these videos show the possibility of taking this violence seriously and reproducing it later. The interlocutors confirmed that the impact of the violent content is a result of the lack of family control and parental guidance. During the individual interview with one of the participants she presented concrete examples of violent content published on social networks: "lately I saw videos of the Taliban, they show a lot of violent practices and behaviors towards others, images that transmit implicit messages. When you see someone who has killed a person, or a child, and if a child looks at this kind of content in social networks, he will reproduce the same acts". Our interlocutors underlined that the diffusion of violence in the virtual sphere impacts teenagers who are not aware of the risk of this content more than adults who can choose content far from violence. For them, the family must take into consideration that control and communication are effective means to protect children and adolescents.

From the point of view of the Ultras "Siempre Paloma" football participants, digital socialization has an impact on the ideas of young people. On the one hand, members of Ultras use various platforms to organize and publish the announcements of the events. We noticed that they are very active in social networks like Facebook where they have created official pages and discussion groups. Social networks in their opinion are a sphere of expression of social needs and a mechanism for transferring messages to policy-makers about the situation of marginality and exclusion and any form of injustice. Digital technology replaces the role of cultural activities for teenagers. We have found that minors spend more than 2 h in video games of a violent nature, such as fights and wars. This is why the participants revealed that the virtual space has become a field of production of violence.

In the case of minors, we observed that violence is exercised in the educational space: the family and the school, where those actors operating in these spaces consider violence as a legitimate behavior. On the other hand, there is always the risk of radicalization through the digital space, as minors have become attached to social networks and violent video games, a phenomenon far from the initial role of the family in orientation and communication. From the focus group of minors, the participants showed their low participation in extracurricular activities and communication within the family, which allows the digital space to become a place to share and exchange with peers. The characteristics of the working-class neighborhoods show how many of the young people live in the margins of society, while a group of them always try to show their belonging to this territory through sports or art.

When asked about violence in the virtual space, the *Adl wal Ihsane* association participants confirmed that violent content has always circulated, particularly during the period of the pandemic, because people have been attached more to social networks. Teenagers who see this content can reproduce it, especially the videos mirroring images of war and fights. From another point of view, a participant emphasized that the images of the war against Muslims represent the pejorative image of the other. She added that the messages circulated in the media and social networks are signs to "sully the image of Islam under the title of terrorism". However, they have found that a significant number of Muslims are victims of physical and symbolic violence: "what happens today is a great international policy against Islam". In this regard, participants consider that the problem of conflict and violence is not limited to the local context, but in their opinion, international policies are building a war against Islam. It is an expression that shows the relationship between national and transnational dynamics. Thus, they see globalization and international politics as a mechanism to eliminate Islam and Muslims. The conspiracy theory is strongly present.

4 Conclusion

We can conclude that violent extremism is not limited to a specific area, but is a phenomenon that cuts across urban and rural areas, and is present in both the public and private spheres of young people. This finding leads us to explore the new positions that young people are taking after their individual experiences with violence. We have been able to notice, based on this empirical work, that members of the three associations have both divergent and similar opinions regarding the factors behind radicalization. For each case study, recommendations were formulated based on the data collected. Participants emphasized the importance of creating infrastructures to help people in schools and universities, as well as sports and meeting facilities in disadvantaged neighborhoods, to promote exchanges and communication between young people.

An effort must also be made to create cooperation between associations and the state to promote the work of integrating young people into the political discourse to make their needs heard. Young people must take part in local and national social and political dynamics. The family must be included in young people's access to the Internet, through communication and attention. Also, access to violence is an enormous challenge regarding social networks, which constitute another space to produce different forms of violence. They facilitate the dissemination of hate speech and discrimination, not only among young people, but also among minors who have access to these platforms through various means of communication.

The goal of this chapter was to analyse the socioeconomic, cultural, territorial, religious and political dynamics that produce radicalization and violent extremism, based on the experiences of young people in different contexts and using meso-scale data. Also, our aim was to make an interconnection between these different factors, to understand the forms of interaction and representation of young people in situations that have a direct and indirect relationship to violence in the various spheres around them.

References

Abouzzohour, Y. (2020). Libya's Tangier Tallks: Why is Morocco getting involved?. Moroccan Institute for Policy Analysis. Retrieved December 2023, from https://mipa.institute/8290.

Azim, S., Er-rifaiy, A., & Mouna, K. (2024). *Report on prevention of extremism, The Case of the Moroccan organisation for childhood and youth in Kenitra and Amal association in El Hajeb*. The European Institute of the Mediterranean (IEMed). Retrieved February 2024, from https://h2020connekt.eu/wp-content/uploads/2024/03/D5.2-COUNTRY.pdf

Bassou, N. (2019). *La Radicalisation chez les Filles. Analyse de Trajectoire Individuelles au Maroc et en France*. PhD thesis, Mohamed V University and Aix-Marseille University.

Daoudi, H., & Alami-Fischer, R. (2020). *Al Adl Wal Ihssane, une Jamaa née dans l'amertume*. Atlas info. Retrieved February 2022, from https://atlasinfo.fr/al-adl-wal-ihssane-une-jamaa-nee-dans-lamertume.html

Haut Commissariat au Plan (HCP). (2020a). *La situation du marché du travail en 2020*. Retrieved May 2024, from https://www.hcp.ma/La-situation-du-marche-du-travail-en-2020_a2650.html

Haut Commissariat au Plan (HCP). (2020b). *Note d'information, les comptes régionaux de 2018*. Retrieved May 2024, from https://www.hcp.ma/region-tanger/attachment/2141567/#:~:text=La%20r%C3%A9gion%20Tanger%2DT%C3%A9touan%2DAl%20Hoceima%2C%20avec%20un%20PIB,de%20Rabat%2DSal%C3%A9%2DKenitra

Kingdom of Morocco. (2021). *Inauguration of the Office of the United Nations Counterterrorism and Training Program in Africa in Rabat*. Retrieved February 2024, from https://www.maroc.ma/en/news/un-office-counter-terrorism-and-training-africa-inaugurated-rabat

Masbah, M. (2019). Transnational security challenges in North Africa: Moroccan foreign fighters in Syria 2012–2016. *Middle Eastern Studies, 55*(2), 182–199.

Mouna, K., Er-rifaiy, A., & Fadil, M. (2021). *Morocco—Macro-drivers of radicalisation and violent extremism*. The European Institute of the Mediterranean (IEMed). Retrieved February 2022, from https://h2020connekt.eu/wp-content/uploads/2021/09/Morocco_CONNEKT_Macro_Drivers.pdfù

Mouna, K., & Mouna, A. (2021). L'enseignement coranique chez les Jbala du Rif occidental. *Revue des mondes musulmans et de la Méditerranée, 150*(10), 10.

Samouni, M. (2017). *Masks of extremism. The origins of religious radicalisation in Morocco*. En toutes lettres. Collection Enquêtes.

Yafout, M. (2017). *The activities of Adl Wal Ihsane in the Neighbourhoods. How to build a 'non-legal'consensus from a 'tolerated'*. Conflict International Development Policy. Retrieved February 2022, from https://journals.openedition.org/poldev/2323

Political Divisions and Narratives of Exclusion in Bosnia and Herzegovina

Muamer Hirkić, Anida Dudić-Sijamija, Sarina Bakić, and Damir Kapidžić

1 Introduction

Bosnia and Herzegovina (BiH) gained independence from Yugoslavia in March 1992, undergoing a 3-year war resulting in approximately 100,000 casualties (BBC News, 2017). The country operates as a consociational democracy with a system of government were three main ethno-religious groups (Bosniaks, Croats, and Serbs) share power, as defined by the Dayton Peace Agreement. The institutional setup of BiH consists of the Federation of Bosnia and Herzegovina (FBiH), Republika Srpska (RS), as well as the Brčko District. FBiH is further divided into cantons, while RS has a centralized government. Asymmetric federalism is combined with ethnic federalism and limited central authority which gives outsized importance to ethnic groups (Kapidžić, 2020). The Office of the High Representative (OHR) played a crucial role in peace implementation since the end of the war. At the state level, there is a three-member Presidency, a government with limited powers, and entity governments with greater autonomy. Elections are held every 4 years, but the dominance of ethnic parties restricts political competition. According to the 2013 population census, BiH has 3.5 million inhabitants. The ethnic composition includes 50.1% Bosniaks, 30.8% Serbs, 15.4% Croats, and 3.7% others. The ethnic structure is clear, with the majority of Serbs in Republika Srpska and the majority of Croats and Bosniaks in the Federation of Bosnia and Herzegovina (Balkan Insight, 2016).

In BiH, the phenomenon of "violent extremism" results from several major events, including the 1990s war, the rise of Salafi preaching linked to the conflict, and the impact of global occurrences like September 11th, the emergence of ISIS,

---

M. Hirkić (✉) · A. Dudić-Sijamija · S. Bakić · D. Kapidžić
University of Sarajevo, Sarajevo, Bosnia and Herzegovina
e-mail: muamer.hirkic@fpn.unsa.ba; anida.dudic@fpn.unsa.ba; sarina.bakic@fpn.unsa.ba; damir.kapidzic@fpn.unsa.ba

C. Torrekens et al. (eds.), *Social Contexts of Radicalization and Violent Extremism in the MENA and Balkans*,
https://doi.org/10.1007/978-3-031-84521-5_6

and the war in Ukraine. These events influenced the understanding of related concepts such as terrorism, extremism, and radicalization in BiH (Hirkić et al., 2022). The traditional perspective ties violent extremism in BiH to religious, particularly Islamist radicalization. Indeed, the war in the 1990s created a conducive environment for the introduction of new ideas, leading to the prominence of Salafi interpretations supported by external influences (Azinović, 2017). While most research focuses on Islamic extremism, identified groups of Serbs and Croats support ethnic, Orthodox, and Catholic extremism. Violence within BiH has not been recorded, but citizens have joined conflicts outside the country, particularly in Ukraine. However, post-9/11, BiH aligned its counter-terrorism approaches with global trends.

In recent years, the narrative has shifted towards the return and repatriation of individuals from the foreign battlefields (Center for Security Studies, 2022). Also, it is important to highlight the emergence of extremism related to political ideologies, ethno-nationalism, and far-right views. BiH is grappling with the evolving nature of extremism, emphasizing the urgency to comprehend and define concepts like radicalization and extremism in the local context. As individuals from BiH become involved in combat activities in Ukraine, various forms of extremism beyond Islamist radicalization are coming to light. Nonetheless, it is important to underscore BiH society's vulnerability due to the recent history and unresolved governance issues. Furthermore, BiH is susceptible to radicalism due to institutional challenges, a frozen conflict, and unclear identity issues (Kapidžić et al., 2020). It is thus crucial to recognize the complexity of radicalization processes, acknowledging different phases and factors that distinguish between different forms of radicalization.

2 Institutional Level of Analysis

The first part of the CONNEKT project explored the macro/institutional level of analysis and showcased its importance for understanding radicalization processes. By starting from the macro level, it is possible to connect institutions to meso/community and micro/individual levels, shedding light on the role of strategic approaches and institutional interactions in shaping priorities and allocating resources. The research focuses on seven potential drivers of radicalization[1] and their correlation with institutional practices, advocating for a comprehensive approach at the macro level. The institutional perspective extends to state institutions, societal actors like religious institutions, civil society organizations and international entities, emphasizing their roles in countering extremism through education, infrastructure development, community policing, communication strategies, and other actions.

[1] Those drivers are territorial inequalities, economic deprivation, political ideas, cultural factors, religion, digital literacy, and transnational dynamics.

Bosnia and Herzegovina is characterized by several actors, both state and non-state, related at different scales to the issue of radicalization among its youth. Previous research (Kapidžić et al., 2021) was carried out with the following question in mind: "Do institutions view radicalization differently, and are some drivers more relevant than others?" By looking into practices of different types of institutions, macro results present a comprehensive overview of institutional drivers of violent extremism, as well as the complexity of C/PVE cooperation between different types of institutions, patterns of support from domestic and foreign actors, and the dynamics of establishing formal and informal communication channels. The research covered state institutions, international organizations, civil society organizations (CSOs), religious institutions, and the media, looking into drivers based on territorial inequalities, economic deprivation, political issues, culture, education and leisure opportunities, religion, digital socialization and transnational dynamics.

Therefore, the study revealed different institutional understandings of radicalization, clarified collaboration patterns among institutions from different sectors, presented the complexity of relationships within institutions and ways of cooperation, and confirmed the roles of formal and informal relationships in communication channels (Kapidžić et al., 2021). Institutions place special focus on the necessity of preventive C/PVE action, and some have separate departments that specifically deal with this topic. CSOs try to fill the gaps created by the work of state institutions, while the media provides space for critical analysis of consequences and causes of radicalization, and foreign organizations usually adopt a multi-sectoral approach with a special focus on young leaders.

Regarding the drivers of violent extremism, the research has shown that not all are considered as equally relevant, but there is no full agreement on this (Kapidžić et al., 2021). The first driver (territorial inequalities) is largely seen to go together with individual perceptions of marginalization and injustice and is no longer linked to a rural-urban divide. It is not seen as an independent driver. Likewise, the second driver (economic deprivation) has been described as an indirect driver manifested on the individual level, functioning in combination with other drivers, such as education. As with territorial inequalities, individual perception, lack of perspective, professional success and low self-esteem play an important role. The third driver (political issues) is primarily reflected through political polarization based on ethnic narratives and vulnerability. Research has shown that radical groups and organizations in most cases do not engage with politics, they do not aim to incorporate their values into the system or produce change but rather seek to replace it (Kapidžić et al., 2021). The fourth driver (education, leisure and cultural factors) primarily relates to the "way of life", which in the context of BiH can be seen through the prism of sub-cultures and ways of identification, but also the issue of toxic masculinity. Speaking of the fifth possible driver (religion), the research has shown that there is significant misuse of religion to legitimize particular opinions and worldviews, foremost the assumption of Islam as the dominant factor of radicalization. Research has repeatedly found this to be a false narrative in BiH, where Islam can even act as a protective factor against radicalization (Kapidžić et al., 2021). The sixth factor (digital socialization) is mostly used to spread radical ideas simply and effectively. It represents a significant challenge to analyze and address because of the different ways individuals consume online content, as well as the inability to find an institutional solution to remove unwanted content from social networks. Finally, the last driver of radicalization (transnational dynamics) is viewed as significant and is manifested both through actions from the immediate neighborhood and from the wider region.

Thus, the seven identified radicalization drivers provide a better understanding of the radicalization process leading to extremist violence but the importance of some drivers varies. This is why, in order to better understand the radicalization process, it is significant to have a closer look at how these drivers play a role within a community, at a meso level. Indeed, the meso approach calls for empowerment of local communities, providing resources for self-governance, and fostering resilience against extremism through tailored solutions. Therefore, three case studies have been conducted. The first one looks into the "two schools under one roof" phenomenon in Central Bosnia Canton; the second explores two football supporter groups in Banja Luka and Mostar, and the last one analyzes youth supporters of online Salafi influencers. These three different meso-level contexts help us to understand which drivers can be perceived as important or triggering for the members of their communities.

Each case study will be present the aim, methodology and the challenges encountered and the results will focus on the seven drivers identified in the CONNEKT project.

3 The Contexts: Case Studies and Methodologies

3.1 Two Schools Under One Roof

The phenomenon of "two schools under one roof" implies two separate schools (pupils, teachers, and technical staff) which use the same teaching space. This is a product of post-conflict Bosnia and Herzegovina, and it reflects one of the major political divisions in the country, namely the divide between Bosniaks and Croats in areas with ethnically mixed populations. The concept of "two schools under one roof" was established as a temporary solution[2] to encourage the return of displaced people, and according to some estimates, there are 56 schools today in BiH labelled as "two schools under one roof".[3] The research was conducted in two high schools labelled as "two schools under one roof" in Central Bosnia Canton. The schools

[2] The concept "two schools under one roof" was born in the context of the devastated education system of 1999 following the years after war destruction in Bosnia and Herzegovina (1992–1995).

[3] More information available on: https://ndcmostar.org/bs/dijalog-o-obrazovnim-politikama/

were divided in a way that lessons in one school are being taught in Bosnian language, and in other in Croatian. The schools share common entrances, common premises (school yard and sport halls), as well as meeting halls. Pupils do not have common teachers nor common activities unless those are initiated by non-governmental organizations or similar actors.

Usually, schools use different "national" curricula (Bosniak and Croatian), a mechanism for institutionalization of educational and social divisions. The consequence that follows is continued negative portrayal of "the Other", rooted deeply in nationalist political correctness, that is, mainstream cultural background, as well as the lack of sensitivity and understanding for anyone who is seen as 'the Other'. The way that political divisions are institutionalized through governing institutions allows radical ideas to emerge and gain prominence. This includes radical narratives of exclusion, segregation and discrimination that can be identified in the education sector and institutionalized through the "two schools under one roof". Thus, the education system is deploying segregation of children on the national basis: in the Republika Srpska teaching is conducted in Serbian language, while in the Federation of Bosnia and Herzegovina there are independent national schools or classes with different national programs—Bosnian and Croatian. This means that the education system in BIH is based on ethnocentrism, exclusivity from dominant ethnic identities and their educational politics, which is an obstacle for multicultural education and intercultural learning (Trkulja, 2017).

Our aim was to analyze the polarized and divisive conditions under which young people socialize, and to investigate the role of political ideas as a driver of radicalization. As political ideas are integrated into the institutional structures of the schools, their built environment, and the separate curriculums, their role is to divide young people and restrict cross-socialization.

Participants in the research were pupils of these two schools labelled as "two schools under one roof". Prior to conducting research, a request of approval for data collection activities was sent to the cantonal Ministry of Education. Upon obtaining the approval, contacts were made with school principals, and agreements were made on how the research should be conducted. The research relied on qualitative methods including group discussions and in-depth interviews. The criteria for participation were the following: (1) participants need to be over 15 years, and (2) participants had varying school performance. The selection of pupils for focus groups and interviews was carried out by school principals and expert bodies.

The implementation of research activities consisted of two phases: the first phase of research included two focus groups with five participants in each school (ten in total). The second phase of the research implied in-depth interviews with a total of five pupils in both schools (two in Croatian language school and three in Bosnian language school).

3.2 Organized Groups of Football Fans

Football fans in Bosnia and Herzegovina are regularly responsible for urban violence, driven by a combination of fan-based subculture and political ideology. Almost all football clubs have a clear ethnic affiliation with ties to a particular nationalist ideology. This includes a culture of hostility especially towards clubs of the ethnic "other". The groups are self-organized, have common views and values, an original or authentic name, a historical presence and institutional/group memory, specific roles, and behavioral patterns. The main reason we have decided to choose football fans communities for this research is that this subculture consists mostly of young people brought together through their shared ties to a football team and general knowledge and adoration for the sport. The intense feelings for a football club can lead to extreme behavior when fans encounter one another. Football fans in Bosnia and Herzegovina also express their feelings of rivalry and hatred in terms of nationalist symbols and nationalist identity. Additionally, this encompasses various forms of socially inappropriate behavioral patterns related to their social rebellion because of their social and economic position within society. Subcultures can be important for multiple studies because subculture groups often develop their own communication styles and social norms. Certain behavioral patterns or values may be mistakenly pathologized by people or groups outside that subculture. Also, certain subcultures may face discrimination from the majority groups within society (Bauman, 2001).

Our aim was to focus on fans' groups that, in many cases, openly advocate nationalism, ethnocentrism, xenophobia, and homophobia, and who carry out violent attacks on various "others". We chose two groups located in the north and south of the country, Banja Luka and Mostar, covering both entities of Bosnia and Herzegovina. Both have very active and visible football clubs' supporters' groups that were reached through requesting for interviews, and both agreed without any preconditions. The main criteria for the selection of participants in focus group and interviews were being active and substantial members of the football clubs' supporters' groups, and their age (following the methodological framework that requires 15 to 30-year-old participants). Unfortunately, gender balance was not achieved and the youngest participants were 19 years, while the the oldest were 31. All participants in the focus groups and interviews were males living in Mostar and Banja Luka. For focus group 1 in Banja Luka, we had four participants and three additional participants for the interviews. For the focus group 2 in Mostar, there were five participants and an additional interview was conducted with two of them.

The main challenge of these research activities was the issue of mutual confidence and trust, especially towards us as researchers, mostly regarding the anonymity of football supporters and handling of potentially sensitive information. Furthermore, these two groups come from totally different cultural and ethnic backgrounds. This was a serious challenge to obtain comprehensive and valuable answers from these specific cultural groups.

3.3 Youth Supporters of Online Salafi Influencers

Several religious lecturers or *da'is*, who have the rank of "superstars" within their online communities on Facebook and YouTube, regularly post sermons and lectures that could include radical messages and views that are often not supported by the official religious institution of the country—the Islamic Community in Bosnia and Herzegovina. This represents an important sociological phenomenon, especially due to the susceptibility of youth to online content (Kapidžić et al., 2021). According to previous research conducted by Balkan Investigative Reporting Network (BIRN), Salafi online influencers are supported by a network of organizations registered as associations for the promotion of 'positive values' and 'original Islam', youth associations, and book clubs (Balkan Insight, 2019).

Metodieva (2021) noted that previously, local and abroad-based influencers maintained their ties through shared activities, such as guest lectures and online discussions. Hesová (2021) believes that this last wave or form of Salafi activity can be characterized as neo-Salafism—which needs to be distinguished from previous Salafi, Wahhabi, and Mujahideen activities in BiH—and which can also be viewed through the prism of online Islamic missionary activism that is mostly based on youth and adult education, religious authority, media activism, and community building.

Digitalization, and especially social networks, were mentioned as potentially relevant mechanisms to spread radical ideas among youth followers. They can also serve as a tool for the socialization of individuals with radical or extremist ideas as an echo chamber where such ideas are amplified. Our aim was, thus, increasing the knowledge on the digitalization-related phenomena in Bosnia and Herzegovina that could correlate with the potential radicalization drivers among youth. Firstly, we will identify prevalent drivers of radicalization in the online Salafi communities and map the principal subjects and topics within the consumed social media content. Finally, we will establish a clear linkage between the findings at the macro-level and the subsequent meso-level analysis.

The selection process was made through the active monitoring of online lectures and educational content of the most popular Bosnian Salafist influencers via YouTube and Facebook platforms. The profiles of the two most prominent Salafi lecturers were selected, which together number around 325 thousand followers on Facebook, and around 46 thousand followers on YouTube.

The researchers conducted a qualitative content analysis of the most popular posts of the two most followed online *da'is* (lecturer) on Facebook and YouTube platforms. The posts were selected according to a criterion of engagement, or more precisely, according to the number of recorded reactions or likes. A total of 20 Facebook posts and 6 YouTube videos were analyzed. The period considered in the analysis is 1 year (from January 1, 2021, to December 31, 2021). The study was done so that the seven defined drivers were coded into the content that Salafi influencers publish to their supporters. The coding method assigned the keywords and thematic units related to drivers to the most popular posts. In this way, posts were classified into adequate categories, which allowed for the observation of followers' reactions and potential matches with the assigned categories. Nonetheless, it was possible to obtain a broad picture of the topics that provoke the most number of reactions, and also to analyze the ways in which such topics are approved, through the comments section below each of the posts.

4 Results

According to CONNEKT aims and goals, each case study has been examined through several drivers: religion, digital socialization, educational, leisure, and cultural opportunities, transnational dynamics, political issues, economic deprivation, and territorial inequalities. Each driver will be displayed in the following sections.

4.1 Religion

Within the "two schools under one roof" case study, participants highlight the fact that religion as a driver of radicalization is, unfortunately, most commonly associated with Islam. Most of the participants who state this perception explain that they often come across notions of "Islamic extremists" in the media, where they are presented as people who harm others in the name of religion. Indeed, some media sources employ the term "Islamic extremism" rather clumsily, stereotypically, or even deliberately describing extremist and theoretical events, thus spreading misinformation by presenting "Islam"—religion—and "Islamism"—political ideology—as synonyms.

Participants from the organized groups of football fans stated that religion in Bosnia and Herzegovina has a positive life influence on individuals and that it has nothing in common with violence. As the participants from the "two schools under one roof" case study, they showed high awareness of political manipulation and misuse of religion within society, in media, and also throughout history in general. They view religion as a positive attitude towards life, but they are also aware that religion is used to create animosities between people and to generate conflicts, or as an excuse for terrorist violence. Moreover, the interviewees emphasized that other religious identities, those of other groups they do not belong to, have never been an obstacle or threat to them. Two participants mentioned that they would defend their religion in case it was threatened, a position that might be misused under certain circumstances.

For a complete understanding of the religious aspect, we captured the prevalent narratives and reasons that lead people to take an interest in online Salafi preaching. The idea of producing online Salafi content and establishing a Salafi network of online influencers is based on the desire to bring followers closer to the interpretation of Islam advocated by such groups. Therefore, most of the Facebook and

YouTube posts analyzed in this study deal directly or indirectly with Islamic regulations and contain religion as a leitmotif, meaning that online Salafi influencers offer interpretations of the regulations in a simple way that is understandable to all followers. The essential reasoning behind their actions is the idea of Islamic authority, authentic Islam, or role modeling for all those who seek knowledge from "authentic" sources. *Da'is* use the Quran, the Hadith, as well as the works of both well and lesser-known authors, interpreters, and scholars—where many of them are from the same or similar Salafi circles. In this way, followers are presented with a dose of legitimacy that supports personal, day-to-day opinions, and thus there is a smaller number of those who could challenge such opinions. Previous macro-level research from the CONNEKT project has shown that most Salafi influencers in Bosnia and Herzegovina completed their formal higher education in states such as Jordan, the United Arab Emirates or Saudi Arabia—meaning that they did not study within the Islamic Community in BiH and, for that reason, they were not allowed to become officials in this institution (Kapidžić et al., 2021). However, online profiles show that Salafi influencers emphasize acquired degrees (master's or doctoral degrees), to give an even greater dose of legitimacy to their attitudes and thoughts. Although formal titles have become an important part of the overall online identity of these individuals, there are also religious ones—where a large number of followers have adopted standardized titles for lecturers such as *da'i* (lecturer), *alim* (scholar) or *sheikh* (honorary title, in line with "His excellency"), and use them daily in comments that express forms of agreement with the stated views. Most supporters' posts and comments are of a purely religious nature and show general agreement with *da'is*. On the other hand, *da'is* previously condemned violent extremism and do not express support for individuals or movements (VOA, 2019).

4.2 Digital Socialisation

Online space is often cited as important in the process of radicalization (Bećirević et al., 2017). The DARE (Dialogue on Radicalization and Equality) project, which examined the role of the Internet and social media in self-radicalization processes, states that young people can be victims of propaganda messages of radical organizations via participating in social networks (Facebook, Twitter, TikTok, YouTube, etc.) intended to build support outside the walls of their followers (DARE, 2020). Given that the media influences and shapes attitudes and behaviors, previous research (such as Hasić et al., 2020) on this issue suggests that young people are particularly vulnerable to radicalization in the age of accessible social media. Participants from the "two schools under one roof" case study revealed that they are aware of the negative effects of the Internet on children and young people, and state that they often come across violent content (texts, games, photos, etc.) on social networks. Such content encourages anxiety and resentment among participants. Most of them claim that they do not understand the attractiveness of this online content and believe that they are sufficiently aware of the risks of potential involvement, so they often report violent content to remove it from social networks.

Participants from the organized groups of football fans case study expressed negative opinions towards violent content on online platforms, when using Facebook, watching YouTube videos, or playing games. This is both on platforms related to football and any other online content. They expressed their concern for the impact of violent media content on children and their development.

Lastly, our analysis of the online content of Salafi influencers shows that the basis of online Salafi missionary work is the possibility of using digital socialization through the establishment of virtual gathering places, where mimicking what is known as traditional socialization in congregations or within places of worship takes place. The content is carefully selected, optimized, and adapted to the latest standards of social networks, thus following the latest audio-visual production trends. Visual appeal and well-produced content bring greater interest and involvement to the younger population, especially in terms of the language, which is adapted to the targeted population. For instance, the language in videos is often simple, with many colloquial terms and humorous, meme-like remarks that are relatable to most "ordinary" people, and this, alone, contributes to the charisma of the lecturers. Additionally, there are on-the-spot Arabic to Bosnian translations of verses from the Quran, which affirm the idea of authority and authentic knowledge.

4.3 Educational, Leisure, and Cultural Opportunities

While certain actors of political socialization have a more significant role for individuals than others, the family remains the most important actor of socialization for young people. The orientation of young people towards family in Bosnia and Herzegovina is extremely high and family is an important part of identity. Therefore, if a family in some way nurtures adversity to other ethnic groups, this can lead to limited communication of young people and avoidance of meeting with members of other ethnic groups (Tzvetkova & Mancheva, 2019). This remains a serious obstacle in producing intercultural experiences among young people. Apart from family, an important agent of socialization for young people is also school. Most young people aside from school activities are also involved in some type of extracurricular activities which are of great importance for building collective identity. In the "two schools under one roof" case study, there are no joint teaching or extracurricular activities that can be attended by students of both schools. Our results show that participants in the research are well integrated into society and feel socially included. However, education that rests on ethnocentrism affects all social spheres of young people: the groups they join and the activities they engage in are entrenched in deep ethnic divisions, which reduces the likelihood of meeting peers from another ethnic group. Thus, even though young people have a wide range of educational and cultural opportunities at their own schools, the insistence on ethnic divisions is an obstacle to multicultural education and creates an artificial world of "us" versus "them".

Regarding participants from the organized groups of football fans case study, all respondents stressed that relations with their families are most important to them, and that they enjoy a very open relationship with mutual understanding. One participant mentioned that he spends most of his time with his daughter. They stated that their leisure time is spent no differently than how other young people do. Most of their free time is spent in cafes and pubs, with their girlfriends, watching football games on TV and going to stadium matches. Respondents from Mostar wish there were more cultural opportunities in the city, especially places to go out and more music concerts. Moreover, it was interesting to hear that the entire group from Banja Luka resented sports betting, while all participants from Mostar stated that they gamble every day and regularly.

While observing the content on Facebook and YouTube platforms, most activities of online Salafi lecturers can be summarized under the category of "lifestyle coaching", as they offer instant advice for everyday life issues. Therefore, Salafi influencers can communicate or promote a tangible product, an ideology, or a message in such a way that followers perceive it as a desirable cultural element and, what is more, as part of a beneficial way of living (Sorgenfrei, 2021). They often emphasize advice related to the position of women in the family; the relationship of spouses; allowed and forbidden daily activities; and social phenomena that are not related to religious teachings. YouTube videos are, in many cases, re-uploaded versions of Facebook Live lectures, which are regularly held on their profiles. Thus, it can be concluded that online Salafi lecturers act as non-formal educational actors, who attempt to deconstruct complex ideas and demanding concepts in a simplified way to all generations and audiences by relying on religious references. Sabic-El-Rayess (2021) confirmed this claim by pointing out that, in a vacuum left by formal education, Salafi mentors provide continuing education for the marginalized through mentorship-based clinics, online programming, podcasts, and face-to-face lectures.

4.4 Transnational Dynamics

In the "two schools under one roof" case study, students attending classes in the Bosnian language have no connection to schools and organizations in neighboring countries. Analyzing the causes of poor cooperation with schools from neighboring countries, the participants who attend classes in Bosnian think that cooperation with Croatia or Serbia would cause unrest. On the other hand, for students attending the Croatian language curriculum, cooperation with schools and organizations in neighboring countries is of great importance. They believe that it is necessary to invest more efforts in keeping up good relations with neighbors, especially with Croatia, which has a great influence on their socialization. They also see the connection with Croatia in the commitment to attend classes exclusively in the Croatian language.

The political and societal complexity of Bosnia and Herzegovina is very noticeable in the responses of focus groups participants from the organized groups of football fans' case study when asked about their sense of belonging to the state of Bosnia and Herzegovina in relation to their national or ethnic identity. Almost every participant emphasized that they have no strong feelings towards Bosnia and Herzegovina as a country such as: "I do not feel any attachment towards Bosnia and Herzegovina". They emphasized this in different ways but always clearly tinted with political statements and opinions, such as: "We are born here, this is our country, but nothing nice is said about us Croats here." Participants from both focus groups expressed that the role of neighboring countries in their life is an important one. In Mostar and Banja Luka this relates especially to the role of Croatia and Serbia, respectively. This role is mostly seen through connections with football fans from those countries, their cooperation and friendship. For all interviewed participants this type of cooperation is very important.

Operating on the Internet, Salafists can dispense with territorial constraints. In Islam, the idea of *Ummah* (community) that transcends nation-state borders plays an important role and thus connects Muslims around the world. This concept represents an important segment of the daily work of online Salafis, which is best seen in posts expressing solidarity and support to various Muslim countries and peoples. For instance, several such posts confirm the strong support that online *da'is* have from the Sandžak region in both Serbia and Montenegro.

4.5 Political Issues

Almost all participants of "two schools under one roof" case study are fully aware of the politicized social relations in the local environment and the disproportionate power relations in Bosnia and Herzegovina, which in general affect both internal and intergroup attitudes and behaviors. Our research shows divided opinions of young people about the significance of ethnicity and nationality: students who attend classes in the Bosnian language feel a sense of belonging to the state of Bosnia and Herzegovina. In the focus group, they stated that they respect ethnicity, but that belonging to the state is more important to them. They believe that the division into "us' and "them", and "ours" and "theirs" is an obstacle to unity and a better state of equal opportunities. On the other hand, students attending classes in the Croatian language do not feel much of belonging to the state of Bosnia and Herzegovina and ethnicity is more important to them. They believe that the state has not given them enough support and that it is more important for them that the people to whom they belong accept and respect them.

This concern is shared with the participants of the organized groups of football fans case study. For some of them, injustice can be seen and felt in every segment of the community, primarily through corruption, persistent unemployment, difficulty of everyday life, inadequate wages, emigration of people from Bosnia and Herzegovina, and lack of life perspectives for young people. On the other hand, two participants from Banja Luka stressed that the greatest injustice happens on the street in interaction with state authorities. They consider that the political system is the biggest cause of injustice in the community underlining persistent police violence. The animosity that members of the groups show towards the political system, represented mostly through police forces, and towards ruling politicians, is the most vivid indicator of potential radicalization.

Much of the online activism of Salafist lecturers on Facebook and YouTube is about everyday events, implying that political events in Bosnia and Herzegovina have some space in their activism. Often, criticism is directed inwards—more precisely towards the policies of Bosniak politicians and parties, as well as towards the Republika Srpska entity and the treatment of Muslims who are a minority there. In their posts, the *da'is* mostly pray for imams working in the Republika Srpska, praising their efforts for Muslim post-war returnees. The analysis showed that online Salafi lecturers do not challenge the political system in a way that implies they want to become part of those structures, or in a way that they want to change that system from within. Therefore, it is possible to conclude that such posts are not among the most popular ones in terms of supporters' engagement, and as such do not represent a significant driver in the context of this study.

4.6 Economic Deprivation

High unemployment rates, growing poverty, inadequate health and social protection, unequal opportunities in education are just some of the causes of high economic deprivation in the country. During the sessions organized within the "two schools under one roof" case study, respondents in both focus groups showed a high level of awareness of the factors that contribute to the low quality of life in Bosnia Herzegovina. One participant in the in-depth interview stated that he was denied the necessary medical assistance only because one of his parents was a member of a certain political party. Due to these circumstances, he feels discriminated against and considers whether the political action of his parents in the future will be an obstacle to the full realization of civil rights and needs.

As mentioned previously, participants from the organized groups of football fans' case study underlined the socio-economic disparity happening in BiH. This kind of socio-economic injustice, related to social class stratifications, ingrained and institutionalized corruption, and resentment towards "young people with rich (politically connected) parents" that our respondents mentioned is particularly revealing concerning the potential causes and triggers for their resentment and enormous bitterness, which can all be a factor for their radicalization.

Within the youth supporters of online Salafi influencers, the case study failed to reveal the impact of "economic deprivation" as a factor in radicalization.

4.7 Territorial Inequalities

No data was found that would indicate that the driver of "territorial inequality" plays an important role in the process of radicalization of young people. Moreover, the data of the macro-level research show that the driver of "territorial inequality" in Bosnia and Herzegovina is not related to the rural-urban distinction, but rather to individual perceptions of marginalization and injustice (Kapidžić et al., 2021). Perry (2016) states that young people in BiH, although they have no previous war experience, express dissatisfaction with the slow pace of change in society, where marginalization, neglect and injustice are common. This is illustrated by the fact that students of "two schools under one roof" subjectively believe that they daily experience some kind of injustice (in the family, school, and local community) and express concern about it. In regards tp territorial inequalities, it is more appropriate here to speak of "inequalities that arise as a result of deep ethnic divisions" which create a subjective sense of injustice, as a participant attending school in the Croatian language described it. Both groups were all quite agree regarding the use of violence in both territories. Most of the respondents claimed that they have experienced violence from the police and from fans of other football clubs in Bosnia and Herzegovina. Other than that, territorial inequalities were not seen as an important driver for this subculture group.

Finally, in the youth supporters of online Salafi influencers case study, the analysis of posts on Facebook and YouTube showed that the driver of territorial inequalities is non-existent in the context of the online Salafi network.

5 Conclusion

Operating under the decentralized system of the Dayton Peace Agreement, BiH functions as a consociational democracy with three main ethno-religious groups: Bosniaks, Croats, and Serbs. On a sub-national level, the country comprises the Federation of Bosnia and Herzegovina, Republika Srpska and the Brčko District. In BiH, "violent extremism" stems from events like the 1990s war, Salafi preaching, and global occurrences such as September 11th, ISIS emergence, and the Ukraine conflict. This has influenced the understanding of terrorism, extremism, and radicalization. While commonly associated with Islamist radicalization, there are identified Serb and Croat groups supporting ethnic, Orthodox, and Catholic extremism. BiH has aligned its counter-terrorism approaches with global trends, and the narrative has shifted towards the return of individuals from foreign battlefields. The country faces challenges with political ideologies, ethno-nationalism, and far-right extremism. The evolving nature of extremism underscores the urgency to define radicalization and extremism in the local context, considering the vulnerability of BiH society due to its recent history and unresolved governance issues.

The CONNEKT project's initial phase delved into the macro/institutional level of analysis, emphasizing its significance in understanding radicalization processes. The research, focused on Bosnia and Herzegovina, explored seven potential drivers of radicalization, examining their correlation with institutional practices at the macro level. The study unveils varied institutional perspectives on radicalization, highlighting collaboration patterns, the complexity of relationships within institutions, and the roles of formal and informal communication channels (Kapidžić et al., 2021).

The goal of this chapter was to bring some answers stated in the macro-level research while opening other questions that could be addressed in future studies. The phenomenon of "two schools under one roof", based on deep ethnic divisions, is the most striking example of ubiquitous segregation, discrimination, and inequality in education. The education model in "two schools under one roof" reflects the cultural specifics of only one ethnicity, does not provide knowledge about the other ethnic groups, and does not treat cultural differences as added values. At the same time, subcultures such as organized football club fans are the target of violent repression from the state which fueled resentment towards it from the members. Consequently, organized groups of football clubs' supporters remain a potential arena for radical and divisive political attitudes, ethnonational polarization, and political instrumentalization. On the other hand, the online space is still institutionally unregulated, which opens the possibility of placing and spreading potentially dangerous content. Online Salafi influencers also have significantly better visibility on social networks than the Islamic Community in Bosnia Herzegovina and thus represent a challenge for the ultimate religious authority and interpreter of religious regulations.

The results of the case studies provide insights into various drivers influencing radicalization in Bosnia and Herzegovina. In terms of religion, perceptions of Islam's association with extremism are shaped by media stereotypes, with football fans emphasizing the positive impact of religion on their lives. Online Salafi influencers, however, focus on disseminating simplified interpretations of Islamic regulations, leveraging digital socialization to create engaging content. The significance of family, education, and cultural opportunities is evident, with ethnic divisions hindering multicultural experiences among youth. Economic deprivation emerges as a driver, with participants expressing resentment toward socio-economic injustices and corruption. Territorial inequalities, while not identified as significant drivers, are intertwined with ethnic divisions, contributing to a subjective sense of injustice among the youth.

The impact of transnational dynamics is observed through the connectivity of football fans with neighboring countries and online Salafis expressing solidarity with global Muslim communities. Political issues, including dissatisfaction with the political system and police violence, are identified as potential drivers of radicalization, especially among football fans. Despite high economic deprivation rates, the youth supporters of online Salafi influencers do not reveal a direct link between economic factors and radicalization. While territorial inequalities are not identified as a driving force, the subjective sense of injustice associated with deep ethnic divisions remains a concern, influencing perceptions of inequality. The findings highlight thus the complex interconnectedness of these drivers, but further micro-level studies are needed in order to bring more precise elements of understanding in those dynamics.

References

Azinović, V. (2017). *Between salvation and terror: Radicalization and the foreign fighter phenomenon in the Western Balkans*. School of Political Science and Atlantic Initiative.

Balkan Insight. (2016, June 30). *Census Reveals Bosnia's Changed Demography*. Retrieved May 6, 2024, from https://balkanin-sight.com/2016/06/30/new-demographic-picture-of-bosnia-finally-revealed-06-30-2016/

Balkan Insight. (2019). *Bosnian Salafist Preachers Calibrate Message to Growing Audience*. Retrieved May 6, 2024, from https://balkaninsight.com/2019/11/08/bosnian-salafist-preachers-calibrate-message-to-growing-audience/

Bauman, Z. (2001). *Community. Seeking safety in an insecure world*. Polity Press.

BBC News. (2017, June 21). *Bosnia war dead figure announced*. Retrieved May 6, 2024, from http://news.bbc.co.uk/2/hi/europe/6228152.stm

Bećirević, E., Halilović, M., & Azinović, V. (2017). *Literature review. Radicalisation and violent extremismin the Western Balkans*. Extremism Research Forum, Foreign and Commonwealth Office British Council. Retrieved February 2022, from https://www.britishcouncil.ba/sites/default/files/erf_literature_review_2017_radicalisation_and_violent_extremism.pdf

Center for Security Studies. (2022). *Disengagement, rehabilitation, and reintegration of foreign terrorist fighters - Country report: Bosnia and Herzegovina*. DRIVE on the right path project. Retrieved December 2023, from https://drive-ontherightpath.eu/wp-content/uploads/2022/05/drive-report-bosnia-23-05-2022.pdf

DARE. (2020). *Country-level reports on drivers of self-radicalisation and digital sociability - Introduction*. Retrieved February 2022, from https://documents.manchester.ac.uk/display.aspx?DocID=58632.

Hasić, J., Mehmedović, M., & Sijamija, M. (2020). Country report: Bosnia and Herzegovina. In *Perception about radicalization by young people in the Western Balkan region*. Bratislava.

Hesová, Z. (2021). Wahhabis and Salafis, daije and alimi: Bosnian neo-Salafis between contestation and integration. *Southeast European and Black Sea Studies, 21*(4), 593.

Hirkić, M., Kapidžić, D., & Turčalo, S. (2022). Strategic policy suggestions for a new approach in countering violent extremism in Bosnia and Herzegovina. In M. Brunelli (Ed.), *Violent extremism in the Western Balkans: Islam, identity and measures countering radicalisation - Perspectives from Kosovo and Bosnia and Herzegovina case studies* (pp. 148–191). L'Harmattan Italia.

Kapidžić, D. (2020). Subnational competitive authoritarianism and power-sharing in Bosnia and Herzegovina. *Southeast European and Black Sea Studies, 20*(1).

Kapidžić, D., Dudić, A., Kadić, V., & Turčalo, S. (2020). *Country reports on national approaches to extremism: Framing violent extremism in the MENA region and the Balkans: Bosnia and Herzegovina*. The European Institute of the Mediterranean (IEMed). Retrieved February 2022, from https://h2020connekt.eu/wp-content/uploads/2021/01/Bosnia_CONNEKT_Approaches_to_extremism.pdf

Kapidžić D., Hirkić M., Dudić, A., Turčalo, S., Bašić, S. & Bakić, S. (2021). Drivers of radicalization and violent extremism in the light of state dynamics in MENA and the Balkans - Bosnia and Herzegovina. : The European Institute of the Mediterranean (IEMed). Retrieved February 2022, from https://h2020connekt.eu/wp-content/uploads/2021/09/Bosnia_Herzegovina_CONNEKT_Macro_Drivers.pdf.

Metodieva, A. (2021). The radical milieu and radical influencers of Bosnian foreign fighters. *Studies in Conflict & Terrorism, 46*(9), 1725.

Perry, V. (2016). *Initiatives to prevent/counter violent extremism in South East Europe - A survey of regional issues, initiatives and opportunities*. Regional Cooperation Council. Retrieved February 2022, from https://www.rcc.int/pubs/38/initiatives-to-preventcounter-violent-extremism-in-south-east-europe-a-survey-of-regional-issues-initiatives-and-opportunities

Sabic-El-Rayess, A. (2021). How do people radicalize? *International Journal of Educational Development, 87*, 102499.

Sorgenfrei, S. (2021). Branding Salafism: Salafi missionaries as social media influencers. *Method & Theory in the Study of Religion, 34*, 511.

Trkulja, A. (2017). *Two schools under one roof in Bosnia and Herzegovina (Mis) understanding of problems and possible solutions [Dvije škole pod jednim krovom u Bosni i Hercegovini (Ne) razumijevanje problema i moguća rješenja]*. Analitika.

Tzvetkova, G., & Mancheva, M. (2019). *Country report: Bosnia and Herzegovina GREASE - Radicalisation, secularism, and the Governance of Religion: European and Asian perspectives*. Retrieved February 2022, from http://grease.eui.eu/wp-content/uploads/sites/8/2019/11/Bosnis-and-Herzegovina-Report.pdf

VOA. (2019). *Followeri selefijskih predavača između ljudskih prava i isključivosti* [Followers of Salafi lecturers between human rights and exclusivity]. Retrieved May 6, 2024, from https://ba.voanews.com/a/followeri-selefijskih-predavaca-izmedju-ljudskih-prava-i-isklju%C4%8Divosti/5160822.html

Propaganda and Misinformation as Drivers of Radicalization in Bulgaria

Stefan Ralchev and Nadya Stoynova

1 Introduction

Far-right extremism in Bulgaria has become increasingly dynamic in recent years. Diverse actors engage in far-right rhetoric or acts, including political parties, non-partisan organizations and informal groups such as skinheads and football hooligans (Traffic News, 2020b). Far-right extremists have inflicted injuries and even death on members of minorities (Hristova, 2018). Civil society has been particularly vocal in emphasizing the threat of far-right radicalization. Far-right extremist rhetoric and actions are espoused by a spectrum of actors in Bulgaria which roughly fall into the following three categories (Dzhekova et al., 2015): political parties, non-parliamentary activist organizations and informal groupings.

The political unrest and widespread protests that the country experienced in 2013–2015, coupled with the migrant crisis, provided a suitable environment for the reinvigoration of some existing far-right organizations and the emergence of new actors, like paramilitary formations that have become known in the public domain for their patrolling activities near the Bulgarian border with Turkey. Similarly, the parliamentary elections of 2017 resulted in the entry into government of the far-right coalition Patriotic Front (PF), which marked the first time that a nationalist far-right formation became a decisive factor in the executive. This presence resulted in a lack of political will to tackle right-wing radicalization, while at the same time intensifying the already present process of normalization of hate speech in the public domain (Ivanova, 2018). Despite the rise in incidents involving right-wing nationalists, behind which formal and informal organizations were visibly sitting, counterintelligence, police, and investigative institutions avoided working against

S. Ralchev (✉) · N. Stoynova
Center for the Study of Democracy, Sofia, Bulgaria
e-mail: stefan.ralchev@csd.eu; nadya.stoynova@csd.eu

C. Torrekens et al. (eds.), *Social Contexts of Radicalization and Violent Extremism in the MENA and Balkans*,
https://doi.org/10.1007/978-3-031-84521-5_7

right-wing radicalism. The last parliamentary elections of November 2021 resulted in the entry into Parliament of another far-right party, Revival (*Възраждане*). In parallel, along with the rise in prominence of political actors in the far-right spectrum, the research underscores the persistence of widespread prejudice against certain minority groups, mainly the Roma and LGBTQI people (Todorov, 2021). Such a prejudice can easily be exploited by right-wing extremist actors. Indeed, political parties in the far-right ideological spectrum use hate speech against different minorities, most often the Roma, but also Muslims, refugees and migrants, and LGBTQI people. Generally, however, political parties and their members eschew engagement in violence or direct calls to violence. The use of violence is largely associated with other, more informal, right-wing extremist actors (the second category mentioned above) but remains very difficult to estimate to its full extent (Amnesty International Bulgaria, 2015; Dzhekova et al., 2017). However, exploiting popular prejudice, political actors proactively organized or took part in inflammatory events such as the protests against the so-called "Roma criminality" which have high potential for resulting in violence.

Previous macro-level analysis for Bulgaria showed that while a number of respondents from law enforcement and the judiciary recognized the threat of far-right radicalization, few measures targeted towards primary prevention or more systematic sanctioning of far-right violence such as hate crimes have been undertaken (Dzhekova & Stoynova, 2019). One reason for this is the notion among representatives of institutions that the far-right lacks mobilization potential towards violence. Problems in the registration, classification, and investigation of potential crimes with discriminatory motives greatly complicate an accurate assessment of the phenomenon's scope (Dzhekova et al., 2017). At the same time, several respondents agreed that there is widespread normalization of far-right rhetoric in Bulgarian society.

With the 2013 refugee crisis, Bulgaria has seen a series of significant changes in the macro-level environment, especially regarding international dynamics and political/social discontent. After the peak of the refugee flow through Bulgaria in 2015, nationalist parties assigned the issue top importance. The two major parties at the time, both the ruling Citizens for European Development of Bulgaria, GERB (*Граждани за европейско развитие на България, ГЕРБ*) and the opposition Bulgarian Socialist Party, BSP (*Българска социалистическа партия, БСП*), adopted many of the nationalist parties' theses on refugees, possibly in an attempt to limit their loss of electorate and the emergence of more radical nationalist parties. With the sharp decrease in the refugee flow in 2017, the topic of the "demographic threat of Muslim refugees" began to fade. The second line of rhetoric of nationalist parties, the one against the Roma minority, also started to diminish in appeal. With the opening up of the European labour market by major countries such as Germany, the United Kingdom, France, and others, a process of intensive emigration began, including in Roma communities, and criminal incidents and social conflicts in the country as a whole declined sharply, bringing attention away from the so-called issue of "Roma criminality". A factor for the diminishing crime rate may have also been the very rapid decline in unemployment and growth in income in the country in the period 2014–2019 (National Statistical Institute, 2024).

However, new divisive issues emerged linked to transnational developments. After the elections in 2017, the victorious party, GERB, formed a government with the new coalition of nationalists, United Patriots. Two initiatives of GERB were the ratification by the parliament of the Istanbul Convention and the adoption of the Strategy for the Child (2019–30). United Patriots stood firmly against both documents. GERB was forced, after a series of shocks, to give in to the nationalist parties to maintain its power, thus encouraging the emergence of a strong anti-European and conservative wave in the country.

With the onset of the pandemic, a macro-level factor linked to political discontent was the opposition to the anti-COVID-19 and vaccination measures. The new opposition formations, fearing that the pandemic would give the GERB government a chance to win the next general elections, openly took sides against lockdowns, wearing of masks and later vaccination. Particularly active in this regard was the nationalist Revival Party. Its entire 2021 election campaign was developed through groups of its supporters on Facebook and against COVID-19 measures.

Other conclusions were that the far right is particularly dynamic, with the rhetoric and tactics used by far-right actors evolving considerably and moving away from violence and towards more veiled influence tactics, especially with the proliferation of online disinformation in recent years. One example can be football supporters, who were especially targeted by prevention measures related to far-right extremism. As shared by a respondent from the security services in the macro-level research, there is no longer a hard core of far-right extremists focused on and gravitating toward the fan clubs. There is a significant change in the profile of members, and the characteristics cited in different research differ substantially (Dzhekova et al., 2021).

Regarding this, Bulgarian institutions' approach to radicalization focused mostly on the threat of Islamic radicalization. The official response can be described as out of sync with actual radicalization dynamics, as far-right radicalization can be described as much more dynamic. Far-right actors were seen as evolving in terms of structure and tactics, as opposed to a largely stagnating and overstated threat of Islamist radicalization. Far-right radicalization is generally overlooked by institutional representatives and prioritized by civil society actors, although some institutional representatives recognize that right-wing radicalization, narratives of the right wing, as well as associations with conservative Christian actors, need to be addressed. However, officially, few measures are taken to counteract far-right radicalization in its various manifestations. Instead, P/CVE measures are overly focused on Islamist radicalization and prioritize law enforcement measures while overlooking the prevention dimension.

Consequently, this chapter focuses on the two case studies that are of particular importance in the context of radicalization and VE in Bulgaria: Online Conservative Communities and Football Supporters. The first case study focused on the intersections between the far-right narratives and actions as expressed in online conservative communities focusing on key novel issues for the far-right, such as protection of traditional family values and opposition to COVID-19 measures. It looked into how macro-level drivers of radicalization and violent extremism, identified previously by CONNEKT, act at the meso level of these communities and their specific social contexts. The issue of violence and the potential for violence was also explored. The report drew on field research carried out in the period between December 2021 to March 2022, and aimed to examine the interaction between macro factors and meso-level community dynamics. Its objectives were to analyze a sub-national community-level environment that is conducive to or at risk of violent extremism and determine factors within the social environment which create conditions for violent extremism.

The case study of football supporters in Bulgaria followed up on a macro-level analysis conducted earlier as part of the CONNEKT project and tried to establish how the relations of meso dynamics are regarding the macro-level drivers within the specific social contexts. Several reports point to alleged violence on the part of football fans against vulnerable groups or the police (Traffic News, 2020b), which indicates risks of radicalization and violent extremism among young football supporters. The targeted communities were online public Facebook groups or pages, and the research was complemented by interviews with football fans of popular clubs. The communities were selected based on previous research by CSD (Dzhekova et al., 2015) and after consultations with stakeholders. Along these lines, the main research objective of this case study was to examine how the drivers of radicalization and violent extremism identified in the academic literature, and also studied by CONNEKT, function in the target communities as a context of social interaction.

2 Case Studies

2.1 Intersections Between the Far-Right Narratives and Actions as Expressed in Online Conservative Communities

Recent developments in Bulgaria have indicated that far-right actors are increasingly engaging in rallying popular support through spreading propaganda and misinformation, both online and offline, and forming alliances with other actors to influence policy-making. The debates around the so-called Istanbul convention and the proposed Strategy for the Child 2019–2030 showcased how the instrumentalization of Russian propaganda and fake news by the emerging nexus of conservative Christian organizations, far-right political parties, and non-partisan organizations can gather momentum online, result into protests and ultimately achieve the goal of derailing policy reforms (Karaboev & Angelov, 2018). Subsequently, similar tactics (spread of Russian and other propaganda, fake news, and disinformation online resulting in protests) by partially overlapping actors were used in opposition to COVID-19 pandemic measures.

The ultra-conservative communities that formed around the defense of traditional family values, and specifically against legislative initiatives considered to undermine these values, most notably the Istanbul Convention and the proposed Strategy for the Child 2019–2030, included many diverse actors, such as far-right political actors, then in government, as well as conservative Christian denominations and associated non-profit organizations (Karaboev & Angelov, 2018). These actors were supported in their opposition by the Bulgarian Orthodox Church (Pravoslavie.bg, 2018; StandartNews, 2019)[1] and the Mufti's office (Eurocom, 2018; Grand Mufti's Office, 2019). Online support was also rallied against the documents resulting in protests. Ultimately, the Istanbul Convention was ruled unconstitutional and the proposed Strategy for the Child was withdrawn. Upon the withdrawal of the two legislative documents, a new issue around which online conservative communities rallied was in opposition to measures taken to combat and manage the COVID-19 pandemic. Nevertheless, a reconfiguration of the opposition against pandemic measures and vaccination was observed in contrast to the Istanbul Convention and the Strategy for the Child issue.

What is specific about informal groups organized around right-wing conservative causes is that they often emerge through social networks around certain causes. Over time these groups around causes begin their own life, find new directions, and often right-wing nationalist parties begin to borrow these new ideas. Two far-right parties emerged as main opponents of all types of measures—the oldest far-right party *Ataka* and, most prominently, the newest far-right party *Vazrazhdane*, which managed to gain seats in Parliament in the last elections held in November 2021 (Webcafe, 2021). In addition, as a journalist investigation by Kirkova, Kostadinova and Marchev for the initiative Factcheck launched by the Alliance of European Journalists in Bulgaria showed, several actors who were active in spreading online misinformation in defense of traditional family values later moved on to do the same concerning COVID-19 measures and vaccination (Factcheck, 2021). The organization behind the conservative communities in focus is different—online or within friends' circles. Usually, there is no clear leadership in the groups, and the inclination to engage in protest actions is spontaneous. They have found sustainability and a sense of belonging in the virtual realm, giving them a specific online social context.

2.2 *Social Networks and Extreme Attitudes Among Football Supporters in Bulgaria*

Previous studies of football hooliganism show that for young people in Bulgaria, the neighborhood is the most decisive factor determining their club allegiance, i.e. where they grew up playing football with their friends, went to school, and saw

[1] Nevertheless, it should be noted that the position of the Bulgarian Orthodox Church against the Strategy for the Child has not been clearly stated. A position against the document was posted on the official website of the Church but was later withdrawn and argued to be a personal position.

graffiti about a football club (Dzhekova et al., 2015). The school environment can be also a factor of youth aggression: "Peer pressure at school and on the streets of the neighborhood and association with juveniles prone to aggression and crime are also important factors leading to radicalization, since as a person prone to aggression displays less aggressiveness when in a group of non-aggressive peers" (Dzhekova et al., 2015, p. 107). By joining a fan club, the supporter experiences belonging to a particular group which they perceive as "family". They seek support, understanding, and the respect of others within the group. The group is deemed to share the same values as the individual—prowess, bravery, honor, and a sense of justice. Furthermore, belonging to a group attenuates the sense of responsibility and makes football fans ready to commit criminal offenses they would be reluctant to commit outside the group. Thus, very often violence at stadiums is a result of minor incidents in which gradually non-aggressive people are embroiled in escalating fights (Dzhekova et al., 2015).

Criminality is strongly linked to the activities of some factions, including drug sales, assaults (including with firearms), usury, etc. (Traffic News, 2020a). Those joining the hooligan scene are aged between 15 and 23 years and young members need to pass certain acceptance ceremonies such as inflicting damage on the enemy club's property, beating up a schoolmate supporting the rival club, "and can escalate into beating up a schoolmate supporting the rival club or member of ethnic minorities" (Dzhekova et al., 2015, p. 107).

Not all fans are organized, though. The majority of people supporting their team at matches go independently, in small groups, and sometimes there are frictions with the organized supporters, who are trying to impose certain behaviors. Both organized and unorganized supporters tend to meet not only on match days but socially. Groups can vary in size and over time: official fan clubs are larger, with several thousand supporters, while factions usually comprise less than a hundred people.

One specific feature of football hooliganism in Bulgaria is that hooligans are often used by political parties for political goals (paid involvement in protests, sabotaging anti-government protests, sparking ethnic conflict) (Dzhekova, 2016). This suggests that institutional responses to far-right radicalization expressed in football hooliganism may be reluctant. In the macro-level analysis for Bulgaria (Dzhekova et al., 2021), one law enforcement representative argued that during the COVID-19 crisis, football fans participated in protests because they honestly wanted to be allowed to attend football games, while dismissing any linkage with fans involved in a recent attack on LGBTI people in Plovdiv, which was reported by the media to have been organized by supporters of a local football team. He believed that football hooligans' aggression is mostly directed at supporters of other teams and what we see is a stagnation in these groups.

Another notable tendency as regards social contexts vis-à-vis football supporters in Bulgaria is that match attendance has steadily decreased since the 1990s. Average attendance has fallen from 6500–7000 in the 1996–97 season to some 2000 in the 2014–15 season (Dzhekova et al., 2015). Interest in football games has dramatically fallen, especially in light of the COVID-19 pandemic, and hard-line supporter groups have become less active. One specific social context linked to this case study are online groups and Facebook pages. They display a sense of group belonging mostly linked to their respective football team and the Bulgarian nation.

3 Methods and Issues

The methodological approach for both the online communities and football supporters involved non-participant observation of public Facebook groups and pages identified using Facebook's instrument CrowdTangle and consultation with representatives of civil society organizations, independent experts, and political parties. The employed method of non-participant or unobtrusive observation of the public posts and interactions of the selected communities was chosen in order to mitigate negative outcomes that are likely to occur in the event of revealing the aim of the research. There is widespread mistrust among the selected communities towards civil society, which is often described as an advocate of the very harmful ideologies that these communities stand against. In addition, non-obtrusive observation allowed the teams to observe the organic development of interactions and narratives within the communities. The selection of interviewees was based on the popularity of the football team they supported and accessibility. Interviewees were selected based on already established contacts of CSD with football fan clubs from previous research efforts. Interviews were held in person. One interviewee sent detailed written responses to the previously approved questionnaire.

For the online conservative communities, interviews included representatives of youth organizations and youth formations of political parties. The research focused on analyzing interactions in online groups and eight semi-structured interviews with representatives of civil society organizations, independent experts and political parties. For the football supporters, four in-depth interviews with fans of specific teams within the age range of 18–30 were carried out. For both case studies, it was decided that only public Facebook groups and pages shall be observed, in line with ethical standards defined by the CONNEKT project. In the conservative communities' study, Facebook' CrowdTangle instrument was used to identify the five most popular ultra-conservative groups in terms of membership and interactions and the five most popular pages in terms of followers and interactions for the period 15 September—15 December 2021. The groups/pages' names directly indicated the affiliation of members with a specific ideology or cause or were active in promoting causes associated with the communities (e.g. traditional family values). CrowdTangle itself suggested associated groups. In parallel, a consultation was held with experts about their view of the most relevant groups/pages, mostly coinciding with the CrowdTangle choice. The groups/pages were organized mainly around two issues prioritized by key far-right political actors, namely the protection of traditional family values from encroachment by liberal "gender ideologies" and opposition to the COVID-19 measures and restrictions.

Interview respondents were selected based on two main criteria: being active in (or at the very least a sympathizer of) the most prominent far-right parties or other conservative civil society organizations and age (12–30 years old). In some cases, the team suspended the second criterion, as prominent figures in these movements are often older. An independent expert, also not within the target age group, was interviewed for additional data triangulation. Nevertheless, the majority of respondents fit both criteria.

In the football supporters' study, Facebook' CrowdTangle instrument was used to identify the five most popular football supporters' groups in terms of membership and interactions and the five most popular pages according to followers and interactions. In parallel, a consultation was held with representatives of the national police and Sofia metropolitan police about their view of the most relevant groups. The Facebook groups and pages unite supporters, mostly youths, of the respective team and contain posts and comments about ongoing matches, transfers of players, relations with the football governing body (the Bulgarian Football Union, BFU), rival teams and supporters, topical political events and patriotic posts about national holidays and figures. The latter two were of specific interest to the observers. Posts and comments on all mentioned topics contained allusions or outright qualifications that could be characterized as racist or discriminatory. The team arrived at the selection of four specific groups/pages: CSKA SOFIA HOOLIGANS (supporters of CSKA Sofia)—by far the most active group in terms of posts—Ultras Levski, National Fanclub of Supporters of PFC Levski and Levski Sofia Zapad (supporters of Levski Sofia)—pages which were much less active, hence their higher number and longer observed period. The first group was observed for the periods 14–25 January and 17–21 February 2022; the three others, less active, were observed for the periods including 11 November 2021–11 February 2022 and 17–21 February 2022. The research team chose to use online group observation rather than face-to-face field activities to collect data because (1) access to an adequate number of respondents for the research would be difficult, given the closed nature of these communities and the suspicion with which they treat scholars and journalists; and (2) in this way it could focus on the increased online presence of football fans over the recent years and correlate it with the digital socialization driver of CONNEKT. The narrower age range for the four in-depth interviews with football supporters ranged from 18 to 30.

Most of the challenges faced by the research team were present in both case studies. The first challenge concerned the limitations of Facebook's tool CrowdTangle for the project's purposes, as it is not able to scrape content from comments under posts, while comments would be the main source of data. Due to that, in both studies, observation was carried out manually, checking all the posts and comments for the designated period. The second challenge was related to the need to reduce the initial 3-month period envisaged for the online observation of Facebook groups due to the large amounts of content generated by the selected groups and pages. As a result, the teams opted to shorten the period to a much more technically feasible one. A third setback restricted to the online conservative communities' case study concerned delays in the data collection due to the Bulgarian parliamentary elections in late 2021 and contamination of some of the staff as well as respondents with COVID-19. It was important to postpone the fieldwork until after the elections as political actors relevant to the research were busy with campaigning. A final difficulty was that some interviews were declined or canceled due to respondents' unwillingness to be associated with the labels "extremism" and "radicalization". Mistrust of project aims was expressed by some prospective respondents upon getting acquainted with the consent form to take part in interviews, and also expressed mistrust towards non-governmental organizations and the aims of scholarly research.

4 Results

By shedding light on the views of community members and local-level institutions and allowing for direct observation of community-level dynamics, the meso-level analysis enabled a more accurate and nuanced understanding of which radicalization/extremism drivers were the most relevant in the specific communities selected, how they manifested and what impact they had on social interactions. Among the seven main macro drivers[2] actualised at the meso level within conservative online communities were political dissatisfaction and transnational dynamics. Another prominent factor was identified, namely the role of social media and social digitalization. In the football fans' communities, the four macro factors identified to play a role at the meso level were digital socialization, political dissatisfaction, territorial differences,[3] and transnational dynamics. One additional driver, nationalism, specific to the context of football supporters in Bulgaria, was identified, often manifesting itself as intolerance to "the other" or xenophobia against Roma, Turks, and the Macedonian nation, often resulting in hate speech in Facebook groups. One conclusion of the meso-level analysis is that social networks serve to amplify extreme attitudes among fans. Another is that violence is considered a legitimate means to achieve an end. These conclusions will help endorse an adequate prevention approach in the future and select appropriate micro paths to individual dynamics and drivers for radicalization and violence among football supporters.

4.1 Political Issues

Narratives were critical to the Bulgarian political elite, referring to its corruption, inability, and execution of foreign actors' agenda (pointed out to be the EU, the United States (US), NATO, Big Pharma, all of which are representations of shadow

[2] Religion, political issues, digital socialization, educational, leisure, and cultural opportunities, transnational dynamics, economic deprivation, and territorial inequalities.

[3] For the purposes of the analysis, territorial differences in this case study are understood as self-perceived distinctive traits or beliefs of certain football club's supporters that sets them apart from a rival club's supporters or from supporters from other cities: e.g. dedication to anti-communism, charitable activities, etc.

global elites). They referred to Russia as a defender of traditional family values, in opposition to the US, the EU, NATO, and their "gender ideology". The pandemic topic was present as well as the idea that it was planned to reduce world population and that it was used to limit individual rights and freedoms. Also, the narrative of international elites controlling and exploiting the Bulgarian population through the corrupt national elite was noted to be well-established and used by far-right extremist actors in the country (CSD, 2019) and elsewhere (Lee, 2021). This narrative of victimization and being under threat is often observed in far-right discourse and has adapted well to opposition to COVID-19-related measures and restrictions. Not only are these national institutions (and by extension their foreign masters) corrupt and not protecting the national interest or humanity's interest, but they are actively undermining it by chipping away at individual freedom to establish an ever-advancing dictatorship.

The more traditional far-right thesis refers to the elite's betrayal not only of the inherent values of the Bulgarian people but also of the economic ruin of the country. The "EU manipulation, the West" but mainly "Germany's actions to subjugate the country", and the "corruption of the local elite through Eurofunds", are some of the elements mentioned by respondents. Similar arguments are presented both online and by respondents regarding traditional family values, which were considered as being under attack. Nevertheless, it should be noted that political dissatisfaction is more strongly pronounced in online settings and among those who are not actively socially engaged in proactively advancing their causes offline. Interview respondents, especially those associated with organizations such as far-right political parties or conservative civil society organizations, are less likely to express very strong feelings of injustice. Still, it appears that getting actively involved in political or civil society organizations tempers more radical views as it provides them with a sense that injustices can be addressed by being socially active.

Political dissatisfaction manifested itself as a radicalization factor in the football supporters' case study along three main lines: (1) negativism towards the current leadership of the football governing body, the Bulgarian Football Union (BFU), which is most of the time linked to the political leadership of the country, previous or incumbent; (2) general indignation against corrupt government and political parties; and (3) calls to protests against the current order, including violence. All three lines were evident in data obtained in the online observation, while interviews demonstrated a negative attitude towards Bulgaria's communist past, disapproval against current political leadership, and a specific attitude towards violence as a legitimate instrument, in some cases, to achieve one's goals. As mentioned earlier, understandably the most exploited topics in the observed Facebook groups/pages were linked to football: the respective teams' performance, transfers of players, and rival teams. However, a clear tendency registered by the research team was to criticize the BFU president, Borislav Mihaylov, and his team, often associated with the general political situation and governance of the country. As his background is from one of the two biggest Sofia football clubs, Levski Sofia, most of the criticism came from the rival team's supporters in the group CSKA SOFIA HOOLIGANS.

However, supporters of Levski Sofia, while criticizing the planned appointment for sports minister of Radostin Vasilev, with a CSKA background, have also expressed a negative attitude towards the BFU leadership, linking it to the political establishment previously in power in Bulgaria. A very strong sentiment across Facebook groups/pages concerns the perceptions of the corruption of football management and the political class. Distrust in political parties and institutions and perceived social injustice in Bulgarian society emerged as shared sentiments in some Facebook comments and throughout interviews made for this research, which were far more intense than statements from respondents.

Regarding violence, what was observed in online comments shows not infrequent calls for its use against officials and the political class. Interview respondents were generally against it but some of them admitted that it can be a legitimate means to an end when other methods fail. Some of the interviewees insisted that violence is not a universal response, and that radicalization in their circles would not differ from the whole society. Yet violence often accompanies the activities of football fans even outside games. For example, in the anti-government protests of the summer and autumn 2020, it was widely believed—including the police—that some violent outbursts and provocations were made by organized fans of major football clubs (Nova TV, 2020).

4.2 *Transnational Dynamics*

While respondents also consider that traditional family values are under threat due to foreign encroachment in Bulgarian politics, conservative online communities tend to be more radical in emphasizing that liberal values of tolerance and respecting and protecting minority rights such as climate change, multiculturalism, feminism, and gay parades, are inherently incompatible with Bulgarian identity but are pushed on the population. Transnational dynamics also manifest in the narratives: arguments and specific content shared in online conservative communities are often imported in ranging from citing foreign sources of information (e.g. a video in Italian showing positive tests, which emphasizes that the most positive results are of people with various rates of vaccination), referring to events happening abroad (e.g. protests in different cities around the world against Covid-19 measures) or through repeating arguments originating from abroad.

Opposition against the Strategy for the Child in Bulgaria spread both online and offline the information that the Strategy will make it possible for children to be more easily extracted from their families and given to gay couples in Norway. An investigation of the Dnevnik newspaper showed very similar allegations were used in other countries in opposition to juvenile justice initiatives (Leshtarska, 2019). Similarly, the Great Reset theory has been spread in other countries and with regard to other disease outbreaks (Fatcheck, 2021).

Another manifestation of the transnational dynamics factor, especially in terms of the protection of traditional values is the presentation of Russia as a defender of traditional values. Nevertheless, there are indications that misinformation about the COVID-19 pandemic originating from Russia has also been spread actively in Bulgaria by one of the most fervent opponents of vaccines and pandemic-related restrictions, Plamen Paskov. Despite being a veterinarian, this opponent of COVID-19 measures was particularly active in Bulgaria but also often appeared on Belorussian TV, where he has been variably represented as a virologist, economist or political scientist (Bedrov & Lavchiev, 2020). As the present research has shown, political dissatisfaction and the use of foreign propaganda and misinformation have been adapted well to support both the causes of opposition to encroachment of liberal values and opposition to COVID-19 measures. On the other hand, the convergence of far-right narratives and religious conservatism has not translated well to the opposition towards COVID-19. There are only limited allusions to religion in online interactions on the topic of the pandemic. On the other hand, religious arguments are often expressed in opposition to encroachment of gender ideologies from the West.

Bulgarian football hooligans have established friendly ties with certain Western European or Balkan football club supporters, visiting games abroad or welcoming their fans to games in Bulgaria, thus exchanging experience and beliefs (Dzhekova et al., 2015). Sometimes local animosities of friendly clubs abroad can be the cause of violence against visiting Bulgarian supporters, leading even to fatalities (See for example Trifonova, 2020). In the football fans case study, transnational dynamics was less observed as a macro factor replicating itself at the meso level. One line of agitation, especially among Levski Sofia fans, is linked to the harmful influence of Russia on Bulgarian society. One interviewee said a lot of money is invested in fake news and that's why the EU is fighting Russian propaganda. Another one mentioned that foreign films about skinheads influenced the culture of his supporters' group, including hairstyle and fashion.

4.3 Digital Socialization

In the online conservative communities' study, the growing reliance on accessing information through social media is coupled with algorithms that promote the formation of echo chambers. This dynamic is exacerbated by the general failure of social media platforms to counter the spread of misinformation related to COVID-19 (Milmo, 2021). This failure is particularly pronounced in tackling misinformation in languages other than English (Rishi, 2021). It should be noted that despite the concerning messages observed in the online community, outright calls for violence are rare. Instead, most actions that the online community calls for fall in the remit of the legitimate—protests, resignation, investigation, and sanctions for the political elite. Protesting as a strategy for achieving goals is particularly referenced both by respondents who are not part of any organization and by the online community, as evidenced by the numerous shared videos and other content on protest actions against COVID-19 measures taking place around the world.

Similarly, interview respondents tend to not view violence as a solution for the problems they identify in Bulgarian society. This more moderate position expressed by interviewees can partially be attributed to several factors—the tendency for people to express more extreme views online (Stern, 2018) as well as the fact that as representatives of more organized far-right actors (e.g. political parties and youth clubs), they would tend to eschew violence in comparison to other far-right actors such as skinhead gangs and hooligans (Dzhekova et al., 2015). Respondents associated with political parties and formal clubs say they do not condone violence and directly oppose it as a means of combating injustice. Instead, more legitimate means are emphasized, such as increased control over and sanctioning unlawful behavior. Some isolated calls for physical violence can nevertheless be found in online interactions, especially directed towards the Bulgarian political elite.

It should be noted that while there are no indications of far-right violent radicalization, the dynamics described above are highly problematic as they bring about and exacerbate already existing societal schisms and polarization. Protest actions, despite being legitimate, do have the potential to escalate into violence if crowd dynamics are not properly controlled or if protesters are riled up by far-right actors. One example is a 2011 protest organized by the far-right party Attack (*Атака*) in front of the Sofia mosque Banya Basi against the allegedly high volume of the loudspeakers during prayer. After escalation and clashes between Attack supporters and Muslims, five policemen were injured and two Attack supporters were arrested (Vesti, 2011). The observation of public Facebook groups and pages of football fans demonstrated the relevance of the social networks phenomenon. The online environment tended to magnify extreme sentiments shared by the target group, allowing them greater anonymity and freedom. This was confirmed in the interviews conducted in parallel as part of the research. All respondents said they actively used social networks and channels for communication, highlighted the easiness of saying things online, and reckoned their influence power on youth.

Digital socialization played a role even before the advent of social networks. One interviewee agreed that the internet certainly contributes to violence, not least because of explicit visuals, and mentioned specific websites where stories were published about fights between factions, confiscated paraphernalia (scarves, etc.) as trophies, and choreography during games. One interesting feature of organized fans was the tendency to engage in sports. One respondent said interest in sports and practicing them was a motivating factor to become a devoted supporter. Another shared that his and other factions of supporters have established fight clubs in Mixed Martial Arts (MMA) to "canalize their energy." He added that football supporters today no longer find it fashionable to drink.

4.4 Nationalism, Xenophobia and Hate Speech

In the football case study, one specific factor has been identified as a meso-level driver of radicalization among football supporters which was not part of the macro analysis. It can be roughly described as nationalism, very often degrading to xenophobia and hate speech (in online groups). As a rule, football supporters in Bulgaria tend to identify with patriotic and nationalist causes (Dzhekova et al., 2015). This was confirmed in this research, with interviewees sharing the importance of the Bulgarian nation when it came to allegiance and loyalty.

In the observed Facebook groups and pages, posts and comments commemorating national holidays and figures have been regular, collecting the greatest number of positive interactions.[4] Controversial historical figures linked to Nazism have also been mentioned. These sentiments are sometimes directed at topical political developments. For example, a visit of Prime Minister Kiril Petkov to North Macedonia in January 2022, aimed to improve bilateral relations and possibly open the way for North Macedonia's launch of European Union accession negotiations, invoked negative reactions and warnings.[5] Sometimes, events from everyday life can provoke strong reactions by football fans, unifying them along ethnic, Bulgarian, lines against other ethnicities. One respondent invoked the mass anti-Roma protests from 2011, when an ethnic Bulgarian youth in the village of Katunitsa was run down and killed by members of a notorious Roma family linked to criminal activity. The protests were attended by fans of all major football clubs alike, expressing indignation at the perceived social injustice.

Nationalism can turn into xenophobia or outright racism among certain factions of supporters. Xenophobia, racism, and hate speech are visible in the observed Facebook groups and pages. Most often, pejorative terms and slurs for Roma people, Muslims, Jews or homosexuals, sometimes combined with threats, are used to express anger at footballers or management.

In conclusion, interviews with participants in conservative informal groups and experts monitoring these processes revealed some common features in the dynamics of the groups. The motivations for their organization in protest actions on the street emerge mainly on Facebook and among friends at the local level. These are heterogeneous groups, and Facebook appears as a platform for their organization. Participants perceive themselves as "different" from the rest of society. There are no expressed leaders, as most are horizontal organizations. There are representatives and supporters of far-right parties, but when an everyday issue of common interest arises, the groups begin to produce content and eventually, a live event such as a protest occurs. In this sense, there are Facebook groups with an ideology on the one hand, and there is a live organization, on the other.

The meso-level analysis shows that the macro drivers also emerging on the meso level are political or social discontent, transnational dynamics, and digital socialisation, as expressed in the essence of the observed online groups. In terms of political discontent, what unites these groups are a few basic statements, the most common being the demand for "justice and punishment of politicians". At the same time,

---

[4] For example, in the observed period, there were posts about the anniversary of Gotse Delchev's birth (4 February) and Vasil Levski's demise (18–19 February).

[5] The national narrative in Bulgaria is that Macedonians have a Bulgarian historical and cultural background, which they fail to recognize, and Bulgarian public opinion is in favor of vetoing North Macedonia for EU membership talks until controversies about the history and the rights of Bulgarians in the country are settled.

sensitive issues in the far-right discourse in society from the recent past (e.g. the "problematic" Roma minority) are no longer relevant in the presence of new issues (such as the Istanbul Convention, the Child Strategy, and COVID-19). Very often, conspiracy theories are involved in the groups' explanation of reality. This is also one of the main lines concerning the transnational dynamics factor. In this light, the interplay of drivers is a central characteristic, with the most frequent combination being political grievances and international influence. One conclusion of the meso-level analysis is that online communities tend to express their disagreements more radically than what was observed in interviews, which is a manifestation of how the digital socialization driver plays into their attitudes. This, and the fact that Facebook is a basic platform for their organization for offline action, makes this factor highly relevant. Another conclusion from both Facebook groups and interviews is that violence tends not to be endorsed as a legitimate means of pursuing one's goals and protests are seen as the acceptable way to go. However, the risk for extreme behavior is present, manifested in specific verbal attacks on vaccination points or tensions at anti-government protests.

For the football fans' case study, the intersection between the above-analyzed drivers and digital socialization was highly noticeable. One observation is that the online environment tends to enhance radical statements and provides a thriving milieu for hate speech: extreme language was missing in interviews and abundant in comments on Facebook. Another intersection concerns political dissatisfaction and nationalism/racism/hate speech: anti-government and anti-establishment statements by football supporters often contain expressions of hate. A combination of territorial differences and nationalism was also observed: one respondent said that "belonging first to the neighborhood, then to the city, and then to the state is fundamental for the group. This affiliation has always been a source of pride. For example, I will give the modern inter-neighborhood wars in our childhood—to defend your neighborhood was a matter of honor. Defending the colors and the name of your city and football club, defeating the enemy on the streets and in the stadium—this is a great reason to be proud. It is the same with our homeland, Bulgaria is in the first place when it comes to a national cause".

As regards prevention, according to the macro-level research, related phenomena such as hate crime, football hooliganism, racism, discrimination, and xenophobia have not been the focus of the dedicated prevention and countering strategy. On the contrary, they are approached within a broader scope of policy themes such as crime, education, protection of human rights, diversity, social policy, and integration. Tackling football hooliganism has been mainly geared toward preventing violence between rival football clubs (Dzhekova et al., 2015). Some representatives of law enforcement, juvenile delinquency services, and the judiciary acknowledge the connections between football hooliganism and far-right extremism. However, other police representatives consider far-right extremism and football hooliganism to be separate issues despite significant overlap identified in studies and numerous attacks against different minorities, including LGBTQI people.

This separation of the issues is also obvious in cases in which institutions different from law enforcement work with football hooligans, such as juvenile delinquency services. Despite the consensus that youths are a particularly vulnerable group when it comes to radicalization, there are no avenues for an approach not dominated by law enforcement or correctional approaches. As long as the issue is seen as related only to sports, the local juvenile delinquency bodies can work on such cases. Once there are indications of radicalization, the case moves to the purview of law enforcement or security services. Drawing from the meso-level analysis, a useful prevention avenue would be to pay particular attention to hate speech in the education system and to try to limit hate speech in social networks.

Moreover, the analyzed data point out that prevention of potential far-right radicalization should address rampant political dissatisfaction, which leads to extreme distrust towards institutions. Decisive actions and a multi-faceted approach on all levels of society are needed to restore some degree of social trust in institutions and the media, diminishing trust in conspiracy theories. In addition, the spread of misinformation needs to be tackled by a multifaceted approach. Regarding youth, fostering critical thinking and media literacy is particularly important. Research shows that critical thinking is insufficiently prioritized at Bulgarian schools, and functional literacy rates in Bulgaria are low (Dimitrov, 2019).

In terms of micro/individual paths, the research on online conservative communities does not indicate that their association with far-right actors might develop significant potential for violent radicalization. On the other hand, the spread of propaganda and misinformation as well as narratives generally espoused by the far-right narratives has the potential to bring about a worsening of societal polarization. Supporters of far-right and pro-Russian party Revival present the highest risk of being radicalized and of taking extreme actions, as demonstrated in several recent anti-government protests organized by the party.

For the majority of interviewed football fans, violence is a determining factor for the identity of hooligans. Violent conduct of some football supporters is sometimes interpreted as being determined by one's 'nature'. Characteristics such as low level of education, poor professional realization, maladjusted behavior in childhood (behavioral problems), and attention difficulties are also predictive of potentially aggressive behavior (Dzhekova et al., 2015). The meso-level research showed that family is a strong determining factor in building up a system of values among fans, especially visible in the interviews. Most respondents shared that "traditional family values" are something they have been brought up with and that family ranks high as an object of their loyalty, together with club and nation. In this light, possible extension into the next level of research could be individual and emotional drivers, including within the family and the specific educational environment. Indeed, according to Bulgaria's Ombudswoman, Bulgaria ranks among the top countries with violence and bullying at school, with 50% of the children having reported psychological violence at school in 2021 (bTV News, 2022).

5 Conclusion

Both case studies tried to identify how CONNEKT's macro-level drivers of radicalization and violent extremism operate on the meso/community level among online conservative communities and young football supporters. Ultra-conservative communities in Bulgaria, online and offline, tend to organize along ad hoc issues of interest, most often "in defense of traditional family values" and against COVID-19 restrictions. Their membership and agenda are often intertwined with that of far-right, populist parties of the day. Facebook is a strong platform for their organization and motivation, including live protests. The relevant drivers from the macro-level analysis, which are manifested at the meso level and are frequently interplaying, are political issues, transnational dynamics and digital socialization. A strong role in the dynamics of meso-level interactions is played by conspiracy theories and Russian propaganda. The Russian influence plays a very different role in the two case studies, as we can note that in football fan groups, Russian influence is seen as harmful to Bulgarian society.

The online observation of public Facebook groups and pages and in-depth interviews with football fans pointed out that risks of far-right radicalization are discernible in the "patriotism" and nationalism cherished by fans and certain factions and shared online. Violence is accepted as a legitimate means to an end. A very important conclusion of the meso-level analysis is that online communication tends to increase extreme sentiments among football supporters' groups, resulting in xenophobia and hate speech. This conclusion is similar to the online conservative communities, as they tend to express their disagreements more radically than what was observed in interviews, which is a manifestation of how the digital socialization driver plays into their attitudes. However, in conservative communities' violence tends not to be endorsed as a legitimate means in pursuing one's goals, and protests are seen as the acceptable way to go. While violence is not endorsed by these groups, a risk for violent action exists linked to protests organized by them, especially those associated with the Revival party.

Regarding prevention, it will be useful to try to limit hate speech in social networks, to pay particular attention to hate speech in the education system, and to improve literacy rates and critical thinking at schools, as a way for youth to be more attentive to fake news and misinformation. A relevant micro-level research would be to investigate the increasing violence, physical and psychological, happening at Bulgarian schools and the psychological and emotional drivers leading to it.

References

Amnesty International Bulgaria. (2015). *Missing the point: Lack of adequate investigation of hate crimes in Bulgaria.* Retrieved June 2024, from https://www.amnesty.org/en/documents/eur15/0001/2015/en/

Bedrov, I., & Lavchiev, N. (2020, December 2). Ветеринар, политолог, вирусолог. Българската звезда в медийната машина на Лукашенко [Veterinarian, political scientist, virusologist, the

Bulgarian star in Lukashenko's media machine]. *Svobodna Evropa*. Retrieved June 2024, from https://tinyurl.com/bdfzrkt3

bTV News. (2022, February 8). Омбудсманът: Пандемията е задълбочила проблема с насилието в училище [The Ombudswoman: The pandemic has deepened the problem with violence at school]. Retrieved June 2024, from https://btvnovinite.bg/bulgaria/ombudsmanat-pandemijata-e-zadalbochila-problema-s-nasilieto-v-uchilishte.html

CSD. (2019). Как крайнодесните послания в интернет достигат и влияят на българските младежи [How extreme right messages in internet reach and influence Bulgarian youth]. Retrieved June 2024, from https://csd.eu/fileadmin/user_upload/events_library/files/2020_07/Propaganda_-_Article__V4_.pdf

Dimitrov, D. (2019, December 6). PISA 2018: Образование с часовников механизъм [PISA 2018: Timebomb education]. *Capital*. Retrieved June 2024, from https://www.capital.bg/politika_i_ikonomika/obrazovanie/2019/12/06/4001542_pisa_2018_uchilishte_za_vchera/

Dzhekova, R. (2016). Theoretical framework and concepts of radicalisation. In O. Shentov & B. Todorov (Eds.), *Understanding radicalisation. Review of literature*. Center for the Study of Democracy. Retrieved June 2024, from https://csd.bg/publications/publication/understanding-radicalisation-review-of-literature/

Dzhekova, R., Mancheva, M., Doichinova, M., Derelieva, L., Bezlov, T., Karayotova, M., Tomov, Y., Markov, D., & Ilcheva, M. (2015). *Radicalisation in Bulgaria: Threats and trends*. CSD.

Dzhekova, R., Ralchev, S., & Stoynova, N. (2021). CONNEKT country paper on macro-level drivers: Bulgaria. In *The European Institute of the Mediterranean (IEMed)*. Retrieved June 2024, from https://h2020connekt.eu/publications/mapping-drivers-of-radicalisation-in-the-light-of-state-dynamics-in-bulgaria/

Dzhekova, R., & Stoynova, N. (2019). Vigilantism against ethnic minorities and migrants in Bulgaria. In T. Bjorgo & M. Mares (Eds.), *Vigilantism against migrants and minorities*. Routledge. Retrieved June 2024, from https://www.academia.edu/42665551/Vigilantism_against_Ethnic_Minorities_and_Migrants_in_Bulgaria

Dzhekova, R., Stoynova, N., Moravec, L., Bláhová, P., & Anagnostou, D. (2017). *Situational assessment of extremist trends*. CSD.

Eurocom. (2018). Главното мюфтийство се обяви против Истанбулската конвенция [The Grand Muftiate declared it is against the Istanbul Convention]. Retrieved June 2024, from https://eurocom.bg/new/glavnoto-miuftiistvo-se-obiavi-protiv-istanbulskata-konvenciia

Factcheck.bg. (2021, May 27). От Истанбулската конвенция, та на „Измамата кОвид-19 [From the Istanbul Convention to the 'Covid-19 fraud']. Retrieved June 2024, from https://factcheck.bg/ot-istanbulskata-konvenciya-ta-na-izmamata-k0vid-19/

Grand Mufti's Office. (2019, April 11). Национална стратегия за детето 2019–2030 или когато пътят към ада бива постлан с „добри" намерения [National strategy for the Child or when the road to hell is paved with good intentions]. Retrieved June 2024, from https://tinyurl.com/3sfznv5c

Hristova, N. (2018, June 14). 49 г. затвор за трима, пребили жестоко мъж—изглеждал им като имигрант [49 years of prison for three who severely beat a man—he looked like immigrant to them]. *dir.bg*. Retrieved June 2024, from https://dnes.dir.bg/temida/49-g-zatvor-za-trima-prebili-zhestoko-mazh-izglezhdal-im-kato-imigrant

Ivanova, I. (2018). *Public attitudes to hate speech in Bulgaria in 2018*. Open Society Institute.

Karaboev, P. and Angelov, G. (2018, February 17). Джизъс срещу "джендъра" - пред кого отстъпи Борисов за конвенцията [Jesus against the 'gender'—whom Borissov acceded to for the Convention]. *Dnevnik*. Retrieved June 2024, from https://www.dnevnik.bg/bulgaria/2018/02/17/3130749_djizus_sreshtu_djendura_-_pred_kogo_otstupi_borisov_za/

Lee, B. (2021). *Narratives of the far-right*. Crest Security Review.

Leshtarska, D. (2019, May 16) Истанбулската стратегия за детето [The Istanbul strategy for the child]. *Capital*. Retrieved June 2024, from https://www.capital.bg/politika_i_ikonomika/bulgaria/2019/05/17/3906609_istanbulskata_strategiia_za_deteto

Milmo, D. (2021, November 2). Facebook failing to protect users from Covid misinformation, says monitor. *The Guardian*. Retrieved June 2024, from https://www.theguardian.com/technology/2021/nov/02/facebook-failing-to-protect-users-from-covid-misinformation-says-monitor

National Statistical Institute. (2024, June). Demographic and social statistics". Retrieved from https://infostat.nsi.bg/infostat/pages/module.jsf?x_2=3&lang=bg

Nova TV. (2020, September 3). НОЩ НА СБЛЪСЪЦИ В СОФИЯ: Десетки ранени полицаи и протестиращи [Night of clashes in Sofia: Dozens injured police and protesters]. Retrieved June 2024, from https://tinyurl.com/bdcmhcv3

Pravoslavie.bg. (2018, January 22). Обръщение на Светия Синод относно Истанбулската конвенция [Address by the Holy Synod on the Istanbul Convention]. Retrieved June 2024, from https://tinyurl.com/2p8mncbn

Rishi, I. (2021, October 26). Facebook has language blind spots around the world that allow hate speech to flourish. *CNN*. Retrieved June 2024, from https://edition.cnn.com/2021/10/26/tech/facebook-papers-language-hate-speech-international/index.html

StandartNews. (2019, February 12). Скандал в Синода по стратегията за детето [Scandal at the Synod on the strategy for the child]. Retrieved June 2024, from https://www.standartnews.com/balgariya-obshtestvo/skandal-v-sinoda-po-strategiyata-za-deteto-384884.html

Stern, A. (2018, May 17). *The psychology of Internet rage*. Harvard Health Publishing. Retrieved June 2024, from https://www.health.harvard.edu/blog/the-psychology-of-internet-rage-2018051713852

Todorov, A. (2021). *Радикализация на неприемането: Групова омраза и дясно-екстремистки нагаси в България* [The radicalisation of non-acceptance: Group hatred and extreme far-right attitudes in Bulgaria]. Friedrich Ebert Stiftung.

TrafficNews.bg. (2020a, April 24) Знакови лица от агитката на Левски зад решетките заради мокри поръчки [Flagship Levski supporters behind bars for ordered hits]. Retrieved June 2024, from https://trafficnews.bg/krimi/znakovi-litsa-agitkata-levski-zad-reshetkite-zaradi-mokri-176414/

Trafficnews.bg. (2020b, September 27). Малките ултраси, вилнели в центъра на Пловдив, скочили заради спонтанен ЛГБТ парад [Young ultras rampaging in the center of Plovdiv jumped because of a spontaneous LGBT parade]. Retrieved June 2024, from https://trafficnews.bg/plovdiv/malkite-ultrasi-vilneli-tsentara-plovdiv-skochili-zaradi-190322/

Trifonova, T. (2020, January 6). Атаката срещу феновете на 'Ботев' Пловдив в Солун била непредизвикана [The assault on Botev Plovdiv fans in Thessaloniki was unprovoked]", *bTV News*. Retrieved June 2024, from https://btvnovinite.bg/bulgaria/fen-na-botev-plovdiv-e-zaginal-v-solun.html

Vesti. (2011, May 20). Сблъсъци пред джамията в София [Clashes in from of the mosque in Sofia]. Retrieved June 2024, from https://www.vesti.bg/bulgaria/politika/sblysyci-pred-dzhamiiata-v-sofiia-3829911

Webcafe. (2021, October 20). Протест против ваксините блокира част от центъра на София [Protest against vaccines blocks part of Sofia centre]. Retrieved June 2024, from https://webcafe.bg/bulgaria/protest-protiv-vaksinite-blokira-chast-ot-tsentara-na-sofiya.html

Addressing and Understanding Youth Radicalization in the Republic of North Macedonia

Lidija Georgieva and Elena Mujoska-Trpevska

1 Introduction

The former southernmost Yugoslav federal unit, now the Republic of North Macedonia (RNM) got its independence after the successful referendum in September 1991. Even though the country survived the Yugoslav wars of the 1990s, a violent conflict between the Macedonian security forces and the Albanian radicals broke out in 2001. After the insurgence, settled with the so-called Ohrid Framework Agreement (OFA), a power-sharing political model was introduced in the state which is now applauded in scholarly literature (Bieber, 2008; Horowitz, 2014; Ilievski & Wolff, 2011).

With the bulk of minority groups' demands institutionalized by OFA in 2001, violent extremism in the state was significantly settled. Yet, the state faced several challenges over the next two decades. The loudest cases involved, anew, Macedonian-Albanian shootouts and were contextualized within the Kosovar-Macedonian cross-national network of radicals. On the 12 April 2012, five Macedonian civilians were killed near the lake of Smilkovci, in the vicinity of Skopje, an attack which the Macedonian Ministry of Internal Affairs defined as a "deliberate terrorist act aimed at destabilizing the country" (Marusic Jakov, 2012). In early May 2015, a shootout between the Macedonian forces and the self-identified ethno-Albanian National

L. Georgieva (✉)
Faculty of Philosophy, Ss. Cyril and Methodius University in Skopje, Skopje, North Macedonia
e-mail: georgieva@fzf.ukim.edu.mk

E. Mujoska-Trpevska
Center for Strategic Research, Macedonian Academy of Sciences and Arts, Skopje, North Macedonia
e-mail: emujoska@manu.edu.mk

C. Torrekens et al. (eds.), *Social Contexts of Radicalization and Violent Extremism in the MENA and Balkans*,
https://doi.org/10.1007/978-3-031-84521-5_8

Liberation Army erupted in the town of Kumanovo, taking the lives of eight policemen and 10 militants and leaving 37 officers hospitalized. As a result, 28 men were arrested and charged with terrorism-related sanctions by the Macedonian authorities (Marusic Jakov, 2015).

The most recent wave of radical groups in North Macedonia was pinned down to the names of two influential imams in Republic of North Macedonia (RNM). According to Qehaja and Perteshi (2018), the two imams have both "embraced a violent form of fundamentalist Islamic ideology and spearheaded the creation of youth groups, bringing in *jamaats* or *parajamaats*,[1] many of the men active in those networks ended up in Syria and Iraq, while the rest continue to spread the fundamentalist ideology through online content" (Qehaja & Perteshi, 2018, p. 12). In 2017, the Soufan Center published a report that counted 135 Macedonian foreign fighters in the Islamic State in Iraq and Syria (ISIS) between 2011 and 2016 (Barrett, 2022). The latest research, conducted in the wake of the disintegration of the ISIS-controlled territory in Syria and Iraq, shows a clear decline in the number of Macedonian foreign fighters from 2017 onwards (Kambovski et al., 2020). These departures "effectively stopped" in 2018, according to Stojkovski and Kalajdziovski (2018).

Even though the state did not, thereafter, ban any political party on the grounds of spreading "anti-democratic ideology and violence"—an active legal mechanism in Macedonian legislation (Casal Bértoa & van Biezen, 2017)—several fringe organizations, which oftentimes evoke violent symbols and use militant discourses and hate speech, are operating in the country.[2] Moreover, as of the mid-2010s, there has been a tendency to register so-called "patriotic organizations" in the national registry of non-governmental organizations (NGOs), many of which were instrumental in the infamous storming of the Macedonian Parliament, also known as "Bloody Thursday". This event happened after the parliamentary majority elected an ethnic-Albanian as a spokesperson on 27 April 2017: 16 persons were found guilty and charged with 211 years in prison for "terrorist threat to the constitutional order and security" (Stojančova, 2019).

The major institutional bodies are aware of these groups, and cooperate with the other relevant institutions, such as the officially registered religious communities and detention centers in North Macedonia by sharing know-how and practices. On a different note, the civic sector experts stressed that the NGOs' work generally focuses on prevention rather than reintegration of the detained foreign fighters. Moreover, experts from the civic sector claimed that the work with the detained

[1] *Jamaats* or *para-jaamats* are usually groups of young individuals, practicing conservative Islamic rituals, outside of the mosques and not subject to the authority of the Islamic association. For example, the crisis of legitimacy in the Macedonian Islamic Community (BFI) particularly in Skopje and Kumanovo has spurred the creation of para-jamaats, especially those divided into the so-called conservative practitioners and radical groups.

[2] Zdravko Saveski notes that the common feature of the "Neo-Nazi and Islamic fundamentalists" is the very fact that they are "very obscure and absent from the public sphere"—while, in recent years, their presence on social media was much increased (Saveski, 2021: 100).

foreign fighters in North Macedonia should be done in cooperation with the relevant NGOs, as an already established practice in the region, to avoid recidivism issues.

It is noteworthy the past few years, particularly from 2017 and the Macedonian government transition to the current one, have been critical for the implementation of a new, redesigned policy toward countering terrorism and the prevention of violent extremism (C/PVE) and security sector reforms. The new state approach is framed in the so-called "soft measures" of C/PVE involving wider social engagement and non-traditional security actors. However, those measures are also accompanied by "hard measures" of C/PVE referring to a set of coercive actions (Huq, 2016). The state's Police Strategy for Development 2016–2020 is a neat illustration in these regards as it clearly denotes the main agent in the fight against terrorism—the intelligence institutions—a prevailing approach in the 2010s. The key institution-building events are the formation of the National Committee for Prevention of Violent Extremism and Counterterrorism (NCCVECT) and the Office of the National Coordinator for CVE and CT (NCoCVECT) in 2017, as well as the subsequent National Strategies for Counterterrorism (2018–2022; NSCT) and Countering Violent Extremism (2018–2022, NSCVE), as well as the National Strategy for Prevention of Violent Extremism (2023–2027, NSPVE). The major institutional body, NCCVECT, aims to cover the whole territory of North Macedonia and now works in 14 municipalities—mostly with a higher multiethnic proportion and in the municipalities with a dominant ethnic group. Following the latest change in the number of municipalities in 2013, North Macedonia has 80 of them. A mere proportion is not a good pointer: for most experts, the territorial dispersion is well covered in the state and the civic sector's work on C/PVE. With the establishment of NCCVECT, as well as the subsequent NSCT, NSCVE and NSPVE, North Macedonia is unarguably catching up with the C/PVE agenda of regional states, predominantly from the Western Balkans.

Furthermore, it is commonplace that North Macedonia had successfully cooperated with its transatlantic partners in the global fight against terrorism before 2017. This cooperation also extends to North Macedonia's membership in MONEYVAL, a Financial Action Task Force (FATF) regional body, North Macedonia's Financial Intelligence Office's membership in the Egmont Group, and the state's approval to join the G-7 24/7 Network. The international partners are also significant as they provide financial means for implementing various C/PVE-related projects in the civic sector and facilitate regional cross-national cooperation in C/PVE. The OSCE Mission to Skopje, the United States Agency for International Development (USAID) and the American and British Embassies in Skopje were instrumental partners in these regards. They helped not only with financial support but also in terms of logistics by bringing the local institutions, NGOs, religious communities and academia into the institution-building process (Arifi, 2019).

The Committee on Relations between Religious Communities and Groups' Affiliates (CRRCG) participated in the formation of NSCT and NSCVE in 2018. CRRCG has actively contributed to national efforts in combating contemporary security threats. According to its 2020 Annual Work Plan Implementation Report, the Committee has played a role in addressing terrorism, violent extremism, and the phenomenon of foreign fighters (CRRCG, 2020). While the concept of radicalization is not extensively detailed, the report highlights the Committee's engagement in international cooperation and initiatives aimed at enhancing security measures in North Macedonia. This shift in focus since 2019 suggests a broader institutional approach, moving beyond interfaith dialogue to direct involvement in counter-extremism strategies. Here, besides the role of a facilitator of the dialogue between the various religious communities in North Macedonia, CRRCG also aims to gather information from the religious communities on the eventual radicalization of individuals or groups and follow the work of the officially registered religious communities, cooperating with the state's security forces.

The situation on the ground reveals that, on the one hand, major religious institutions are working in the direction of C/PVE, while on the other, religious-based violence and "radical interpretations" exist (Saveski & Sadiku, 2012). Two tendencies were linked in several reports: the Macedonian Center for International Cooperation in the course of early 2010s, as well as, more recently, the Association for Democratic Advancement Democracy Lab, in cooperation with the Berlin-based Berghof Foundation, noted that the Islamic Religious Community of North Macedonia (ICM) is losing support among its constituencies, which in turn paved the way for "nontraditional" interpretations of the traditional-in-North-Macedonia Hanafi school of Islam (Morina et al., 2019). Thus, we identify North Macedonia's most recent C/PVE policing as a hybrid model of normative and coercive isomorphism, as it draws on the professional knowledge of a broader set of stakeholders while also benefiting from the aforementioned international support.

The European project CONNEKT explores the factors contributing to radicalization and violent extremism in the MENA region and the Balkans, focusing on seven identified drivers: religion, political, territorial inequalities, economic deprivation, transnational dynamics, education, cultural, and leisure opportunities, and digital socialization.

It examines the connections and importance of these drivers across three levels of analysis: macro (broad), meso (community), and micro (individual). The project aims to gradually build a comprehensive understanding of radicalization, integrating findings from each level into the next. As a result, three case studies have been conducted in different areas. The first one covers the Commemorations of the 2001 Macedonian conflict in Tetovo, the second one covers football fan groups in Tetovo and Skopje and the third one covers the prisons and correctional and educational facilities in Volkovija. In the following section, each case study will be described in terms of socio-geographic elements. Results will be then displayed regarding the seven radicalization drivers selected and mentioned above.

2 Case Studies and Methodologies

2.1 *Commemorations of the 2001 Macedonian Conflict in Tetovo*

Commemorative events, as such, bear moral and emotional dimensions, with communities continually choosing who and what is worth remembering and, by the same token, who and what is not, while heavily relying on symbols and cultural artifacts as means of representing the past. Commemorative events in general are also considered as "one of the steps in a radicalization process used for recruitment" although such events could be related to events that are perceived as disrupting for one and cheering for another community at some point involved in conflict (Suttmoeller et al., 2011 cited in Lowe et al., 2013, p. 84). Nonetheless they also offer the opportunity to look at the wide and complex set of social actors engaged into mnemonic activities of victims of terrorism and terrorist attacks. The commemorations of the terrorist attacks in Europe as of the mid-2000s are thus an example of many "spontaneous" practices of the communities, which can oppose, complement, or go hand-in-hand with official memory politics, policies and discourses (for an overview, see Milošević, 2017).

We argue that such a perspective on North Macedonia can provide a better understanding of several social and political developments related to the aftermath of the 2001-armed conflict in the state, as commemorations of the 2001 conflict in North Macedonia, often organized by ethnic or political groups, function as platforms for community interaction and potential radicalization. Although the former southernmost Yugoslav state managed to avoid the bloodshed of the Yugoslav wars of the 1990s, the inter-ethnic tensions between the two largest ethnic communities in the state—the Macedonian and the Albanian one—escalated in early 2001, soon after the end of the war in the neighboring Kosovo. More precisely, on January 22, 2001, the so-called National Liberation Army (NLA), mostly consisted of ethnic Albanian rebels from Kosovo, then Yugoslavia and Macedonia, attacked the police station in Tearce, in the vicinity of the city of Tetovo, thus provoking a clash with the state security forces. The shootings between the NLA fighters and the state security forces escalated in March 2001 and lasted up to August that year, resulting in more than 200 casualties and over 100,000 internally displaced persons (Ackermann, 2002; Bellamy, 2002; Brunnbauer, 2002; Daskalovski, 2004; Ortakovski, 2001; Phillips, 2002). The 6 months conflict was settled with the Ohrid Framework agreement (OFA): a peace agreement signed by the leaders of the largest domestic parties from the two dominant blocks—Macedonian and Albanian—and the international brokers, which paved a way for a major institutional restructuring of the Macedonian state (Bieber, 2008; Georgieva et al., 2011; Horowitz, 2014; Ilievski, 2007; Ilievski & Wolff, 2011).

Although OFA was a blueprint for the new power-sharing model, it also paved the way for the establishing of a peculiar ethno-centric "citizenship regime" where the citizens "realize their rights, obligations and participate in the public and political spheres exclusively as members of ethno-national and religious communities" (Spaskovska, 2012, p. 101; see, as well Janev, 2011).

Thus, we postulate that the legacy of the 2001 conflict presents one of the most heated memory-related topics in the domestic public discourse and unarguably the most contested issue from the history of Macedonian-Albanian interethnic relations in North Macedonia. The memory discourses over the 2001 conflict were yet primarily discussed as part of the symbolic conflict between the two largest ethnic communities in the state, while the scholars traced either the pre-history of these tensions or their embeddedness in the post-conflict setting (see, for instance, Ragaru, 2008; Dimova, 2013). Neofotistos's study (Neofotistos, 2012) on the construction of the Albanian memory culture in North Macedonia after 2001 remains the most elaborate attempt to grasp its bottom-up formation and annual development (see, as well, the recent take by Reef, 2018). A 2021 research project mapped the commemorations of the 2001 conflict in the state (Trajanovski & Georgieva, 2022) while several oral history publications on 2001 appeared since 2019 (Stojanov et al., 2019).

Violence during and after commemorative events in contemporary Macedonian society is not a novelty per se: in the past years, we observed contestations along religious, ethnic and national lines in and beyond Skopje, about themes that stretch from the recent to ancient history (Trajanovski, 2021). The local contexts beyond Skopje did not get the same attention and treatment as the developments in the capital city. This is certainly the case with Tetovo, the third most populated city in the state, which was the major theatre of some of the most intense shootings in 2001. In short, the armed clashes in Tetovo started in March 2001, when several rebels opened fire on the Macedonian police from the Kale suburb and attacked the nearby village of Selce. Today, Tetovo is a multi-ethnic city of more than 84,770 inhabitants (alongside its vicinity), out of which 15.529 of ethnic Macedonian (mostly Orthodox Christian) and 60.460 of ethnic Albanian origins, mostly Muslim (State Statistical Office of the Republic of North Macedonia, 2022). Even though the city holds a history of peaceful coexistence that dates back long beyond the 2001 conflict, interethnic tensions reappeared after 2001.

Ever since 2001, the local municipality in Tetovo is led by Albanian political parties; in particular, the ethnic Albanian party Democratic Union for Integration (DUI) up to 2021.

Hence, we depart from the hypothesis that the commemorative events related to the 2001 conflict are used as platforms for promoting exclusivist and ethno-centric agendas which, in turn, mobilize individuals and, eventually, can fire up inter-ethnic tensions. More precisely, we assume that these events can trigger ethnic and religious hatred at individual and community levels and re-enhance the borders between the two dominant communities in public discourse. We also believe that a closer look at the local context of Tetovo will provide a better understanding of the institutional work, the bottom-up dynamics and the legacies of the inter-ethnic past at a meso-level.

First, we analyzed media texts on the commemorative events in and around Tetovo as of 2001. Secondly, we organized two focus groups with Tetovo vicenarians of Macedonian and Albanian ethnic backgrounds. Thirdly, we conducted four semi-structured interviews with relevant stakeholders regarding the commemorations of 2001 in the city and the state. The rationale behind this approach was to get as multivocal perspective as possible, taking under consideration the factual and diachronic developments over the last two decades (via the media texts), the voices of the local youth of the two largest ethnic communities in the city (via the focus groups), and the standpoints of the stakeholders that are actively participating, organizing or following the commemorative dynamics in the city in the state from both the sides (via the interviews).

The two focus groups were organized in Tetovo, in February 2022, and both had five discussants each. As we already mentioned, we aimed to speak with a generation of Tetovars who were born during or immediately after the conflict, so they could not have a direct memory of the conflict but have as much experience with the annual commemorations of 2001 as possible. Hence, the Macedonian discussants are born from 2001 to 2002, while the Albanian ones are all born in 2001.

As for the interviews, we managed to speak with a former member of the Macedonian security forces and a high representative of a war veteran organization, a high representative of the Macedonian army, a former high representative of the Ministry of Interior (MoI), and a former high representative of the Ministry of Defense (MoD) and expert on the Albanian commemorations.

2.2 *Football Fan Groups in Tetovo*

In the ex-Yugoslav post-conflict region, a large portion of the recent scholarship links football fandom with various nation and identity-building processes before and after the Yugoslav demise (Čolović, 2002; Đorđević, 2015; Mills, 2012; Vrcan & Lalić, 1999). Here, sports—and especially football—are considered to be major rituals of popular culture that contribute to establishing the symbolic borders between the nations (Brentin & Cooley, 2015), while the well-documented football fans' involvement in the war activities of the 1990s hints at their actual inputs in the establishment of the physical borders between the nation-states (see, for instance, Kelly, 2019; Hodges, 2019; Međedović et al., 2020).

The critical background of this debate was—and still is—the changing institutional and legal environments for battling violence at sport events in post-Yugoslav Macedonia. Signatory of the 1985 European Convention as a Yugoslav federal state, the Republic of Macedonia passed its first Law on the Prevention of Violence and Indecent Behaviour at Sports Events in 2004.

The Law on Sports (first adopted in 1996) underwent a series of changes: in 2002, conditions were created for sports associations to be transformed into commercial companies. The changes from 2004 enabled the decentralization of sports and their financing by local governments according to their financial potential, while sports associations and sports clubs continue to depend on the budgetary support of the state. The Law on the Prevention of Violence and Indecent Behaviour at

Sports Events regulates these issues and establishes measures for their prevention. The goal is to protect the safety of spectators, competitors and other participants in sports competitions from acts of violence (introducing and displaying banners, flags and other objects with text, images, signs or other symbols, as well as singing songs or throwing messages that cause and incite hatred or violence based on racial, national and religious affiliation or other characteristics). However, the law is not gender sensitive and lacks provisions on gender-based violence and gender-based hate speech at sporting events. The research with focus groups resulted into a shared perception that violence and hate speech are part of female football competition as well, but receives less attention.

This trajectory of developing the legal and institutional infrastructures towards prevention and towards cooperation with relevant social stakeholders can be identified as related to the development of the holistic C/PVE approach in the state as of the mid-2010s, discussed in the two CONNEKT national reports for North Macedonia (see Kambovski et al., 2020, 2021).

The above contexts lead us to assume that football fan groups might present critical social milieus that facilitate the radicalization of the Macedonian youth. Sociologists say that hate speech at sporting events, even if isolated, can easily disrupt inter-ethnic relations (Ameti et al., 2023; Đorđević & Scaturro, 2022). The clashes between Bulgarian and Albanian fans in Skopje before the football match between Skhupi and Levski resulted in an official reaction of the Ministry of Foreign Affairs of Bulgaria. The Macedonian minister of foreign affairs stated that involving different ethnic groups and communities has occurred historically, and he has always believed that fan behavior should not be used to assess community relations. He emphasized that the fan world is separate, and such events should not be viewed in the context of political relations within or between states (MIA, 2023).

The rivalry between fan groups is not limited to sports, but also includes offensive and hateful speech based on religion and nationalism. In the area of Tetovo municipality, during a football match between teams of "Shkendija" and "Tetex" from Tetovo, the members of the fan groups "Balisti" and "Vojvodi", usually use hate speech, insults and threats on national and religious basis.

The most recent examples of reconciliation failures demonstrate this dynamic and its impact on inter-ethnic dialogue at various levels, paving the way for future collisions. In this case study, we focus on the city of Tetovo. Even though the city has a history of peaceful multiculturalism and tolerance, the recent two post-conflict decades were marked by the process of cleaving along ethnic lines. For this study purposes, we conducted two focus group discussions with members and sympathizers of the two largest football fan groups in the city of Tetovo—Vojvodi and Ballistët—and four in-depth interviews with experts-practitioners from the field (from Skopje and Tetovo). Each focus group was composed of four participants. We spoke with a generation of football fans who are above 18 years old, but are young adults, as the youngest participant in the focus groups was born in 2002, while the oldest in 1996. The four in-depth interviews present a qualitative addition to the argument as they all refer to particular and important aspects triggered during the two focus groups. Therefore, after the completion of the two focus group discussions, we conducted semi-structured interviews with a legal scholar, a legal practitioner, a football coach, and a CSO expert, all of them have vast experiences with the football fandom and sports scene in the state, as well as various phenomena related to football-related violence.

Vojvodi Tetovo was founded in 1988 and primarily supports football club Teteks and basketball club Teteks, but also all Macedonian sports clubs in Tetovo, including football club Ljuboten, volleyball club Bamikor, and others. Their recognizable logo is a hand with a cross, which represents Orthodoxy in the group. Cheering in Tetovo has existed since FC Teteks competed in the Second Yugoslav League in the early 1980s, but there was no organized cheering until 1988. The cheerleading group has a Presidency, which includes a Board of Directors, a Statute, and a membership card. Their flag "With faith in God, Dukes to the grave" also symbolizes religious attachment. They are the initiators of the unification of all fan groups in Macedonia with the motto "Under one name and one flag". The goal of this initiative is to organize and unite cheering of the Macedonian national teams in football, basketball and handball. Their fan group Facebook is followed by more than 8000 followers.

Supporters of KF Shkendija—Ballisti, use the name of the nationalist movement Bali Kombëtar from the Second World War. The club was founded in 1979, in the former Yugoslavia, and was banned for using nationalism. When Shkendija joined the Macedonian Football League, the support club was re-founded as Ballisti in 1992. The group is also known for their extreme nationalist, sometimes separatist rhetoric, expressing pride in their Albanian heritage and intolerance towards other ethnic groups in North Macedonia.

Conditions that contribute to sports matches, especially football ones, being a source of violence that can turn into violent extremism are systematized into two key drivers with negative impacts (Georgieva et al., 2024).

Young people may face sociocultural and communication barriers that keep them away from active participation in PVE activities. Processes of radicalization or peer pressure can drag them into negative activities such as sports violence or hooliganism. The absence of educational programs and lack of awareness can prevent young people from understanding the importance of preventing violent extremism and getting involved in it. In parallel, unemployment and socio-economic challenges can distract young people from PVE activities. Lack of opportunities to acquire appropriate skills and employment can make them vulnerable to negative activities.

The institutional weakness and lack of control/monitoring and evaluation tools is also raised. In the last 2 years, the central government has no concept for the development, financing and control of the funds invested in sports. The manipulations of organized individuals and groups, installed in the administrations of sports clubs and national sports federations, reflect on the sport as a whole. Driven by personal and family interests, they abuse them as an additional and only source of financing. At the same time, they are disguised in the form of associations of citizens, as private clubs or federations.

Weak local capacity is also a phenomenon that needs to be taken into account. The local government does not allow real dedicated financing of sports in accordance with the law, while the main principle in financing is the realization of narrow party goals. Therefore, sports and sports activities can be a source of violence and violent extremism, as well as extreme nationalism, in certain environments, but also serve certain daily political goals of individuals, groups and political parties. The impact of the measures to prevent violent extremism is felt, especially at the institutional level, but in our opinion, it is necessary to undertake or develop activities and measures to bridge the gap between the institutions and the local population.

The non-engagement of young people in activities that contribute to their professional and personal growth and development, on the one side, and the political situation, on the other, are considered as preventing youth from active participation in decision-making processes at different levels.

2.3 Prisons and Correctional and Educational Facility Volkovija

We believe that radicalization as a phenomenon in RNM occurs in prisons, particularly among young men aged 18–24. When they are imprisoned, a variety of groups, individuals, and ideologies already present in the prisons may radicalize them, whether through nationalist or religious ideology or in other ways. Consequently, this case study examines the radicalization potential in the prison system in North Macedonia. It focuses on the correctional-educational facility (CEF) for juveniles that exists in Volkovija, in the vicinity of Tetovo, as it provides a good case of meso-level context of interactions. We conducted two focus group discussions with members of the State Council for the Prevention of Juvenile Delinquency (8 participants) and children sent to CEF Volkovija Tetovo to serve the "referral to a correctional facility" measure, i.e. children—protégés[3] (15 children)—and three in-depth interviews, with relevant experts. Following that, to obtain a comprehensive understanding of prison conditions and young people's perspectives on radicalization, we introduced an entirely different group of participants into the study. Thus, we conducted research with young people and practitioners who had never been involved in criminal activities, highlighting education as a fundamental principle in mitigating the process of radicalization that culminates in violent extremism. Finally, three semi-structured interviews were held with one faculty professor of law, a public prosecutor employee and a former director of the Intermunicipal Center for Social Affairs—Skopje (Mujoska-Trpevska, 2024).

We conducted two focus group discussions in February 2022: one with members of the State Council for the Prevention of Juvenile Delinquency (8 participants) in

[3] The term "children—protégés" is recognized in Macedonian law and refers to a distinct group of children, in this case those who are in conflict with the law, but under the protection of the CEF Volkovija and the Directorate for the Execution of Sanctions.

Skopje and another with 15 children—protégés from CEF Volkovija Tetovo serving the "referral to a correctional facility" measure. These groups were selected to assess the Council's understanding of radicalization, given their role in promoting children's rights, and to gather insights from children in correctional facilities. Participants came from various ethnic backgrounds Additionally, we conducted three in-depth interviews with experts: a legal professor and president of the State Council for Preventing Juvenile Delinquency, a legal practitioner and head of the Treatment department at Correctional and Educational Facility, and a representative from the Council of Europe. These interviews provided qualitative insights, highlighting key themes from the focus group discussions and offering expertise on working with at-risk youth and radicalization-related issues (Mujoska-Trpevska, 2024).

In the second phase of the research in 2023, we held a focus group with ten high school and college students, selected based on criteria such as age (18–29), education, gender balance, and geographic diversity. This phase aimed to explore the views of young people not involved in criminal activities, emphasizing the role of education in preventing radicalization. Finally, three additional interviews were conducted with key figures (a law professor, a public prosecutor employee, and a former director of the Intermunicipal Center for Social Affairs) to gather insights on current practices addressing youth violence and radical ideologies, as well as institutional responses to violent extremism and the need for improvements in these areas (Mujoska-Trpevska, 2024).

In terms of institutional structure, the State Directorate for Execution of Sanctions (DES) has joined the NCCVECT to continue working with legal prosecutors and other ministries to design and implement measures to address identified signs of radicalization in prisons. Among the activities undertaken so far are training of prison staff to prevent and protect convicts from the effects of radicalization, as well as direct outreach to prisoners who may be radicalized and pose a risk to themselves and other inmates (National Strategy for Countering Violent Extremism, 2023–2027).

The drafting of the new National Strategy for Penitentiary System Development (2021–2025) aimed to succeed the previous one (Council of Europe, 2021). This new National Strategy is an important milestone expected to contribute to ensuring a more secure and humane treatment of detained and sentenced persons, respecting and protecting their fundamental rights, in line with European values and standards. To be more exact, the new Strategy continues to promote and upgrade the penitentiary system in accordance with current standards, by establishing a modern penitentiary system for dealing with persons deprived of liberty in a safe environment, with dignity and respect, proper education and professional training, support for their personal development, constructive use of their free time, and support for their reintegration back into society after serving their sentence. This is one of the main strategic goals of Macedonian current penitentiary policy addressing radicalization leading to forced extremism in prisons (Mujoska-Trpevska, 2022).

When it comes to youth protection and education, both governmental institutions and civil society recognize that children are particularly vulnerable to terrorist associations and groups' messaging, delivered through social media. Even more so, when it comes to children at risk or in conflict with the law. Countering violent extremism by engaging frontline school workers (teachers, principals, and administrative officials) is a particularly effective method of addressing violent extremism among youth, because education, or lack thereof, is a critical component in determining whether someone will develop extremist views in their lifetime (see also Stojkovski & Kalajdziovski, 2018). The role of primary and secondary schools, as well as faculties and higher education schools is critical in developing knowledge and mechanisms of resistance in young people to radicalization that leads to VE (Mujoska-Trpevska, 2024). Additionally, in terms of C/PVE, the National Committee placed a premium on youth participation. Representatives from the Ministry of Education and Science, as well as the Agency for Youth and Sports, which are the two leading institutions involved in activities with the youth target group, are members of the Committee.

3 Results

Now that the case studies have been presented, the results will be displayed by each selected radicalization drivers, i.e. that are religion, political grievances, territorial inequalities, economic deprivation, transnational dynamics, education, cultural and leisure opportunities, and digital digitalization.

3.1 Religion and Ethnicity

Football fan groups in Tetovo see ethnic, cultural, and religious identity as powerful motivators, which are frequently used to mobilize ethnic groups or spread hate speech. Although identity issues are not the only motivators for joining a football fan group, fan group activities in the past and present help to strengthen symbolic boundaries between North Macedonia's two dominant ethnic and religious communities.

In particular, we found that young members and sympathizers of Skhendia (Balisti) see local and state institutions as distant (specifically law enforcement institutions or football associations) while those of Teteks (Vojvodi) see local authorities as hostile, mostly due to negative perceptions as a result of a lack of political representation of ethnic Macedonians on local level. The space left by local governance and sports institutions is often filled by international actors who perceive sports and fan groups in the country in several ways: as a means of social reconciliation of different groups, but also as platforms for possible radicalization. International partners are significant as they provide financial means for implementing various C/PVE-related projects in the civic sector and facilitate the regional cross-national cooperation in C/PVE. Besa Arifi (2019), professor of criminal law at the South East European University and an expert in violent extremism, considers the OSCE Mission to Skopje, the USAID and the American and British Embassies in Skopje were instrumental agencies in these regards. They offered not only financial support but also logistical resources by bringing the "local institutions, civil society organizations (CSOs), religious communities and academia" into the institution-building process (Arifi, 2019, p. 29).

As for the meso-level, members and sympathizers of football fans have ambivalent attitudes towards radicalization and VE: the groups perceive the violent behavior of the group itself to be presented as an attitude of defense of the group and, often, its members use heroic tropes and references of ethnic and religious identity markers to support these and similar behaviors. We see these meso-dynamics in line with macro-level findings regarding the drivers of cultural, ethnic and religious salience. However, some differences can be noted about the role given to ethnicity at the macro and meso levels. As for the findings at the macro level, the dominant perspective on football fan groups in North Macedonia—among scholarship, the media and the general public—is that the main axis of contestation is the ethnic one. However, we argue that this approach overlooks intra-ethnic conflicts between fan groups, which are equally dangerous.

On the other hand, participants in the Volkovija case study on Prisons, Correctional, and Educational Facilities emphasize the importance of religion as a driver. Most children's respondents believe that radicalism and religion are directly linked. There is one answer from a protégé who, when he hears the term radicalization, usually through media "thinks of faith and religion". Regarding the State Council focus group findings, the role of religion and political views in the emergence of violent extremism or radicalism stands out. Another important driver is the religious education, which can play a big role. Religious education is increasingly recognized as an instrument for the prevention of violent extremism. Religious education should enable students to gain knowledge and understanding of the influence of religions on people's and societies' lives, contribute to students' spiritual and moral development, raise students' awareness of life's fundamental issues, and encourage them to explore, reflect on, and provide answers to such questions in light of the world's great religious teachings and ethical traditions (Mujoska-Trpevska, 2022). In this frame, the Commission for Relations with Religious Communities and Religious Groups is a local actor in RNM with the greatest potential to increase the positive impact of C/PVE while limiting its negative impact.

In short, we can state that religion in the context of Macedonian society holds a significant place in terms of being in touch with and influencing the religious practice of young people. Considering that religion and ethnicity overlap, it should be taken into account that their connection with political grievances and territorial organization can make young people vulnerable to radicalization attempts. Of course, the process of migration and emigration, which has been present for a long time, relatively changes the demographic structure of the country as a whole, but especially in multi-ethnic areas such as the capital and the northwestern part. In that direction, the sensitivity of multi-ethnic and multi-religious environments to the influences of ethno-political mobilization or radicalization remains high.

3.2 Political Grievances

During the Commemorations of the 2001 Macedonian conflict in Tetovo case study, discussions suggest that Tetovo youth have a nuanced understanding of the notion of radicalization: considering it both as a negative category (such as in terrorism, physical aggression and war) and a positive practice (such as in radical reforms, mentioned by the Macedonian group, or the political radicalization of Martin Luther King and Nelson Mandela, mentioned by the Albanian group). Moreover, both groups identified the state's political parties as the major proponents of interethnic tensions in North Macedonia.

It has already been mentioned that political organization and political parties are based not only on political ideology and values but also on ethnicity. Although there are examples in the parties of other members, different in terms of ethnicity and religion, they still remain monolithic. In that way, the political competition is also held as an ethnic one, which leads to frequent conflict situations related to access to resources, participation in local and state government, identity issues, that is, language use issues. Since the independence of the state in 1991, all the composition of the Government includes representatives of Macedonians and Albanians and smaller ethnic communities. After 2001 and the change of the Constitution, non-majority ethnic communities are protected from majorization through the so-called Badenter's rule, which requires consent on a number of issues important to them on different levels of decision making. Polarization in perceptions results from the fact that a series of abuses related to corruption and abuse of positions in the implementation of policies puts ethnic communities in a privileged or subordinate position.

In sum, North Macedonia's political landscape is shaped by a mix of ethnic tensions, historical grievances, identity struggles, and challenges related to corruption and governance. These issues have created a highly polarized political environment that often hampers progress toward greater stability and integration with Western institutions like the EU and NATO. In addition to the internal ones, there are also grievances in the process of EU membership negotiations due to the dispute with Bulgaria over the Macedonian identity and history, while the dispute with Greece over the name wepe overcome by the Prespa Agreement. Although it is becoming more important for neighborly-bilateral relations, disputes and solutions also affect internal political relations due to the different perceptions of which concessions and solutions are acceptable and with what consequences.

As per the interviews we conducted, the memory of 2001 is instrumentalized by political parties. This is done by the high party officials, who use the commemorative events to mobilize the party base, and by the lower party echelons, who use them to pledge loyalty to the party. Thus, these perceptions of the Tetovar youth suggest that the political grievances driver may be seen as one of the most potent means for radicalization and violent extremism in their city.

We find the focus group discussions on the topics of extremism, radicalization and violence incredibly telling in these regards: similarly to the political agendas of- and influences over the fan groups, the participants in the two focus groups showed awareness of the global phenomena of violent extremism, radicalization and terrorism. Yet, when asked about the violence at sports events, they scapegoated the rival fan groups as the "aggressive" ones and agreed upon the fact that their group acts only when attacked. The same discussion revealed, as well, that the focus group participants were certain in their definitions of radicalization and violent extremism as a set of deviant beliefs and activities that are opposed to the state norms and values, and even the football fandom and fan culture in general.

Finally, according to one interviewee in the Prisons and Correctional and Educational Facility Volkovija case study, many of the young men expressed feelings of marginalization and frustration due to the lack of social mobility, inadequate educational opportunities, and political exclusion. These grievances are intensified by their immediate surroundings, including poor living conditions in prison, limited access to rehabilitation, and a social environment filled with cultural tensions. These negative factors create a sense of injustice and helplessness, which pushes vulnerable individuals down the path of violent extremism. CEF Volkovija's political grievances are worsened by a lack of social support, reinforcing the belief that violence is a legitimate outlet for their frustrations.The social and political developments in Republic of North Macedonia in the aftermath of the 2001-armed conflict are thus closely related to their radicalization potential (Georgieva et al., 2021).

3.3 Territorial Inequalities

The Commemorations of the 2001 Macedonian conflict in Tetovo case study illustrate the impact of territorial inequalities on VE between Macedonian and Albanian groups. Starting with the Macedonian group, the discussants pointed out the commemorative activities in Lešok and Karpalak as the most significant ones, or the ones that they follow the most; yet, without paying much attention to the annual developments. They identified the demolishing of the memorial plaques placed in memory of the fallen during the 2001's conflict as a "provocation" by the local Albanians, stressing that such activities are common only in the areas inhabited by Albanians and are likely to happen in the future as well. They also agreed upon the argument that no Macedonian has ever demolished a commemorative plaque of NLA (National Liberation Army) in the last years. Moreover, the group also define as an eventual "provocation" the scenario in which an ethnic Albanian attends a commemoration of Macedonians killed in 2001.

The Albanian group, on the other hand, stated that the commemorations of the war casualties and civil victims are important, yet acknowledged the fact that smaller and radical groups are responsible for fueling tensions before and after certain commemorative events. Even though the group was not as open as the Macedonian one when discussing these topics, they stressed that the general constellation of ethnic hate speech from both the communities in the state, alongside the slow economic development in general—"nothing has changed since 2001"—contributes to escalating and manifests as a demolishment of memorial artifacts.

The young Macedonians participants hold that their Albanian peers lack a basic knowledge of—and fail to understand the Macedonian national history and history narratives—a process which, as per the same focus group discussion, works in both cases and for both groups. Thus, the case study of Tetovo showcased that the memory of the 2001 conflict in North Macedonia impacts the everyday dynamics both at local and national levels.

The Football Fan Groups in Tetovo case study highlights the social context of Tetovo, and its vicinity was unanimously identified as "unique" and/or "different" than the other cities or regions in the state in the two focus groups that we conducted, primarily due to the abovementioned population structure and the recent history of inter-ethnic relations in the city. Tetovo, as already mentioned, is one of the rare ethnically divided cities in the state—beside Skopje—that hosts more than two competitors in the top two national football leagues. Yet, the most recent turmoil between the two largest local fan groups of Ballistët and Vojvodi, leads us to assume that the tensions in Tetovo are ever-growing and get to occupy new discursive domains with time. In November 2018, for instance, members of the two groups were accused of ethnic hate speech performed at two separate events during a single weekend in the city.

The perception of territorial inequality and, more precisely, state absence and the low—or even nonexistent—trust in the central institutions, was presented by the members and sympathizers of Ballistët. This point was further enhanced by the articulated shared perception of police brutality over KF Shkëndija fans, improper treatment of the club and the fan group by the Football Federation of Macedonia (FFM) and, finally, by the very fact that the fanbase of the club is ethnically uniform and thus prone to nurture its ethnic Albanian identity and relations with the neighboring Kosovo and Albania.

The territorial inequalities do not seem to be a relevant driver of radicalization for the Prisons and Correctional and Educational Facility Volkovija case study. However, as a social context, territorial inequality is a significant motivator for education and socialization among young Macedonians. For example, many young students, particularly those who wish to pursue their education, must relocate from their hometowns to Skopje, as it is the only city that provides all opportunities for education, employment, or training. From an early age (16–17 years old), young people are forced to leave their homes and families to continue their education in the capital. The impact and danger of negative influence is twofold: on the one hand, young people are separated from their parents and families, which represents fundamental corrective for their behaviors, and, on the other hand, they begin a new life without adequate parental/family supervision and are easily the target of unwanted influences, including radical ones (Mujoska-Trpevska, 2022).

3.4 Economic Deprivation

The Football Fan Groups in Tetovo case study demonstrates that both groups of discussants agreed that these acts of radicalization are not solely related to the legacies of the 2001 conflict, but also resonate with the economic situation and political affiliations of the participants. Nonetheless, differences between discussants were observed. For the Albanian group, commemorative-related violence is not a mere result of inter-ethnic tensions and sometimes occurs as a reaction to the unfavorable economic situation in the city and the state. However, according to the Macedonian group, one of the major issues related to the commemorative-related violence is the lack of understanding of the Macedonian national narrative by the Albanian peers in Tetovo.

The participant in the first focus group (Vojvodi) pictured the average member of the football fan groups, within the Football Fan Groups in the Tetovo case study, as being in a 'dependent economic situation"—either living with their parents or working for a salary that is close to the state's minimal one. This precarious socio-economic situation is perceived as a potential radicalization driver.

Finally, the Prisons and Correctional and Educational Facility Volkovija case study does not present enough evidence of the economic driver as a radicalization driver because the respondents could not recognize this driver and therefore could not answer this question in particular. However, according to ICM, the official Islamic religious community in Macedonia, one of the reasons for radicalization is the high rate of unemployment and the overall poor economic situation of Macedonian youth. When young people see no hope for a better tomorrow, they become more vulnerable to manipulation. According to our research (Mujoska-Trpevska, 2022), when the economic driver is introduced, young people from low-income families are more vulnerable to radicalization and VE than those from higher-income families. Dysfunctional, larger, economically challenged, and less educated families are viewed as surroundings where this behavior can emerge.

3.5 Transnational Dynamics

The research did not bring enough evidence to consider this driver of radicalization relevant within the Commemorations of the 2001 Macedonian conflict in Tetovo and the Prisons and Correctional and Educational Facility Volkovija case studies. On the other hand, the Football Fan Groups in Tetovo case study presents some interesting facts regarding this driver.

Thus, it is noteworthy is that the transnational dimension and the digital tools were differently understood during the two focus groups. More precisely, the more successful Football Club Shkëndija's fans viewed transnational dynamics via the optics of their club's international fixtures, while Football Club Teteks' ones referred to the national teams' matches and the major developments in the regional fan scenes. We want to underline that the two discussant groups viewed the local events as more significant than the regional and international ones.

3.6 Education, Cultural and Leisure Opportunities

Once again, the research did not offer enough evidence to consider education, cultural and leisure opportunities—and their lack thereof—as a driver of radicalization relevant within the Commemorations of the 2001 Macedonian conflict in Tetovo and the Prisons and Correctional and Educational Facility Volkovija case studies. However, the Football Fan Groups in Tetovo case study pictures the education, cultural and leisure driver through some examples. As mentioned earlier, the animosities which these histories of inter-ethnic (predominantly ethnic-Macedonian and Macedonian-Albanian) tensions in Tetovo are perpetuating in the cultural, educational and leisure domains are also visible when observing the two dominant football fan groups' behaviors and cultures in the city. The Law had several amendments ever since—in 2008, 2011, 2014 and 2015—which projected better cooperation in security terms between the state Ministry of Interior (MoI), the Football Federation Macedonia (FFM), the Agency of Sport and Youth (AMS), and the sport events' organizers and conveners, as well as set of soft measures for cooperating with fan groups (Doda & Mklelan, 2020; Petrevski & Stanojoska, 2014). Some of the most recent activities in these regards are Agency for Youth and Sport newly established cooperation with the National Committee for C/PVE and two Skopje-based high schools within the platform of an EU-funded project entitled "Youth Civic Education Platform for Countering Radicalization". It is important to mention that the MoI was also targeting high school pupils in Tetovo and Gostivar as an age group that is "present the most at the sport events and participates the most in the incidents between the fan groups" and organized several "preventive educational" workshops in the early and mid-2010s (Samardžiev, 2014).

Macedonian educational programs fail to align with the latest developments in global education (Mujoska-Trpevska, 2022). In general, schools do not engage in continuous preventive activities to prevent the emergence of social problems, such as radicalization and violent extremism. This is due in part to the lack of provisions in primary and secondary education laws regarding preventive activities in schools. The role of primary and secondary schools, as well as faculties and higher education schools, is critical in developing knowledge and mechanisms of resistance in young people to radicalization that leads to VE. In addition, stakeholders can use relevant handbooks and guidelines to combat radicalization. One of the most important findings from the Prisons, Correctional and Educational Facility Volkovija case study was that more education for children at risk with the law and professionals working in this field is needed. The Macedonian government should immediately review educational programs and devote significant resources to raise awareness of the importance of radicalism and violent extremism, as well as the consequences of these trends.

3.7 *Digital Socialization*

Within the Commemorations of the 2001 Macedonian conflict in Tetovo and the Prisons and Correctional and Educational Facility Volkovija case studies, this driver did not stand out particularly. However, the Football Fan Groups in Tetovo case study pictures the social digital socialization driver through some examples.

In connection with transnational dynamics, members and sympathizers of football fan groups, particularly Vojvodi, use social media to stay informed about global sports events and the latest developments in fan culture worldwide. They also follow current trends in fan activism and actions through these platforms. The other focus group discussion (Ballistët) showcased that the fans and sympathizers of the football club KF Shkëndija are aware and follow—predominantly online—the latest political developments and news related to the football fan groups in the region. However, they all agreed that the local and national developments are the dominant triggers for tensions with the other rival fan groups. Again, we can juxtapose these findings with the empirical evidence from the scholarship: a 2016 study of the social media activities of 54 football fans in the state revealed that more than a half of the informants used various social media platforms for hate speech and discrimination (Anastasovski & Nanev, 2016). Similarly to the findings of the macro-level research on digital literacy (Kambovski et al., 2021), we identify that the online attitudes and behaviors of the fan group members in the country are not responded with the proper treatment.

4 Conclusion

It is obvious that that some drivers of radicalization are more relevant than others in the Macedonian context. Political grievances, economic deprivation, territorial inequalities, and transnational dynamics seem to be more relevant drivers of radicalisation and VE than religion for instance. Although the former southernmost Yugoslav state managed to avoid the bloodshed of the Yugoslav wars of the 1990s, the inter-ethnic tensions between the two largest ethnic communities in the state—the Macedonian and the Albanian one—escalated in early 2001, soon after the end of the war in the neighboring Kosovo and can be considered as roots for the drivers of radicalization at a national and regional level.

The research showed that the memory of cultures and practices related to the 2001 conflict influence public discourse, especially regarding inter-ethnic relations. Such relations, as well as the ethnic identities, cultures and the history of inter-ethnic dynamics were already identified as one of the dominant drivers of radicalization and violent extremism at the state level. On the one hand, during the events to mark and pay respect to the victims of violence, the narrative of a winner or a loser is favored, while on the other hand, there is a subdivision of the memorialization of the victims, i.e. each ethnic group feels sorry for its own victims. Joint commemoration is an exception, and no messages of reconciliation or forgiveness are sent to the public. Although the solution to the conflict is embedded in the Constitution, the politicization of ethnicity and identity and the political narrative is dominant in terms of gaining merits for the realization of interests. Moreover, we noted and argued that there is a certain discrepancy between the fan groups' self-perceived religiosity and their affiliation to the organized religious groups in the state and the city. More precisely, even though the main and official religious institutions are promoting activities that aim at reconciling, the fan groups—arguably, do not act upon these messages with an increased interest in communicating with the other religious groups. A similar tendency was mapped regarding the partisan influences and the impact of the cultural norms and ethnic communities in general. There is a tendency to self-ascribe a meaning of group identity that is not necessarily in line with the identity markers of the cultures and ethnic communities on a local and national level (Trajanovski & Georgieva, 2022). Threats from violent extremism are ever-changing, taking various forms and manifestations, so continuous education on the topic is essential in countering this phenomenon.

Finally, re-socialization, rehabilitation, and reintegration of radicalized individuals and members of extremist groups continue to be a major challenge in North Macedonia, given the poor conditions in prisons and the lack of effective re-socialization programs. Radicalization in prisons remains a major issue in North Macedonia (Mujoska-Trpevska, 2022). Specialized preventive programs, financial resources, and protocols must be established at the state level to support and oversee the collaboration between the local community, non-governmental organizations, health, social, and educational institutions.

References

Ackermann, A. (2002). On the Razor's edge: Macedonia ten years after independence. *OSCE Yearbook, 2001*(1).

Ameti, E., Mamuti, F., & Rexepi, A. (2023). Football fans and sports events: FC Shkendija-Tetovo. *International Journal of Sport Sciences and Health, 10*(21–22), 49.

Anastasovski, I., & Nanev, L. (2016). The Internet and social networks as opportunities for fans to spread hate speech and discrimination in sports. In V. Kambovski et al. (Eds.), *The dialogue between civilizations and the challenges of tolerance in the digital age* (pp. 144–157). Macedonian Academy of Sciences and Arts. Retrieved June 2024, from https://manu.edu.mk/wp-content/uploads/2024/02/04-Dijalog-megju-civilizaciite.pdf

Arifi, B. (2019). Drivers to violent extremism in Southeastern Europe—The North Macedonian context. *Journal of Penal Law and Criminology, 7*(1).

Barrett, R. (2022). Beyond the Caliphate: Foreign fighters and the threat of returnees. *JSTOR Security Studies Collection.*

Bellamy, A. J. (2002). The new wolves at the door: Conflict in Macedonia. *Civil Wars, 5*(1).

Bieber, F. (2008). Power-sharing and the implementation of the Ohrid Framework Agreement. In S. Dehnert & R. Sulejmani (Eds.), *Powersharing and the implementation of the Ohrid Framework Agreement* (pp. 7–40). Friedrich Ebert Stiftung—Office Macedonia. Retrieved June 2024, from https://library.fes.de/pdf-files/bueros/skopje/06357.pdf

Brentin, D., & Cooley, L. (2015). Sport and nationalism: A review of the literature. *Studies on National Movements, 3*.
Brunnbauer, U. (2002). The implementation of the Ohrid Agreement: Ethnic Macedonian resentments. *Journal on Ethnopolitics and Minority Issues in Europe, 1*.
Committee on Relations between Religious Communities and Groups (CRRCG). (2020). *Report on the Implementation of the Annual Work Plan for 2020, Committee on Relations between Religious Communities and Groups (CRRCG), n/a*
Casal Bértoa, F., & van Biezen, I. (2017). Party regulation and party politics in post-communist Europe. *East European Politics, 30*(3).
Čolović, I. (2002). *The politics of symbols: Essays on political anthropology*. C. Hurst & Company.
Council of Europe (2021). *National strategy on the Development of the Penitentiary system in the Republic of North Macedonia 2021–2025*. Retrieved June 2024, from https://rm.coe.int/national-strategy-penitentiarynorth-macedonia-eng/1680a4618c
Daskalovski, Z. (2004). The Macedonian conflict of 2001: Between successful diplomacy, rhetoric and terror. *Studies in Post-Communism*, Occasional Paper no. 7.
Dimova, R. (2013). *Ethno-baroque: Materiality, aesthetics, and conflict in modern-day Macedonia*. Berghahn.
Doda, A., & Mklelan, M. (2020). *Promoting a multi-stakeholder approach in the process of preventing and countering violent extremism and radicalization leading to terrorism. Summary report on the discussions held at the grassroots level for the National Strategy for Countering Violent Extremism in the Republic of North Macedonia*. OSCE Mission to Skopje. Retrieved June 2024, from https://www.osce.org/files/f/documents/e/5/467109.pdf
Đorđević, I. (2015). *Anthropologist among fans*. Biblioteka XX vek.
Đorđević, S., & Scaturro, R. (2022). Dangerous games. Football hooliganism, politics and organized crime in the Western Balkans. *Global Initiative Against Transnational Organized Crime*. Retrieved August 2024, from https://globalinitiative.net/wp-content/uploads/2022/06/Football-hooliganism-politics-and-organized-crime-in-the-Western-Balkans-GITOC-SEEObs.pdf
Georgieva, L., Kambovski, V., Mujoska-Trpevska, E., & Trajanovski, N. (2024). *CONNECT country papers on micro-level drivers: Drivers of radicalisation and violent extremism in the light of individual dynamics in MENA and the Balkans, North Macedonia*. The European Institute of the Mediterranean (IEMed). Retrieved June 2024, from https://h2020connekt.eu/publications/north-macedonia-country-paper-on-micro-level-drivers/
Georgieva, L., Mehmeti, A., & Musliu, A. (2011). Patterns of conflict resolution in the Republic of Macedonia. *IBIS Discussion Paper*, 8.
Georgieva, L., Trajanovski N., & Kambovski, V. (2021). *CONNECT macro approaches to the study of radicalisation and violent extremism: A view from the Balkan region: An overview of the regional dynamics and patterns of radicalisation and violent extremism (VE) in four Balkan states: Bulgaria, Bosnia and Herzegovina, Kosovo, and North Macedonia*. The European Institute of the Mediterranean (IEMed) Retrieved June 2024, from https://h2020connekt.eu/publications/balkans-macro-approaches-to-the-study-of-radicalisation-and-violent-extremism/.
Hodges, A. (2019). *Fan activism, protest and politics: Ultras in post-socialist Croatia*. Routledge.
Horowitz, D. (2014). Ethnic power-sharing: Three big problems. *Journal of Democracy, 25*(2).
Huq, A. (2016). The uses of religious identity, practice, and dogma in 'soft' and 'hard' counterterrorism. *Public Law and Legal Theory Working Papers, 610*.
Ilievski, Z. (2007). *Country specific report on actors and processes of ethnomobilization, violent conflicts and consequences: Macedonia*. European Academy of Bozen/Bolzano.
Ilievski, Z., & Wolff, S. (2011). Consociationalism, centripetalism and Macedonia. *Crossroads. The Macedonian Foreign Policy Journal, 2*(4).
Janev, G. (2011). What happened to the Macedonian Salad: Ethnocracy in Macedonia. *Ethnologia Balkanica, 15*(1).
Kambovski, V., Georgieva, L., & Trajanovski, N. (2020). *CONNEKT country reports. National approaches to extremism: North Macedonia*. The European Institute of the Mediterranean (IEMed). Retrieved June 2024, from https://h2020connekt.eu/publications/north-macedonia-country-report-on-national-approaches-to-extremism/

Kambovski, V., Georgieva, L., & Trajanovski, N. (2021). *CONNEKT country reports on macro-level drivers: North Macedonia*. The European Institute of the Mediterranean (IEMed). Retrieved June 2024, from https://h2020connekt.eu/wp-content/uploads/2021/09/North_Macedonia_CONNEKT_Macro_Drivers.pdf

Kelly, L. (2019). *Overview of research on far-right extremism in the Western Balkans. K4D help-desk report*. Institute of Development Studies.

Lowe, D., Turk, A. T., & Das, D. K. (2013). *Examining political violence: Studies of terrorism, counterterrorism, and internal war*. CRC Press.

Macedonian Information Agency (MIA). (2023). *Osmani: Fan relations not linked with interstate relations*. Retrieved March 2025, from https://mia.mk/en/story/osmani-fan-relations-not-linked-with-interstate-relations

Marusic Jakov, S. (2012, April 19). Unsolved killings raise fears of Macedonian Turmoil. *Balkan Insight*. Retrieved August 2024, from https://balkaninsight.com/2012/04/19/unsolved-killings-raise-fears-of-macedonian-turmoil/

Marusic Jakov, S. (2015, May 10). Macedonia declares mourning for police killed in Gunbattles. *Balkan Insight*. Retrieved August 2024, from https://balkaninsight.com/2015/05/10/macedonia-mourns-for-killed-policemen-while-shootout-continues/

Međedović, J., Kovačević, U., & Knežević, G. (2020). Militant extremism mind-set in Serbian football supporters: Relations with the adherence to extremist social movements. *Behavioral Sciences of Terrorism and Political Aggression, 14*, 312.

Mills, R. (2012). 'It all ended in an unsporting way': Serbian football and the disintegration of Yugoslavia, 1989-2006. *The International Journal of the History of Sport, 26*(9).

Milošević, A. (2017). Remembering the present: Dealing with the memories of terrorism in Europe. *Journal of Terrorism Research, 8*(2).

Morina, E., Austin, B., Roetman, T. J., & Dudouet, V. (2019). *Community perspectives on preventing violent extremism*. Research report. Retrieved August 2024, from https://www.berghoffoundation.org/fileadmin/redaktion/Publications/Other_Resources/WB_PVE/CTR_PVE_WesternBalkans_Research_Report.pdf

Mujoska-Trpevska, E. (2022). Prisons and correctional and educational facility Volkovija. In T. Chirchi (Ed.), *North Macedonia—Meso level drivers of radicalization and violent extremism*. The European Institute of the Mediterranean (IEMed). Retrieved June 2024, from https://h2020connekt.eu/wp-content/uploads/2022/12/CONNEKT-MESO-N-MACEDONIA.pdf

Mujoska-Trpevska, E. (2024). Prisons & education. In T. Chirchi (Ed.), *Country based national reports on prevention of extremism*. The European Institute of the Mediterranean (IEMed). Retrieved June 2024, from https://h2020connekt.eu/wp-content/uploads/2024/03/D5.2-COUNTRY.pdf

Neofotistos, V. (2012). *The construction of Albanian Martyrdom in the Republic of Macedonia*. NCEEER Working Paper.

Ortakovski, V. (2001). Interethnic relations and minorities in the Republic of Macedonia. *Southeast European Politics, 2*(1).

Petrevski, B., & Stanojoska, A. (2014). *Prevention of spectator's violence and misbehavior at sport events: The need of institutional cooperation before penal sanction*. Faculty of Security.

Phillips, J. (2002). *Macedonia: Warlords and rebels in the Balkans*. I.B. Tauris.

Qehaja, F., & Perteshi, S. (2018). *The unexplored nexus: Issues of radicalisation and violent extremism in Macedonia*. Kosovar Centre for Security Studies.

Ragaru, N. (2008). Macedonia: Between Ohrid and Brussels. *Cahiers de Chaillot, 1*.

Reef, P. (2018). Macedonian monument culture beyond 'Skopje 2014'. *Südosteuropa, 66*(4).

Samardžiev, A. (2014, December 9). Middle school students learn how to be proper fans. *RS Evropa*. Retrieved from https://www.slobodnaevropa.mk/a/26732121.html

Saveski, Z. (2021). Country North Macedonia. In J. Mulhall & S. Khan-Ruf (Eds.), *State of hate: Far-right extremism in Europe 2021*. HOPE not hate Charitable Trust—Amadeu Antonio Stiftung—Expo Foundation.

Saveski, Z., & Sadiku, A. (2012). *The radical right in Macedonia*. Friedrich Ebert Stiftung.

Spaskovska, L. (2012). The fractured 'we' and the ethno-national 'I': The Macedonian citizenship framework. *Citizenship Studies, 16*(3–4).

State Statistical Office of the Republic of North Macedonia. (2022). *Total resident population, households and apartments in the Republic of North Macedonia, census 2021*. Retrieved June 2024, from https://www.stat.gov.mk/publikacii/2022/POPIS_DZS_web_MK.pdf

Stojančova, P. (2019, March 15). For "Bloody Thursday" total of 211 years in prison. *Radio Slobodna Evropa*. Retrieved from https://www.slobodnaevropa.mk/a/29823553.html

Stojanov, D., Kocevska, J., Recica, V., Bernhardt, D., Ashtalkovska Gajtanoska, A., & Jakomovska, I. (2019). *Revisiting 2001*. forum ZFD.

Stojkovski, F., & Kalajdziovski, N. (2018). *Community perspectives on the prevention of violent extremism in Macedonia*. Berghof Foundation.

Trajanovski, N. (2021). A patriotic act for Macedonia? The mnemohistory of Mara Buneva's commemorations in Skopje (2001-2018). *Contemporary Southeastern Europe, 8*(2).

Trajanovski, N., & Georgieva, L. (2022). Football fan groups in Tetovo. In T. Chirchi (Ed.), *North Macedonia—Meso level drivers of radicalization and violent extremism*. The European Institute of the Mediterranean (IEMed). Retrieved June 2024, from https://h2020connekt.eu/publications/north-macedonia-meso-level-drivers-of-radicalisation-and-violent-extremism/

Vrcan, S., & Lalić, D. (1999). From ends to trenches, and back: Football in the former Yugoslavia. In G. Armstrong & R. Giulianotti (Eds.), *Football cultures and identities* (pp. 176–185). Macmillan.

Meso-Level Analysis of Multireligious Contexts and Community Resilience in Kosovo

Lulzim Peci and Agon Demjaha

1 Introduction

Radicalism and violent extremism (VE) in Kosovo are depicted as a complex picture, with many factors and dynamics. In a general perspective, the struggle against VE has been taking place in two dimensions. The first dimension is related to security-centered measures that aim to prevent and combat VE through the conventional rule of law mechanisms. The second dimension pertains to countering radical religious preaching at the doctrinal and ideological levels. The Ministry of Internal Affairs and the Kosovo Police lead the efforts in the first dimension, whereas the Islamic Community of Kosovo is at the epicenter of the second dimension (Peci & Demjaha, 2020).

This introduction briefly presents the main institutional stakeholders related to VE and the most important recent developments. In terms of institutional approaches, it pays particular attention to certain practices and norms of the Ministry of Internal Affairs and the Islamic Community of Kosovo, which hold a leading role in countering violent extremism (CVE).

Several public institutions play a major role in countering and preventing violent extremism (C/PVE) in Kosovo. This includes the Office of the Prime Minister (OPM), the Ministry of Internal Affairs (MIA), the Kosovo Intelligence Agency (KIA), the Security Council of Kosovo (SCK), the Ministry of Justice (MoJ), the Ministry of Education, Science and Technology (MEST) and the Ministry of Labor and Social Welfare (MLSW). The coordination of the implementation of the Strategy on the Prevention of Violent Extremism and Radicalism Leading to Terrorism 2015–2020 (SPVERLT) is the responsibility of the Security Council of

L. Peci (✉) · A. Demjaha
Kosovar Institute for Policy Research and Development, Pristina, Kosovo
e-mail: lulzim.peci@kipred.org

C. Torrekens et al. (eds.), *Social Contexts of Radicalization and Violent Extremism in the MENA and Balkans*,
https://doi.org/10.1007/978-3-031-84521-5_9

Kosovo (SCK) and its Secretariat oversees harmonizing all activities of state institutions regarding the prevention of VE. The OPM has a primary role when it comes to the implementation of all state policies in Kosovo, and is responsible for supervising the progress made, in close cooperation with the SCK (Peci & Demjaha, 2020).

The most important recent development was the government's decision in March 2020 to merge the SPVERLT and the Counterterrorism Strategy of Kosovo into a single strategy. Since then, a designated interministerial body has been working on drafting such a strategy, but no further information is available. This decision was part of the arrangement to implement the Joint Action Plan on Counterterrorism for the Western Balkans, signed between the EU Commissioner for Migration, Home Affairs and Citizenship, Dimitris Avramopoulos, and the Minister of Internal Affairs of Kosovo, Ekrem Mustafa, in October 2019 (European Commission, 2019).

Another important development was the decision of Kurti's government on 12 February 2020 to abolish the post of the National Coordinator against Violent Extremism and Terrorism (Government of Kosovo, 2020a). Later, the new government of Prime Minister Hoti, on 14 July 2020, appointed the Minister of Interior Affairs as the National Coordinator for the Prevention of Violent Extremism and the Fight against Terrorism (Government of Kosovo, 2020b). The newly elected government of Kurti, 2 April 2021, charged the Minister of Interior with this task (Government of Kosovo, 2021).

The MIA is mandated to advance legislation and the policy framework in the field of security issues, whereas the MoJ is responsible for the implementation of reintegration and deradicalization programs within the Kosovo Correctional Services (KCS). In terms of security institutions, the Kosovo Police (KP) is the only institution in Kosovo with a solid capacity to deal with issues related to VE and terrorism. The KIA also plays a crucial role in collecting and disseminating information to the government of Kosovo and security institutions concerning any activity that might be detrimental to the national security of Kosovo. The main developments related to the responses of the institutions in Kosovo were a consequence of the changing context of VE, at a domestic and global level. During the period 2012–2016, almost all activities were directed to prevent individuals from Kosovo from going to war zones in the Middle East. However, during the years 2017–2019, the focus and priorities shifted towards the returning of Kosovo citizens from the war zones and the security challenges that this process entails. It is worth noting that, during this time, the KP in cooperation with the KIA has prevented four planned terrorist attacks in Kosovo (Peci & Demjaha, 2020).

At the local level, municipalities of Kosovo are entitled to play an important role in preventing violent extremism (PVE), according to the SPVERLT. The Municipal Community Safety Councils function within all municipalities. They are led by the mayors and with the participation of the representatives of municipal assemblies, local governments, security institutions, ethnic communities, religious communities, civil society, media, and business (Ministry of Local Government Administration, 2014). In 2016, the first C/PVE Referral Mechanism was established as a pilot project in the municipality of Gjilan, which proved to be a success story. In this context, the main development is the proposal to replicate such mechanisms in three of the regions most targeted by the VE (Peci & Demjaha, 2020).

Other relevant stakeholders include civil society and local experts in Kosovo, international governmental and Non-Governmental Organizations (NGO), and the Islamic Community of Kosovo (BIK). Civil society organizations (CSOs) in Kosovo undoubtedly represent one of the most important stakeholders in awareness-raising, deradicalization, and PVE. The international community mainly has a capacity-building and advisory role. It must be emphasized that they contribute to the major share of funding of local CSOs combating radicalization and VE. The most active international actors in combating violent extremism in Kosovo are the US Embassy, followed by the Organization for Security and Cooperation in Europe (OSCE), the International Organization for Migration (IOM), the European Union (EU), as well as some other individual countries (Peci & Demjaha, 2020).

As the main institution representing the Muslim community, the Islamic Community of Kosovo the BIK plays an important multifaceted role in different aspects linked to VE. Within the Muslim community, there are two prevalent traditions of practicing Islam, namely the Sunni Islam and the Bektashi order. On the other hand, the Christian community is traditionally Serbian Orthodox, Catholic, although there is also a small Protestant community. The involvement of the BIK in all activities aiming to prevent extremism and deradicalize individuals remains essential. Indeed, religiously motivated extremism strives against the particular (mis)interpretation of the religious tenets, which creates a fake religious cause of a holy war against "injustices" and "victimhood". Consequently, efforts to counter VE involve a sharp ideological/doctrinal counternarrative. Competing theological interpretations of religious tenets are at the crux of the battle to counter religiously inspired VE. BIK has been at the forefront of this battle. However, it must be noted that some of the respondents from the macro-level study have argued that ethnoreligious extremism, particularly among certain segments of the Serb community in Kosovo, is no less a threat. BIK is involved in the efforts to counter VE in two aspects: first, it has been part of the major national interagency activities to counter VE. Thus, it participated in the adoption of national strategies against VE and terrorism, in the coordinating bodies (including within the KSC), in programs of deradicalization in prisons, in the consultative religious council convened under the umbrella of the NATO-led KFOR mission, and was also part of local initiatives and mechanisms against VE (Peci & Demjaha, 2020).

In this context, a study conducted on the institutional responses in Kosovo highlights three crucial findings. First, at the initial phase, the institutional response to VE was rather reactive and was triggered by the high number of Kosovars joining terrorist groups in the Middle East. The institutional responses undertaken in this phase entailed classical security-oriented measures. These measures were based on the existing legal and policy framework, such as the Criminal Code, Code of Criminal Procedure, and the Counterterrorism Strategy. In August 2014, police searched 60 locations throughout Kosovo and arrested 40 Kosovar citizens suspected of having joined terrorist organizations in Iraq and Syria. Until January 2015, an additional 80 people were arrested under similar charges including several influential radical imams (Peci & Demjaha, 2020).

In the second phase, the legal and policy frameworks were consolidated with the adoption of the Law on Prohibition of Joining Armed Conflicts outside State Territory, the SPVERLT, and its respective action plan. In this phase, the efforts in C/PVE were diversified in terms of measures and actors involved, including religious communities, CSOs, and international donors. Regarding diversification of measures, the focus was expanded to include activities that involved countering the extremist interpretations of Islam on ideological grounds. In addition, efforts were made towards curtailing transnational Islamic radical movements in Kosovo and using digital platforms for building counternarratives to extremist interpretations of religion.

The third phase is characterized by three parallel developments. Firstly, the nature of the threat has changed and is shaped by the potential threat from the foreign terrorist fighters and their families who were repatriated from the war zones, and the changing of the modus operandi of the extremist religious groups who went underground. Secondly, the efforts to adopt an all-inclusive national strategy against VE and terrorism—which has been agreed with the EU Commission—have not been concluded. Thirdly, the institutional gap because of the abolition of the professional post of National Coordinator against Violent Extremism and Terrorism, and the transfer of his tasks to the Minister of Interior, has not yet been addressed.

As we see, the efforts done by the Kosovo state and the different (local, national, and international) stakeholders to counter violent extremism and disarm the drivers of radicalization are important. Our aim in this chapter is to see how the different selected municipalities, which are the Municipality of South Mitrovica, the Municipality of Gjilan, and the Municipality of Gjakova, deal with VE and try to counter it through a multireligious dispatch between Islamic, Catholic and Orthodox communities. The chosen case studies were based on the distinctive characteristics of the municipalities. South Mitrovica was selected for its historical evolution from an industrial, multiethnic city to an ethnically divided, economically challenged area after the 1999 war, leading to ethnopolitical tensions. Gjilan was chosen to investigate the impact of transnational dynamics at the meso level, given its proximity to the Kosovo—North Macedonia—Serbia cross-border triangle and the significant diaspora in Switzerland and Germany. Finally, Gjakova was selected due to its diverse religious landscape, featuring coexisting Sunni and Bektashi within Islam, alongside Catholicism, Christian Orthodoxy, and the emerging presence of Protestantism following the Kosovo War of 1998–99.

Therefore, this chapter will expose the three case studies that have been conducted to test the radicalization drivers on a meso-level scale. Each case study will be displayed in terms of the socioeconomic and geographic situation and the selection of participants and challenges encountered will also be explained. Finally, the results will be exposed per each of the drivers.

2 Case Studies and Methodologies

2.1 The Municipality of South Mitrovica

Mitrovica is a city divided along ethnic lines where the Municipality of South Mitrovica and the Municipality of North Mitrovica are almost entirely monoethnic and monoreligious, Albanian and Muslim, and Serbian and Christian Orthodox, respectively. As such, it represents a neuralgic point of ethnopolitical tensions in the country in which political grievances are inevitably linked with economic deprivation and ethnic radicalization.

The data from the last population census conducted in 2011 show that the Municipality of South Mitrovica had 71.909 inhabitants (Kosovo Agency of Statistics, 2017). According to the ethnic background, 96.7% of the municipality's inhabitants were Albanians, 0.9% were Ashkalis, 0.7% were Turks, 0.7% Roma, and 1% belong to other ethnic groups (Kosovo Agency of Statistics, 2017). In terms of religious background, 99.3% of the population declared themselves as Muslim, 0.05% were declared as Catholics, 0.015% as Orthodox, and 0.635% were declared without religious affiliation or preferred not to answer (Kosovo Agency of Statistics, 2011a, 2011b). The largest number of young people (63.3%) live in the urban areas, whereas the other part (36.7%) live in the rural areas of the municipality (Kosovo Agency of Statistics, 2011a, 2011b). The Municipality of South Mitrovica has a total of 33 preschool, elementary, and secondary educational institutions, as well as the public University "Isa Boletini" and the International Business College Mitrovica (Peci, 2019b).

The fieldwork led in this municipality is based on qualitative primary sources, such as focus groups with youth of 12–30 years and, in order to get a comprehensive picture, three semi-structured interviews with seasoned civil society activists of the Municipality of South Mitrovica having an in-depth knowledge of the city's evolving social context in the last three decades. The criteria used for sample selection were based on gender, religion, and urban-rural balance.

All participants belonged to the Albanian ethnicity. When it comes to gender, urban-rural representation, and religious affiliation, out of 27 individuals who participated in this research, 15 were male and 12 female, all of them were Muslims, 18 were from urban and 9 from rural areas (Peci & Demjaha, 2022).

More precisely, the focus group of young participants aged 12–15 years consisted of eight individuals, four of which were female and four were male. All of them belonged to the Muslim religion. Three were originating from rural and the other five were from urban areas of the Municipality of South Mitrovica. The focus group of young participants aged 15–18 years consisted of eight individuals, four female and four male, all Muslims. Three originated from rural and the other five from urban areas of the Municipality of South Mitrovica. The focus group of young participants aged 18–30 years consisted of eight individuals from 18 to 27 years old, four female and four male, all Muslims, with five of them originating from urban and the other three from rural areas of the Municipality of South Mitrovica. The three interviewees were males 35–56 years old, all of them from the urban area of South Mitrovica (Peci & Demjaha, 2022).

Regarding the challenges encountered, this research was initially planned to cover the entire district of South Mitrovica, which also includes three other municipalities. Nevertheless, since South Mitrovica is a part of the ethnically divided city of Mitrovica, the political issues are considerably higher than in other municipalities of this district that are not confronted with such problems that affect the lives of people on a daily basis. This was the reason why the focus groups and the interviews were limited to the Municipality of South Mitrovica only.

2.2 *The Municipality of Gjilan*

The data from the last population census conducted in 2011 show that the Municipality of Gjilan had 90.178 inhabitants (Kosovo Agency of Statistics, 2017). In terms of their ethnic background, 97.4% of the municipality's inhabitants were Albanians, 0.1% were Turks, 0.6% Serbs, 0.4% Roma, 0.1% Bosnians and the rest belonged to other ethnic groups (Kosovo Agency of Statistics, 2017). Concerning religion, 98.6% of the population declared themselves as Muslims, 0.7% as Christian Orthodox, 0.05% as Catholics, and the rest were declared as other, without religious affiliation, or preferred not to answer. (Kosovo Agency of Statistics, 2011a, 2011b). The largest number of young people (59.5%) live in urban areas, and the rest (40.5%) live in rural areas of the municipality (Kosovo Agency of Statistics, 2011a, 2011b). The Municipality of Gjilan has 52 preschool, elementary, and secondary, educational institutions, besides the Public University "Kadri Zeka" and a few campuses of private colleges (Peci, 2019a).

This study is based on qualitative primary sources, such as focus groups with 12–30-year-old youngsters, and interviews with two seasoned civil society activists of the Municipality of Gjilan. The selected sample is based on balanced gender and urban–rural representation (Peci & Demjaha, 2022).

The criteria used for sample selection were based on gender, religion, and urban-rural balance, as well as coverage of young participants aged 12–30. In addition, there were two interviews conducted with seasoned former and current institutional representatives, with in-depth knowledge of the evolving social context in the last three decades in the Municipality of Gjilan, to get a comprehensive picture. All participants in this research belonged to Albanian ethnicity. Regarding gender, urban-rural representation, and religious affiliation, out of the 19 individuals who participated in this research, 10 were male and 9 female. All of them were Muslims, and 13 were from urban and 6 were from rural areas (Peci & Demjaha, 2022).

The focus group of young participants aged 12–15 years consisted of six individuals, four females and two males. Two were from rural, and the other four were from urban areas of the Municipality of Gjilan. The focus group of young participants aged 15–18 years consisted of six individuals, three females and three males. Two were from rural, and the other four were from urban areas of the Municipality of Gjilan. The focus group of young participants aged 18–30 years consisted of five individuals aged 18–27 years, two of them were female and three male. Three participants were from urban, and the other two were from rural areas of the Municipality of Gjilan. The two interviewees are male, from 50 and 55 years old, and both were from the urban area of Gjilan (Peci & Demjaha, 2022).

This research was initially planned to cover the entire district of Gjilan, which also includes five other municipalities. Nevertheless, given the fact that the Municipality of Gjilan in per capita terms had the largest number of foreign terrorist fighters in this region that joined the conflicts in the Middle East and that its citizens have considerable family ties with ethnic Albanians in Preshevo Valley (Serbia) and in Skopje and Kumanovo (North Macedonia), the fieldwork conducted with the focus groups and the interviews was limited to this municipality only.

2.3 *The Municipality of Gjakova*

According to the last census in Kosovo of 2021, the Municipality of Gjakova has 94.556 inhabitants, 42% of them living in urban and 58% in rural areas (Kosovo Agency of Statistics, 2011a, 2011b). The ethnic composition of the municipality is predominantly ethnic Albanian (92.7%), followed by the Egyptian community (5.4%), Roma (0.78%), Ashkalis (0.65%) and Serbs (0.017%) (Kosovo Agency of Statistics, 2011a, 2011b). In religious terms, the population largely belongs to Islam (81.7%), followed by Catholics (17.20%), whereas members of other religions and atheists compose 1.1% of the population (Kosovo Agency of Statistics, 2011a, 2011b). 39.6% of the population is economically active, the employment rate is 51%, the percentage of people dependent on social assistance is 4.4%, and on pensions 6.5%, whereas 5.8% of the population is supported by remittances (Kosovo Agency of Statistics, 2011a, 2011b). The municipality has 60 pre-elementary, elementary, and secondary schools, as well as a public university (Kosovo Agency of Statistics, 2018).

This study is based on qualitative primary sources, such as focus groups with youth aged 12–30 years and semi-structured interviews with seasoned civil society activists of the Municipality of Gjakova. Again, the criteria used for sample selection were based on gender, religion, and urban-rural balance, as well as coverage of young participants from 12 to 30 in focus groups. In addition, there were three interviews conducted with seasoned local civil society activists, with in-depth knowledge of the evolving social context in the last three decades in the Municipality of Gjakova (Peci & Demjaha, 2022).

The focus group of the young participants aged 12–15 years was comprised of eight individuals, four female and four male participants, of whom five belonged to Muslim, and three to Catholic religion. Four were originating from urban and the other four from rural areas of the Municipality of Gjakova. The focus group of the young participants aged 15–18 years was comprised of six individuals, three female and three male participants, of whom four belonged to Muslim and two to Catholic religion. Three came from urban and the other three were from rural areas of the Municipality of Gjakova. The focus group of the young participants 18–27 years was comprised of seven individuals, six females and one male participant. Five belonged to Islam and two to the Catholic religion. Four were originating from urban and the other three from rural areas of the Municipality of Gjakova. The three interviewees were males aged 54–65 years old, and they were an Atheist, a Muslim and a Catholic, all originating from the urban area of Gjakova. In total, 24 individuals participated in this research, 11 of which were male and 13 female; 15 were Muslims, 8 were Catholics, and one Atheist; 14 were from urban and 10 were from rural areas (Peci & Demjaha, 2022).

Regarding challenges encountered, this research was initially planned to cover the entire district of Gjakova, which also includes three other municipalities. Nevertheless, due to the level of the plurality of religions and religious interpretations in Gjakova, which is incomparably higher than in other municipalities of this district, the focus groups and the interviews were limited to the Municipality of Gjakova.

3 Results

Mobilizing the seven identified drivers of VE, known as religion, economic deprivation, territorial inequalities, digital socialization, political issues, culture, educational and leisure opportunities, and transnational dynamics, results will be displayed by each driver.

3.1 Religion

Although participants in this research have different opinions about religion as a driver of extremism in South Mitrovica, the research results show that religious preaching by several local Muslim clergy is a source of religious extremism. In this regard, an interviewee considered that religion is not a problem and is only one of the factors that can be used to develop different political agendas. According to him, the most important factor that can drive people towards extremism is nationalism, which is also the most fertile soil for developing different political agendas. Another interviewee thought that religion is not the main factor of extremism, because economic problems are above religion in driving people towards emigration to Western Europe in their pursuit for a better life. Similarly, another interviewee claimed that economic deprivation and unemployment are the most important factors that may push individuals towards religious and other forms of radicalism (Peci & Demjaha, 2022).

Furthermore, extreme cases of psychological manipulation through religious interpretations of local Muslim clergy were also witnessed by some participants of the age group from 15 to 18 years. Thus, a participant observed religious preaching delivered by an imam that had as a topic the existence of a *jinn*[1] that can possess the body or control it. According to him, in the Muslim religion, the existence of jinns is a topic that not everyone can cope with. In some respects, it can cause mental disorders for certain people, as well as depression or stress. He also argued that to cope with these topics one needs to be mentally prepared, otherwise certain individuals can very easily face serious psychological problems. On the other hand, based on their personal experience and perceptions, few participants in this research who practice religion have expressed their high regard about local imams, particularly those of the age group from 12 to 15 years (Peci & Demjaha, 2022).

When it comes to religious practices in the Municipality of Gjilan, in addition to general religious tolerance, there are also cases of religious hatred and extremism. In this regard, one of the interviewees observed that in this municipality, in general, traditional Islam is practiced, but some mosques are under the control of imams and congregations that propagate Muslim *Ummah*,[2] who give primacy to religious affiliation before the national one, and are usually intolerant towards other religions. According to him, in the Council of the Islamic Community of Gjilan, some imams are known for their radical ideas. These imams are elected by their congregations and control 5–6 mosques. Moreover, even the head of the Islamic Council of Gjilan was in the past connected to people who joined the war in Syria. Furthermore, another interviewee claimed that certain congregations prefer radical imams and refuse to pray in the mosques in which moderate imams preach following the program of the Islamic Community of Kosovo. According to him, there were also cases where congregations fueled by radical ideologies have exercised physical violence against moderate imams (Peci & Demjaha, 2022).

On the other hand, the young participants in this research have different opinions on this matter. A participant of the age group from 12 to 15 years assessed that there are prejudices among some Muslims in Gjilan towards persons of other religions, which, according to him, is a consequence of ignorance and lack of knowledge about other religions (Peci & Demjaha, 2022).

Regarding the Municipality of Gjakova case study, the participants of this research aged from 12 to 14 years in general emphasized the lack of religious differences in social relations with their schoolmates or with their peers in the communities where they live. However, they pointed out that the conversion of religion is in certain cases accepted with uneasiness by many of their peers, and that interreligious marriages are still viewed with prejudices. Similar attitudes were noted among the participants of the age group from 16 to 18 years, who also emphasized the lack of religious differences in their social relations, and their close friendships with their peers of other religions (Peci & Demjaha, 2022).

---

[1] Jinns are in Islam intelligent beings created by God that men cannot perceive with their own senses. There are good and evil jinns and they interfere in the life and decisions of humans (Gómez García, 2009).

[2] The Community of Believers in Islam. It is an ideal that nurtures the communitarian identity of all Muslims above their social or cultural diversity (Gómez García, 2009).

According to one participant, religion is not the primary identity pattern of individuals in this municipality, and it is generally perceived by society as somehow neutral, while another participant observed an increasing trend of interreligious marriages nowadays, although in the past they were somehow "forbidden". By the same token, one of the interviewees considered that social practices of religion in Gjakova are liberal. According to him, whoever chooses to go to the *tekke*,[3] mosque, or church can do it without any obstacle. The Gjakova Municipality is well known for its religious coexistence within the Albanian population despite of being one of the places with the highest percentage of members of the Catholic faith. Especially during the times of the Yugoslav/Serbian regime, religious tolerance has been nurtured and strengthened over the years and was pursued with fanaticism. This has also continued after the war in 1998–99, since the Municipality of Gjakova, although a vast majority of its population nominally belongs to Islam, has elected a mayor of the Catholic faith in two terms, 2007–2013. In addition, the Catholic community comprises only 17.2% of the population but is over-represented with around 30–40% in the decision-making structures of the local government (Peci & Demjaha, 2022).

An interesting finding of this research is that most of the young participants do not follow religious preaching in the religious places of worhsip, and they do not identify themselves with religious leaders. On the other hand, several participants considered that a certain number of clergymen are not worthy of the posts they hold, affirmed that they are corrupt, and that they should be licensed by the state, expressing thus huge mistrust in them (Peci & Demjaha, 2022).

3.2 Economic Deprivation

The Municipality of South Mitrovica is characterized by varying levels of ethnically-based political tensions due to the division of the city, which de facto occurred immediately after the end of the war in Kosovo, in June 1999. The division of the city was formalized a few days after the Declaration of Independence of Kosovo, with the adoption of the Law on Local Self-Government, on February 20th, 2008 (Assembly of the Republic of Kosovo, 2008). Nowadays, both, the Municipality of South Mitrovica and the Municipality of North Mitrovica are almost entirely mono-ethnic and monoreligious, the South being Albanian and Muslim, and the North being Serbian and Christian Orthodox, respectively. Against this background, the impact of the driver of (ethnically based) political grievances, intertwined with the driver of economic deprivation, is viewed by most participants in this research, as a cause of several severe consequences for the citizens of this municipality. Due to such a position, Mitrovica is a place of attack of many extremist policies which tend

[3] Oratory or building that belongs to an Islamic brotherhood or Sufi *tariqa*. It is the Turkish equivalent of the *Zawiya* (Gómez García, 2009).

to develop different political processes in the region and beyond (Peci & Demjaha, 2022).

The main narratives related to the concerns of the local community are poverty and insecurity since people do not have a clear perspective on sustainable peace and development. Once the richest city during the 1970s and 1980s, Mitrovica has become the poorest city in Kosovo, and consequently in Europe. Thus, the local political context has also affected the impoverishment of many families, which represents one of the main problems in the South Mitrovica, that may lead to politicization and, eventually, to radicalism. Similar views on the impact of economic impoverishment and the high level of unemployment on radicalization and extremism, also combined with the disappointment from politics at the national and local level are shared by some participants of the age groups from 15 to 18 years, and from 18 to 30 years. However, some of the participants considered that dissatisfaction and disappointments with political elites do not directly drive people toward extremism (Peci & Demjaha, 2022).

The research has shown that although political dissatisfaction is very high in Gjilan Municipality, most of the research participants do not relate it directly with radicalism and extremism. However, some research participants also claim that career progress as well as finding a job depends heavily on family social and political status. Thus, nepotism and corruption might drive certain socioeconomically deprived individuals towards radicalism and extremism. Furthermore, few participants consider that unemployment, lack of job prospects, and limited access to a decent level of social welfare might push some youth in the Gjilan Municipality towards Islamic religious radicalized and extremist groups. A participant in the age group from 15 to 18 years claimed that social and economic conditions are sources of injustice. According to him, youth belonging to wealthier families are better positioned when applying for a job, and in school, they get also higher marks without merits. A participant in the age group from 18 to 30 years claimed that injustices are widespread. According to her, injustices start in the family, first and foremost because females are discriminated in the division of inheritance. In addition, she claims that the children of those who hold political offices, without any merits, are treated better and evaluated higher than other youth in schools. However, another participant of this age group thought that the justice system creates a balance against many forms of injustices that people might experience (Peci & Demjaha, 2022).

Nevertheless, one of the participants also noted cases in which people with very good socioeconomic status joined the conflict in the Middle East. Another interviewee had a similar opinion and claimed that the socioeconomic situation has not had an important impact on extremism, given that, according to him, this is an ideological matter. He admits that there were cases when some individuals with very good economic situations joined the conflict in Syria, but there were also cases when individuals with harsh economic conditions joined as well (Peci & Demjaha, 2022).

The research findings in the municipality of Gjakova case study show that drivers of economic deprivation and the education sub-driver are of special importance regarding social resilience to radicalism and violent extremism. In this context, although seven inhabitants of Gjakova joined the ranks of ISIS, an interviewee claimed that there is no radicalism and extremism in the municipality, but believed that the existing social resilience could be threatened by the low level of education and socioeconomic development. He argued that some "charity organizations" from the Middle East have, through the provision of humanitarian aid, computer courses, and other benefits, managed to recruit some youth to join the war in Syria, by misusing their poor economic conditions for their political aims (Peci & Demjaha, 2022).

3.3 Territorial Inequalities

A participant in the age group from 12 to 15 years stated that, over time, the tolerance between Albanians and Serbs in Mitrovica has started to prevail. According to him, during the period 2000–2005 the situation was more critical, whereas nowadays, there is a good tolerance between them. On the other hand, a participant in the age group from 15 to 18 years observed that life in South Mitrovica is a little different and harder than in other cities of Kosovo, first and foremost because citizens do not feel secure visiting North Mitrovica. A participant in the age group from 18 to 30 years assessed that the issue of the North is a problem of the whole of Kosovo, and, consequently, it is a problem of the national government as well. She considered that Serbia controls the North through different parallel mechanisms and criminal groups, projecting this part of the country as its own, although it should function under the sovereignty of Kosovo. This fact, according to her, affects radicalism, because now the young Serbs who are in the North can be very easily influenced by these structures, and that may lead to physical violence between communities (Peci & Demjaha, 2022).

However, the research findings provide no evidence that the driver of territorial inequalities, seen as the urban-rural divide, has any impact on radicalization and violent extremism in both municipalities of Gjilan and Gjakova (Peci & Demjaha, 2022).

3.4 Digital Literacy and Digital Socialization

Regarding the Mitrovica Municipality case study, one of the participants stated that she heard about extremism from TV news and social media, and she added that she has discussed it with her closest people. She stated that there is a difference between extremism and violence because violence is manifested only after extremism is rooted. Another participant claimed that in addition to TV and social media, she has learned about extremism from different reports and workshops on the topic of extremism. According to her, extremism is the behavior that is projected, or the idea of certain individuals, towards certain social groups, whereas violence, which is not necessarily limited to the physical one, is the materialization of those attitudes or ideas. Most participants confirm that youth spend a considerable amount of time being engaged with social media. In this regard, participants in the age group from 12 to 15 years state that social media are part of their daily life, the main source of their information, as well as for playing video games and for communicating with their social circles. However, participants in the age group 12–15 years remained silent on whether they have encountered religious or extremist content by using them. On the other hand, participants from the age group of 15–18 years pointed out that they have encountered such content on social media. According to a participant, especially during the month of Ramadan, when videos on social media related to religion appear constantly. A participant from the age group 18–20 years claimed that for some time now, she has not come across any content that calls for extremist ideas, which was quite prevalent during the war in Syria. In addition, she affirmed that this format of presentation of religious discourse is useful since people do not need to go to the mosque to hear what the imam says but can listen to it wherever they are (Peci & Demjaha, 2022).

The research has shown that youth participating from the Gjilan Municipality, especially those of the age groups from 12 to 15 years and 15 to 18 years, spend a considerable part of their free time on digital social media. In doing so, they receive most of the information about religion as well as radicalization and violent extremism through digital social media. In this way, the driver of digital socialization becomes the key mechanism of transmission of ideas, values, and identities to youth in the Municipality of Gjilan. A participant in the age group of 12–15 years noted that his classmates have discussed extremism with their teacher during the "Civic Education" courses and that they have conducted internet research on this matter (Peci & Demjaha, 2022).

This research has provided sufficient evidence that digital socialization is rapidly shaping the way of life of youth in the Gjakova municipality, and that it is an important driver that intertwines with the drivers of religious interpretations and transnational dynamics. In this regard, most young participants in this research have declared that they spent many hours of their free time engaging with social media, which has also been confirmed by the interviewees. Furthermore, most of the youth participants admitted that they acquire most of the information about religion via social media. In this regard, a participant in the age group 12–14 years said that she enjoys different people talking about their religions on social media (Tik Tok and Instagram). Similarly, another participant confirmed that social media have a lot of religious content and that by using them she learns about religions, whereas another participant said that she uses YouTube to learn and listen to religious preaching. On the other hand, a participant of this age group observed that when different people post about their religion on social media, often others question their religion. Sometimes, they even argue that their religion is not a true one, which, according to her, is an issue of lack of respect for religious plurality. Finally, another participant has claimed that she uses social media not only to learn about her religion but also to learn about other religions. Thus, there is no doubt that information technologies have increasingly served as an amplifier for disseminating radical extremist messages. Research findings have confirmed that some young participants have witnessed cases in which extremist elements used digital technologies to spread their extremist ideologies and to recruit individuals for their aims (Peci & Demjaha, 2022).

3.5 Political Issues

One of the participants of the South Mitrovica Municipality case study thinks that the local environment does not produce radicalization but rather that radicalization is a consequence of the influence of other external factors, like the political war between Prishtina—Belgrade, and the struggle for geopolitical influence in the region. But as we have seen earlier, the local political context has also affected the impoverishment of many families, which represents one of the main problems in South Mitrovica, that may lead to politicization and eventually to radicalism. Similar views on the impact of economic impoverishment and the high level of unemployment on radicalization and extremism, also combined with disappointment with politics at the national and local level are shared by some participants of the age groups from 15 to 18 years, and from 18 to 30 years. However, some of the participants considered that dissatisfaction and disappointments with political elites do not directly drive people towards extremism. A participant in the age group of 12–15 years stated that over time, the tolerance between Albanians and Serbs in Mitrovica has started to prevail. According to him, during the period 2000–2005 the situation was more critical, whereas nowadays, there is a good tolerance between them (Peci & Demjaha, 2022).

Participants of 12–15 years old from the Gjilan Municipality think that corruption is the biggest problem that hinders perspectives of Kosovo from joining EU and the free movement of its citizens in the Schengen zone. Whereas one of them considered that political dissatisfaction can be used by extremists to spread their ideas, the other one thought that there is no interrelation between political grievances and extremism. A participant in the age group of 15–18 years thinks that political dissatisfaction is very high in Gjilan, and according to him, this is not related to extremism, but rather to emigration. Another participant assessed that, in several cases, political dissatisfaction is related to economic deprivation and might drive certain individuals to move towards extremism since they are more vulnerable due to their harsh economic conditions. Similar views are shared also by the participants in the age group of 18–30 years. Against this backdrop, participants of 12–15 years old do not have any opinion about youth from Gjilan that joined ISIS, because they were children when this phenomenon occurred in this municipality (Peci & Demjaha, 2022).

Finally, within the Gjakova Municipality case study, one of the interviewees claimed that, to a large extent, Bektashian sheiks have an overwhelming authority and influence in the community. According to him, there are well-documented cases in which the sheiks have influenced the elections of mayors of the municipality through their congregations. Furthermore, he affirmed that although they have twice supported a Catholic candidate to become a mayor of the municipality, this was not a virtue of their open-mindedness, but rather a consequence of their desire to interfere in local politics by aligning with the Alliance for the Future of Kosovo (AAK), a party led by prominent figures from the top ranks of the former Kosovo Liberation Army (KLA). He further claimed that the local population often sees religion not solely as faith, but also as an interest or as an activity of certain groups that makes personal benefits, meaning less religious and more business-oriented (Peci & Demjaha, 2022).

3.6 Education, Culture and Leisure Opportunities

South Mitrovica suffers from a low level of education, very limited leisure, and almost inexistent cultural opportunities. In this regard, an interviewee observed that due to the irregular urban planning in the city, which did not envisage sufficient free spaces and parks, the public infrastructure for leisure is very limited. The problems imposed by the limitations of the public infrastructure are used by the private sector which offers additional spaces for sports activities, but such opportunities are available only to youth with good economic conditions. Regardless of these deeply-rooted problems, the sports infrastructure has improved significantly in the last few years. Participants in the age group of 18–30 years claimed that the very strong cultural identity of Mitrovica has declined almost completely. On the other hand, the research findings show that very few of the participants of the age groups from 12 to 15 years, and from 15 to 18 years, are engaged in sports and cultural activities (Peci & Demjaha, 2022).

Several participants in the Gjilan Municipality case study, especially those from 18 to 30 years, believed that it is easier for radical imams who preach fundamentalist Islamic beliefs to manipulate certain individuals who lack a proper level of education. On the other hand, an interviewee considered that a higher level of education and knowledge could, in some cases, contribute to building community resilience to prevent radicalization and violent extremism (Peci & Demjaha, 2022).

Participants in the Gjakova Municipality observed that nowadays youth have sufficient access to sports, culture, and other leisure activities and premises. Nevertheless, different age groups have expressed the wish to change the routine of their free time. Some participants from 12 to 14 years would prefer to work with NGOs dealing with human rights or technological innovation. Others, belonging to the age group from 15 to 18 years, prefer to spend more time in practical work related to their future professions. Finally, most participants from the age group of 18 to 27 years would prefer to travel abroad, especially to Europe, but the lack of visa liberalization for Kosovo citizens hinders such desire. The interviewees also confirmed that sports and cultural facilities in Gjakova have improved in the last years, but they noted that despite that, youth do not participate in large numbers in these activities (Peci & Demjaha, 2022).

3.7 Transnational Dynamics

The transnational dynamics driver in the Mitrovica Municipality case study intersects with religion through foreign influence from the Gulf States that often results in the changed perceptions of youth about religions, and pushes them towards radicalization and violent extremism. Namely, several organizations from Saudi Arabia and other Gulf countries that came to Kosovo after the war have openly challenged traditional practices of Islam and have instead tried to impose alien interpretations of Islam (Peci & Demjaha, 2022).

One of the participants from the age group of 15 to 18 years from the Mitrovica Municipality stated that people joined ISIS because of propaganda and inaccurate information that was spread on the war in Syria, which according to him, not only was wrong but was not even a religious justification for it. She claimed that her parents played a major role in explaining and guiding her on what was going on at that time. Individuals who joined ISIS were driven exclusively by religion, and they were so much brainwashed that they not only sacrificed themselves, but even their families for this cause. In this regard, another participant affirmed that religious brainwashing can be so deep, which he illustrated by the case of a woman in South Mitrovica who lost her husband in the war in Syria and decided to remain faithful to ISIS, refusing to be repatriated together with her children to Kosovo (Peci & Demjaha, 2022).

By preaching radical forms of Islam, imams from North Macedonia have contributed to increased religiosity of the community and radicalization and extremism in the Gjilan Municipality. On the other hand, imams from this country have not only preached radical forms of Islam in mosques of Gjilan, but they have also spread their extremist ideologies through digital social media. In both cases, these interactions weaken the ethnic identity of the Albanian population as an important factor in building community resilience and could thus create a social context permissive to radicalization and violent extremism (Peci & Demjaha, 2022).

According to one of the participants, families with democratic and liberal orientations are generally leaning towards the West. On the contrary, families impacted by religious ideologies are sometimes influenced by radical groups. However, another interviewee observed that there are some cases when several radicalized youths came from very patriotic families that have not had anything to do with extremism. According to him, these cases are a result of the change of the traditional role of the family that occurred after the war of 1999, and of the opening of Kosovo to the world, as well as of the distortion of the educational system. On the other hand, a young participant stated that religions at the global level play a role, because they may get nations closer to one another, but, also, nations may fall apart because of them (Peci & Demjaha, 2022).

One participant noted that years ago, in the mosques in Gjakova, several charity organizations from the Middle East distributed "humanitarian aid" to some local worshipers, who, after some time, went to Syria and died there. Another participant mentioned that some years ago, some Arab organizations were distributing leaflets with religious content that, among other things, were also propagating radicalism and supporting violent extremism. Furthermore, an interviewee pointed out a case where several imams from Gjakova participated in a protest organized by the elements of the Muslim Brotherhood in Kosovo that took place in Prishtina more than 10 years ago. Against this background, according to an interviewee, the number of Muslim believers joining the congregations in the mosques of Gjakova is quite small. He pointed out that, on Friday prayers a maximum of 1000 believers in total worship in the 11 mosques left from the Ottoman Empire (Peci & Demjaha, 2022).

4 Conclusion

It is obvious that some drivers are more relevant than others, according to the case studies. The South Mitrovica case study converges with the impact of macro-level drivers (Peci & Demjaha, 2021), by specifying religion as the most influential driver of violent extremism that is strongly interrelated with the drivers of social digitalization and transnational dynamics. Furthermore, the research findings show that the political issues driver has rather a peripheral importance concerning radicalism and violent extremism. It has been highlighted that the ethnic tensions between Albanian and Serbian communities have not been transformed into a conflict with an interreligious character. On the contrary, radicalism and violent extremism in South Mitrovica, as elsewhere in Kosovo, is a part of global extremist political Islam that has not originated from the local circumstances, but those circumstances have been misused by several organizations from the Gulf countries and certain local radical imams to introduce and strengthen these tendencies.

The Gjilan and Gjakova Municipality case studies also converge fully with the impact of macro-level drivers (Peci & Demjaha, 2021), by specifying religion as the most influential driver of violent extremism that is strongly intertwined with the drivers of transnational dynamics and digital socialization. Furthermore, the research findings show that other drivers have rather marginal or non-existent importance to radicalism and violent extremism.

The research findings have provided evidence that after the war several global extremist movements from the Middle East and some imams connected to them from North Macedonia have penetrated Gjilan. This has had an impact on the change of general culture by strengthening Islamic religious affiliation at the expense of the traditional secular national identity of Albanians in this municipality. Nevertheless, the consequence of this impact was the changed behavior of the local political elite that started to flirt with the leaders of the Municipal Islamic Community, because of their electoral interests, in contradiction with the past, when politics was strongly separated from religion.

Regarding Gjakova Municipality, the research analysis indicates that religion is the key driving factor of violent extremism in comparison with other drivers. Nevertheless, since the information about religions by youth is mainly obtained from social media, on the one hand, and given the strict monoreligious knowledge of local clerics, on the other, religious education under such circumstances can hardly play any role in preventing violent extremism. Furthermore, the research findings indicate that participants of this research, and youth in general, do not identify with existing local religious leaders, and several of them question their professional credentials.

In sum, the meso-level research indicates that certain drivers hold greater significance compared to others, although they are interconnected in various ways. To gain a more nuanced understanding of how these drivers impact individuals, it would be beneficial to pursue further investigations at the micro-level scale.

References

Assembly of the Republic of Kosovo. (2008). *Law on local self government*. Retrieved May 2024, from https://mapl.rks-gov.net/wp-content/uploads/2017/10/Law-On-Local-Self-Government.pdf

European Commission. (2019). *Counter-terrorism: The Commission to sign an arrangement with Kosovo as part of Joint Action Plan for the Western Balkans*. Retrieved May 2024, from https://neighbourhood-enlargement.ec.europa.eu/news/counter-terrorism-commission-sign-arrangement-kosovo-part-joint-action-plan-western-balkans-2019-10-30_en

Gómez García, L. (2009). *Diccionario de islam e islamismo*. Espasa.

Government of Kosovo. (2020a, February). *Decision 02/02*. Retrieved May 2024, from https://kryeministri.rks-gov.net/wp-content/uploads/2022/05/Vendimet-e-mbledhjes-se-2-te-Qeverise.pdf

Government of Kosovo. (2020b, July). *Decision 08/14*. Retrieved May 2024, from https://kryeministri.rks-gov.net/wp-content/uploads/2022/05/Vendimet-nga-mbledhja-e-14-te-e-Qeverise.pdf

Government of Kosovo. (2021, April). *Decision 03/03*. Retrieved May 2024, from https://kryeministri.rks-gov.net/wp-content/uploads/2022/05/Vendet-e-Mbledhjes-se-3-te-te-Qeverise-se-Republikes-se-Kosoves.pdf

Kosovo Agency of Statistics. (2011a). *Popullsia sipas moshave dhe llojit të vendbanimit* [*The population according to age and the type of habitat*]. Retrieved May 2024, from https://askdata.rks-gov.net/pxweb/sq/ASKdata/ASKdata__Census%20population__Census%202011__3%20By%20Municipalities/Pop%20by%20age%20type%20of%20area%20(urb-rur)%20and%20munic.px/

Kosovo Agency of Statistics. (2011b). *Popullsia sipas gjinisë, religjionit dhe komunës* [*Population according to gender, religion and municipality*]. Retrieved May 2024, from https://askdata.rks-gov.net/pxweb/sq/ASKdata/ASKdata__Census%20population__Census%202011__3%20By%20Municipalities/population%20by%20religion,%20sex%20and%20age%20mnicipality.px/table/tableViewLayout1/

Kosovo Agency of Statistics. (2017). *Vlerësim, Popullsia e Kosovës* [*Assessment, the population of Kosovo*]. Retrieved May 2024, from https://askdata.rks-gov.net/pxweb/en/ASKdata/ASKdata__Census%20population__Census%202011__3%20By%20Municipalities/tab%205%204.px/table/tableViewLayout1/

Kosovo Agency of Statistics. (2018). *Pupils by gender in public education in municipalities by year, municipality and gender 2017/2018*. Retrieved May 2024, from https://askdata.rks-gov.net/pxweb/en/ASKdata/ASKdata__Education__09%20Annex/edu35.px/table/tableViewLayout1/

Ministry of Local Government Administration, Republic of Kosovo. (2014). Manual: Municipal Community Safety Councils. Retrieved May 2024, from https://mapl.rks-gov.net/wp-content/uploads/2017/10/Udhezuesi-per-KKSB_14-janar-2015-gj-angleze-1.pdf

Peci, L. (2019a). *Municipalities of the Gjilan region: Socio economic profiles*. Kosovar Institute for Policy Research and Development (KIPRED). Retrieved May 2024, from https://www.kipred.org/repository/docs/Socio-Economic_Profile-_Gjilan_Municipalities_742608.pdf
Peci, L. (2019b). *Municipalities of the Mitrovica region: Socio economic profiles*. Kosovar Institute for Policy Research and Development (KIPRED). Retrieved May, 2024, from https://www.kipred.org/repository/docs/Mitrovice_-_Raporti_i_Konferences_-_Anglisht_157780.pdf
Peci, L., & Demjaha, A. (2020). *Country report on national approaches to violent extremism*. The European Institute of the Mediterranean (IEMed). Retrieved May 2024, from https://h2020connekt.eu/wp-content/uploads/2021/01/Kosovo_CONNEKT_Approaches_to_extremism.pdf
Peci, L., & Demjaha, A. (2021). *Kosovo: Macro drivers of radicalization and violent extremism*. The European Institute of the Mediterranean (IEMed). Retrieved May 2024, from https://h2020connekt.eu/wp-content/uploads/2021/09/Kosovo_CONNEKT_Macro_Drivers.pdf
Peci, L., & Demjaha, A. (2022). Meso-level drivers of radicalization and violent extremism. In *The European Institute of the Mediterranean (IEMed)*. Retrieved May 2024, from https://h2020connekt.eu/wp-content/uploads/2022/12/CONNEKT-MESO-KOSOVO.pdf

Conclusion: Stressing the Role of Social Contexts for Countering Violent Extremism and Radicalization

Tasnim Chirchi, Corinne Torrekens, and Lurdes Vidal Bertran

Related to radicalization and violent extremism, security studies are often focused on the macro-level of the state and institutions dimensions, overlooking significant social interactions at the meso and micro levels in everyday life. Such a focus allows only for a limited understanding of the complexity and dynamic processes of phenomena such as radicalization and violent extremism where sub-national communities' dynamics are key in understanding the interaction between the macro (institutions), meso (communities) and micro (individuals) levels of social reality. From theory to practice, whether in policymaking or civil society and community levels, security appears as a liminal concept necessitating approaches that help manage both its situatedness as well as its normative and interpretive dimensions.

Taking stock of the various and changing meanings of security necessitated that we adopt research methodologies allowing to capture the complexity and the polysemic and situated understandings of it. The present collective book is the result of innovative research, bringing a multi-level and multi-disciplinary study of radicalization by adopting a dynamic approach embracing the intricacy of the social/political/economic contexts studied. Moving away from unidimensional and security-centered research on the topic, the various chapters share the outcomes of participatory and inclusive approaches engaging communities/youth/women as

T. Chirchi (✉)
Ibn Khaldun University, Istanbul, Turkey
e-mail: director@jasminefoundation.org

C. Torrekens
Université libre de Bruxelles, Brussels, Belgium
e-mail: LourdesVB@blanquerna.url.edu

L. Vidal Bertran
Blanquerna-Universitat Ramon Llull, Barcelona, Spain
e-mail: corinne.torrekens@ulb.be

C. Torrekens et al. (eds.), *Social Contexts of Radicalization and Violent Extremism in the MENA and Balkans*,
https://doi.org/10.1007/978-3-031-84521-5_10

significant stakeholders in building a better understanding of the dynamics of the radicalization of youth in the Balkans and the MENA regions.

The present book is a collection of case studies that were part of the project CONNEKT (Contexts of Extremism in MENA and Balkan Societies) whose main objective is "to provide a comprehensive, fully documented and empirically contrasted identification of contexts and drivers of radicalization and violent extremism in the Balkans and MENA".

The contexts of the emergence of radicalization and VE in the Middle Eastern, North African (MENA) region and the Balkans were studied in relation to seven pre-identified drivers: religion, economic deprivation, political grievances, culture and leisure opportunities, digital literacy, territorial inequalities, and transnational dynamics.

The CONNEKT project examined radicalization and VE across MENA and Balkan countries at three macro, meso, and micro levels. The meso-level phase of research presented in this book focused on diverse communities potentially vulnerable to radicalization, offering key insights into the drivers behind these phenomena.

Through case studies, the different contributions investigate various social contexts such as schools, football clubs, children facilities and online communities, identifying the precise role played by the different meso-level drivers explored by CONNEKT as well as their potential intersections.

This conclusion will first highlight the key patterns and insights regarding the drivers of radicalization and present key targeted policy recommendations for prevention, emphasizing the critical role of meso-level analysis in understanding and addressing radicalization.

1 The Drivers of Radicalization: The View from the Meso-Level

When we intersect the findings from both the MENA and Balkan countries, we observe a complex interplay between religion, political grievances, and governance models. More precisely, one of the central combinations of drivers at this level is the interconnectedness of individual political grievances, economic deprivation, and territorial inequalities as central contributors to radicalization. This interconnectedness has been described as the "triangle of anger" (see especially the chapter on Tunisia in this book) which highlights its key role in creating and fueling radicalization and violence in both regions. The different case studies highlight central related issues such as youth alienation, and under-representation which are key in activating the drivers of radicalization in the contexts under study.

The research also emphasizes the importance of alternative spaces, digitalization and leisure/education opportunities, particularly stressing the role of fan cultures and online radicalization mechanisms. Furthermore, transnational dynamics, external influences, and the involvement of diaspora communities and digitalized relationships are identified as crucial factors.

1.1 Summary of the Findings in the Balkans

Table 1 summarizes the case studies selected at the meso-level to examine the drivers of radicalization in the Balkans.

Through the case studies explored in Bosnia and Herzegovina, Bulgaria, Kosovo, and North Macedonia, the most significant drivers of radicalization appear to be the combination of religion, economic deprivation, territorial inequalities, and political grievances.

The cases examined in Bosnia and Herzegovina (Bakic et al., 2022), Bulgaria (Ralchev & Stoynova, 2022), and Kosovo (Peci & Demjaha, 2022), more

Table 1 Case studies for each Balkan country under study[a]

	Bosnia and Herzegovina	Bulgaria	Kosovo	North Macedonia
Case study 1	Two schools under one roof: influence of the political context on radicalization mechanisms and existing segregation dynamics	Online conservative communities: rallying popular support via propaganda and misinformation	Political Grievances in South Mitrovica: city experiences and ethnonational political tensions	Commemorations of the 2001 Tetovo Conflict: Holds importance as a memory-related topic in public discourse
Case study 2	Organized groups of football fans: public displays of violence throughout history	Football supporters: political instrumentalization of hooligans by political parties	Transnational dynamics in Gjilan, a city situated at the triangle border of Kosovo, North Macedonia and Serbia	Football fans groups in Tetovo: ethnic divisions within the local football scene
Case study 3	Young supporters of online Salafi influencers: celebrity status within online communities	/	Religious interpretations in Gjakova: plurality of religious practices encompassing Sunni and Bektashi traditions as well as Catholicism and Orthodoxy	Prisons and the Volkovija correctional and educational facility: specificities of closed environments related to radicalization risks and women facing stronger barriers to education and employment

[a]Based on Hirkic et al. (2024)

specifically highlight the significant role of the influence of Salafi ideologies, particularly through social media.

In the Balkans, one of the main combinations of drivers examined by the researchers was that of religion and political grievances. The findings show that they indeed intersect as potential drivers of radicalisation and violent extremism: animosity towards the political system and institutions increases the perceptions of inequality while the sentiment of injustice linked to deep ethnic divisions encourages exclusive worldviews. However, these findings also significantly challenge the view that religion is the main cause of radicalization. They show for instance that religion can also play a noticeable role in the prevention of radicalization as illustrated by the role of religious organizations which are involved in preventing and countering VE. The case studies show that in countries like Bosnia and Herzegovina (BiH) and North Macedonia, cooperation between religious communities and the state has become institutionalized, while in others it remains informal. In BIH, religious organizations like the Islamic Community have even developed their own P/CVE strategies.

Across the region, state-recognized religious groups are seen as less vulnerable to radicalization than unofficial groups. In North Macedonia, officials question whether religion is a significant driver of violence. Instead, the various stakeholders interviewed emphasize the role of political grievances, such as lack of political representation and governance issues, as critical in understanding the social dynamics of radicalization, thus suggesting that religion is no longer seen as the dominant factor at play in this phenomenon (Bogdanova, 2024).

The findings at the community level in the Balkans also highlight the role of digital literacy and transnational dynamics. Through the case studies, it appears that digitalization has enabled the spread of radical ideas in Kosovo, Bosnia and Herzegovina. Indeed, online disinformation has become prominent especially during the COVID-19 pandemic as far right messages spread among youth for example in Bulgaria, while North Macedonia witnessed widespread "infodemics" (Kapidžić et al., 2023). Like in the MENA region, findings highlight that the lack of critical thinking skills makes communities vulnerable to such narratives. This means that the intertwined influence of digital networks and transnational dynamics, including foreign extremist ideologies, further shape radicalization risks.

Socioeconomic challenges have been mostly present as significant vulnerability factors in Bulgaria, Kosovo, and North Macedonia as they often lead vulnerable individuals to seek refuge in Salafi communities (Kapidžić et al., 2023). Territorial inequalities and transnational dynamics appear to be key contributors to radicalization, with the most visible manifestations observed in football fandom in Bulgaria and North Macedonia. The case studies also point to the role of foreign propaganda and misinformation circulating on social media in exacerbating radicalization, particularly within conservative communities in Bulgaria (Ralchev & Stoynova, 2022). Political grievances further deepen divides through the education system in Bosnia and Herzegovina, fueling far-right ideologies in Bulgaria, sustaining the legacy of armed conflict in Kosovo and straining ethnic relations in North Macedonia.

1.2 Summary of the Findings in the MENA Region

Reports from the MENA region emphasize the complex nature of radicalization, stressing the importance of understanding both the social contexts as well as the dynamic relationship between ideology and context. Table 2 summarizes the meso-level case studies led in each country of the MENA region.

Meso-level findings reveal that multi-layered marginalization lies at the heart of economic, social, and political grievances, characterized by high rates of unemployment, inadequate political representation, and restricted access to social services. Moreover, these various forms of exclusion faced by different groups of youth are also illustrated and exacerbated by patterns of urban polarization fueling radicalization (Chirchi & Ghribi, 2023).

The research on radicalization and violent extremism in the MENA region reveals both common trends and specific differences across countries. At the macro level, most countries rely heavily on security measures to address VE, with limited focus on softer approaches like civil society engagement and education. This security-centric approach, particularly in addressing political and social grievances, has led to stricter policies impacting youth and their access to rights.

The findings stress the complex interplay between local grievances, transnational factors and ideological influences in driving radicalization. While conflicts in Syria, Iraq, and Palestine and other global trends contribute to VE, local grievances remain crucial, with religion and ideology often serving as vehicles for expressing deeper

Table 2 Case studies for each MENA country under study[a]

	Egypt	Jordan	Morocco	Tunisia
Case study 1	The Christian community of Al-Warraq: high unemployment rate and low educational achievements	Karak area: limited opportunies, inequality, and strained relationship with the state.	Amal organization: an NGO which goal is to help transforming violence into alternative discourses	Feriana: proximity to Algerian border and high youth unemployment
Case study 2	Bahtim Informal Community: rapid transformation from agricultural to urban area	Refugees in Northen Jordan: scarcity of opportunities in education, employment and social integration	Ultras Siempre Polama football supporters: a platform for youth expressing discontent with political institutions	Hammam-Lif: area with high crime incidence among youngsters
Case study 3	Alexandria University: site of frequent protests	Ma'an female preachers: a loose structure for informal preachers with high unemployment rate	Childhood and youth organization: the ideological socialization of youngsters within a group	Sidi Abdelhamid: socioeconomic polarization in the governorate

[a]Based on Hirkic et al. (2024)

systemic issues. The role of religion is determined by a combination of drivers which is key in understanding the social dynamics of radicalization phenomena. Indeed, in certain cases, religion is used to contest the legitimacy of national political institutions and articulate a political contestation such in Morocco while in other contexts (such as in Jordan or in Egypt) religious institutions can fill the gaps left by the state public services in deprived communities. Consequently, the case studies suggest that youth radicalization in the MENA region is strongly influenced by a combination of economic deprivation, social exclusion, and political grievances, which are exacerbated by urbanization and territorial inequalities such as in Tunisia. The lack of critical thinking skills and proper platforms for political participation also leaves marginalized youth vulnerable to radical narratives. The case studies underscore the importance of addressing systemic state failures, social injustices, and the need for substantial socio-political changes as central to effective prevention efforts. The findings also highlight the role of digital socialization, drug use, and the absence of religious education as contributing factors to radicalization. In summary, the research provides a nuanced understanding of the diverse drivers of radicalization in the MENA region, stressing the need for comprehensive and context-specific prevention strategies.

2 Common Patterns and Themes in Both Regions

The research methodology through the case studies selection allowed for local contextualization as each study considers the specific historical, cultural, and socio-political contexts of the region or community under examination. Throughout these cases studies in the MENA and Balkans, the researchers engaged with local stakeholders, including community members, policymakers, and civil society organizations, to gather diverse perspectives and insights. This has allowed the research to build a broad security framework going beyond traditional military and state-centric security concerns to address a broader understanding of security covering dimensions such as human, environmental, urban, cyber, and gender security.

By employing this more complex and contextual approach, the case studies methodology provides a more comprehensive and nuanced analysis of security issues, preparing the ground for more effective and sustainable solutions tailored to the unique challenges of each context addressing its specific needs and conditions. This is more specifically required as there is no single or automatic causality between one driver and the phenomena of radicalization and VE, but rather complex combinations of drivers whose effects can be activated in conjunction with specific social contexts or can alternatively be mitigated thanks to local community resilience factors that need to be explored and strengthened.

2.1 *The Elephant in the Room: Governance Models in Combination with the Drivers of Radicalization*

Beyond the local contexts and specificities influencing in differentiated but also common ways the dynamics of radicalization, the case studies have uncovered some findings that were not taken into account at the start of the research such as the role of the models of governance in combination with the already considered seven drivers.

At the start of research, comparison of the MENA and Balkans mainly noted differences such as population size and religious demographics (Bieber & Pollozhani, 2021) as MENA countries are predominantly Muslim, while the Balkans have diverse religious populations. While the researchers started with the assumption that both regions face various forms of radicalization (Bieber & Pollozhani, 2021), empirical findings highlight deeper similarities in the social contexts of radicalization, thus underscoring common issues of disenchantment and frustration amongst youth.

The case studies' findings from both the MENA region and the Balkans indicate that the meso-level dynamics of radicalization and violence need to be understood in connection with deeper systemic and macro-level dynamics such as the deeper systemic crisis in the relationship between the state and its citizens, necessitating solutions that address human development conditions and advocate for substantial economic, social, and political reforms.

This points to a contextual factor that is at the center of the various social contexts under study and drivers: the quality of governance systems and their impacts on communities and citizens. The way these systems are experienced and perceived by communities and more specifically by youth has been crucial in the perception of multi-dimensional grievances. This makes governance systems relevant as an underlying context for these issues interacting with drivers like religion and political grievances in significant ways. Across the case studies in the two regions, multiple political grievances are present including a widespread disenchantment with political elites.

It is worth noting that the Balkan countries are categorized as democracies with varying degrees of freedom, while MENA countries have seen significant changes post-2011. With significant economic and social reforms in Morocco's, while countries like Egypt and Tunisia have faced setbacks, notably Tunisia's democratic decline since July 2021, which impacted the civic space and the human rights situation. According to Freedom House's Freedom in the World report (2023), only Bulgaria is classified as free, with most others being partly free or not free, including Jordan and Egypt. The rise of the far right in the Balkans and authoritarian drives in the Balkans are threatening universal freedoms, leaving marginalized communities vulnerable. It is important to take these contexts into account while understanding radicalization trends in relation to youth to address a significant gap in policy-making in this regard.

One of those significant policy gaps highlighted throughout the case studies is that officials focus on Muslim radicalization is overlooking far-right and nationalist extremism prevalent in the Balkans (Bieber & Pollozhani, 2024a). The presence of such trends was especially observed in countries such as Bulgaria and North Macedonia. In general, the case studies led in the Balkans highlight that ethnic politics and nationalism drive far-right extremism, intertwined with xenophobia and racism. While in the MENA region, ongoing conflicts like the Israel-Palestine war require further research to understand their impact on narratives of injustice. These deeply rooted issues are challenging but they need to be taken into account for effective policies in the P/CVE field.

Research findings also point out two other noticeable issues in P/CVE policies: those centered around traditional securitized approaches mostly exclude civil society and academia from development strategies. This prevents them from taking into account the complex nature of radicalization as well as its social and community dynamics as they tend to only focus on religion and security aspects.

It is also noteworthy that P/CVE policies are sometimes used to restrict civic space and suppress opposition, as evidenced by Freedom House rankings indicating limited freedoms in some countries (Tunisia, Egypt, Jordan) (Freedom House, 2023). This environment fosters censorship and self-censorship, limiting the ability of researchers and interlocutors to fully discuss radicalization and extremism.

2.2 *The Nexus of Alienation: Political Grievances, Economic Deprivation, and Territorial Inequalities*

Throughout the case studies in both the MENA and Balkans regions, governance models breeding social exclusion and alienation appear to foster youth vulnerability to radicalization and violent extremism. More precisely, the dynamics of alienation are the results of the interaction of three main drivers: political grievances, economic deprivation and territorial inequalities.

The outcomes of this "nexus of alienation" are determined by factors such as the level and opportunities for peaceful political and civic participation leading to the lack of trust in institutions, to withdrawal from formal political frameworks and to political apathy, as well as by the role of education.

Similarly to the radicalization dynamics in the MENA, economic deprivation in the Balkans plays a central role in making youth vulnerable to radicalization. The case studies in Bulgaria, BiH, and North Macedonia, highlight how economic deprivation is linked to poverty, exclusion, and unemployment, contributing to radicalization. However, while experts recognize the role of economic deprivation, there is no direct or automatic causality between economic deprivation and radicalization. Case studies show, indeed, that economic hardship is rarely found to be the sole driver. It appears to be mostly activated as a driver of radicalization in combination with other factors such as education as in BiH, where poverty indirectly increases vulnerability when combined with education. In contrast, Kosovo's P/CVE policies downplay economic challenges, as many radicalized individuals are not from poor backgrounds (Bieber & Pollozhani, 2024b).

Radicalization appears from this point of view as deeply political as already highlighted by previous research. The case studies led throughout both the MENA and Balkan region show that radical narratives draw on frustration with state policies and with perceived corruption of political elites. Moreover, several case studies (Bosnia and Herzegovina, Bulgaria and Morocco) underscore resentment toward arbitrary state violence and exclusion (Bakic et al., 2022; Ralchev & Stoynova, 2022; Mouna & Er-Rifaiy, 2021, Chirchi & Ghribi, 2023).

This alienation is further rooted in territorial and economic disparities. For example, the Roma communities in Bulgaria face state and far-right violence, exacerbated by discriminatory policies (Ralchev & Stoynova, 2022).

2.3 Alternative Spaces: Digitalisation and Leisure/Education

As a result of these alienation dynamics and lack of inclusion, youth in the case studies examined seemed to turn towards alternative spaces of socialization. Bosnian and Bulgarian football fans find alternative socialization in stadiums and fan cultures (Bieber & Pollozhani, 2023), while Moroccan youth engage through semi-formal groups like the Amal Association and Ultras, who use sports as a form of protest (Mouna & Er-Rifaiy, 2021). The same dynamics has been observed in Tunisia with the ultras group or with the underground music groups in Hammam Lif (Chirchi, 2024a).

The lack of physical spaces in the MENA region also leads to dangers like drug use among youth (Tunisia, Egypt). Also, because of the same reasons, socialization often shifts towards digital spheres (Tunisia). In both the MENA and Balkans regions, young people use the Internet daily, navigating censorship through VPNs.

Digital spaces facilitate the spread of radical ideas and the formation of transnational alliances, exemplified by foreign fighters from the Western Balkans and Kosovo joining Daesh or fighting in Ukraine (Bieber & Pollozhani, 2021). Online Salafi influencers in Bosnia and female preachers in Jordan further illustrate how digital spaces and networks (Bakic et al., 2022) facilitate the spread of radical ideas.

The COVID-19 pandemic worsened these trends, with far-right groups using disinformation to promote violence (Ralchev & Stoynova, 2022). The U.S. and the EU remain the most influential foreign actors in both regions, fueling radical narratives amid youth disenchantment (Chirchi, 2024b).

It is worth noting, however, that empirical findings help nuance the traditional view of the internet as mostly a risk factor for radicalization. While online spaces can be platforms for community-building and narrative construction, this potential cannot only be mobilized by radical groups, but can help young people to be informed and connected as well as foster PVE efforts. In this sense, the view from the meso-level brings nuance to understanding the role of digital platforms.

2.4 Gender Dynamics

The findings of the case studies also help shed light on the specific characteristics of youth as a social group and the many facets of its social experiences, representations, and emotions. Instead of the various stigma associated with their experiences of exclusion and marginalization, such situated knowledge should help better address their disenchantment and better engage them in effecting real change.

In the frame of the CONKKEKT project, the research examined youth as a main target exploring their social context for radicalization as well as the policies aimed at them. Gender was not the main focus of the research but was considered throughout the case studies. However, the various research report's discussions of gender were limited to male/female dichotomies, with few insights into power relations (Bieber & Pollozhani, 2023). Some of these insights include references to toxic masculinity in Bosnia and Herzegovina (Kapidžić et al., 2021) as well as in Tunisia (Chirchi, 2024a) as well as the role played by female religious preachersin Ma'an, Jordan, and Syrian refugees in Jordan (Mhadeen et al., 2021).

In conclusion, the case studies undertaken at the meso-level, confirm that radicalization and violent extremism are complex occurrences that cannot be understood through the old security lenses. These phenomena are typically framed at the institutional level as a security issue, with little exploration of socioeconomic and political causes, and civil society dynamics is often excluded from the process. In some cases, the label of "radicalization" is used to stifle dissent. However, the cases studies examined through the chapters of this book highlight that there is no simple and direct cause predicting radicalization, nor manifesting uniformly across regions.

The case studies' findings and analysis presented here establish the framework for the necessary debate on social-political issues in the MENA and Balkans. While religion is often assumed to be central to radicalization, the case studies show that radical and violent behaviors need to be understood in connection with their social contexts. Political systems and the degree of civic and political openness and inclusion play a crucial role in this regard.

From the meso-level perspective, the findings of qualitative participatory and inclusive research within local social context described in this book emphasize the crucial role of contexts in understanding VE narratives and drivers of radicalization in both regions. The case studies examined across both regions emphasize the combination of political grievances, economic deprivation, and territorial inequalities as major drivers of alienation, particularly for youth. In many cases, there are no local spaces for young people to engage positively, pushing them into alternative spaces such as online communities or radical groups. Although digital spaces can provide community and counteract alienation, the lack of digital literacy and oppressive realities in some regions allow radical ideas to flourish, often driven by transnational networks.

It is noteworthy that transnational networks of radicalization and violent extremism seem through the case study to be activated as a driver of radicalization only in combination with the local social and political contexts of alienation. From this point of view, and examined from the community perspective, radicalisation does not appear an inevitable outcome of exclusion and alienation, and most youth who experience these issues do not radicalize. Successful PVE should not just focus on individuals who turn to violence but take into consideration the broader social contexts of radicalization as well as its structural causes (Chirchi, 2022, 2024a, 2024b; Kapidžić et al., 2021; Mhadeen et al., 2021).

3 Recommendations

The structural issues and numerous social vulnerabilities outlined in the findings cannot be dealt with through ad-hoc short-term measures and programs and certainly cannot be contained exclusively through the security approach. They necessitate strategies addressing the development of governance models where all stakeholders (state agencies, civil society, experts, local communities) can participate in co-designing a common vision, strategies and programs that help strengthen the national, regional and local resilience to current social vulnerabilities.

3.1 Policy Recommendations for the Balkan Countries

3.1.1 Local-Level Recommendations

Support Local NGOs: Provide financial and institutional resources to local CSOs, and not only in major cities, to support their role and initiatives in preventing radicalization.

Collaboration Among Community Stakeholders: Address radicalization tendencies, especially within football fan communities by fostering partnerships between sports clubs, schools and civil society groups.

Community Engagement: Support CSOs initiatives that enhance the leadership skills of community members as well as youth positive belonging by organizing forums, workshops, and events.

Promote Inclusive Sports Culture: Promote a positive sports culture by encouraging sports events that emphasize inclusivity to counter violence and hate speech.

Targeted Socioeconomic Policies: Design targeted programs that address unemployment and poverty. The focus on education, employment, and skill-building can be harnessed to counter radicalization.

School-Employer Partnerships: Facilitate smoother youth transitions into the workforce by strengthening connections between schools and local employers.

Investment in Community Centers: Address the inequalities in access to leisure and culture by supporting the creation of community centers, especially in disadvantaged areas. Besides access to leisure, these community centers can become hubs for educational and cultural activities. Informal education through arts should be given priority in the activities of these centers.

Youth Awareness Campaigns: Design and support programs raising awareness about nationalism, xenophobia, racism, and hate speech. Young people should lead initiatives addressing these issues.

3.1.2 National-Level Recommendations

Education Reform: Reform education curricula to emphasize critical thinking and diversity while also improving discipline, engagement, and respect among adolescents.

Media Literacy Programs: Help youth identify and resist misinformation and extremist content by including media literacy into school curricula since primary education.

Interfaith Dialogue and Religious Literacy: Encourage and support national initiatives that encourage interfaith dialogue and religious literacy. Discussions on non-violence, tolerance, and cooperation should engage religious leaders.

Mutual Exchange Programs: Address territorial inequalities by implementing exchange programs to foster regional interaction, especially between economically and ethnically diverse areas.

3.1.3 International-Level Recommendations

NGO Collaboration: Strengthen capacity-building efforts to ensure local NGOs can operate sustainably beyond project-based funding and are not driven solely by donor agendas. Promote international partnerships between NGOs to share best practices, resources, and expertise.

Interregional Sports Initiatives: Foster interregional partnerships in sports through cross-border collaborations, particularly among football clubs, to exchange preventive strategies and address shared challenges.

International Cooperation on Fan Behavior: Support the creation of positive sports environments by facilitating global collaboration to manage fan behavior at sports events and sharing effective practices and strategies.

Social Media Information Sharing: Counter the role of social media in misinformation and radicalization by establishing regional networks for transnational cooperation to enhance information sharing and public media awareness.

3.2 Policy Recommendations for the MENA Region Countries

3.2.1 Local Level Recommendations

Youth Empowerment Projects: Launch long-term grassroots initiatives (3–5 years) that help youth develop a sense of agency through the creation of spaces for building trust and meaningful and safe debate and consultation.

Community-Centric Public Services: Ensure better access of marginalized communities, and the overall population, to better local public services, particularly in education and healthcare.

Promote inclusive urban policies that address community-specific needs and involve residents in decision-making.

Local Employment Opportunities: Offering youth practical skills and employment opportunities by creating programs that connect schools with local employers.

Remove bureaucratic barriers and provide resources for youth-led ventures in support of youth entrepreneurship.

Open Civic Spaces: Strengthen youth engagement in civic life by investing in accessible civic education and collaborating with civil society.

Youth Trust Projects: Foster trust with youth and local communities by encouraging local communities to co-design public policies and implement long-term grassroots projects that focus on building and sustaining trust between youth and local governments.

3.2.2 National-Level Recommendations

Education and Employment Policies: Focus on education and employment to address socioeconomic challenges through relevant national policies. Improve youth employability by strengthening connections between educational systems and industries.

Quality Public Education: Ensure equal opportunities for all by investing in quality public education. Enhance curricula by incorporating experiential learning, critical thinking, and platforms for youth-led discussions on social, economic, and political topics.

Youth Inclusion in Public Policies: Promote youth participation in policymaking, providing channels for youth to express frustrations and grievances peacefully. This can be done through national policies and programs in collaboration with CSOs and education institutions.

Youth Political Engagement: Support programs and initiatives encouraging youth participation in political processes—such as party youth wings, government internships, and youth parliaments. They foster positive inclusion and the effective channeling of youth grievances by empowering them to become active political actors and participate in decision-making, rather than engage in violence.

Civic Education Programs: Collaborate with civil society and educational institutions to promote civic education principles and skills and incorporate them into the national curriculum. Such initiatives can be sustained by creating spaces for dialogue in schools and youth centers at the national level.

Tax Incentives and Administrative Facilitation: Offer tax incentives and simplify administrative processes to encourage investment in underdeveloped regions and make projects more accessible to marginalized communities.

Inclusive Urban Policies: Adopt inclusive and participatory approaches to national urban policies and planning to reflect the true composition of cities and effectively address issues like transportation, leisure, cultural facilities, and marketplaces.

Quality Public Services: Improve the quality of public services, including education, healthcare, and access to cultural spaces. Special efforts need to be devoted to enhancing accessibility for marginalized populations.

3.2.3 International-Level Policy Recommendations for the MENA Region

Transnational Collaboration: Counter the role of social media in misinformation and radicalization by establishing regional networks for transnational cooperation to enhance information sharing and public media awareness.

Global Economic Support: Foster equitable economic and human development that achieves human security and social stability by encouraging investments in underdeveloped regions and establishing international twinning processes to connect marginalized areas with global communities and foster human, cultural, and economic ties.

International Educational Partnerships: Exchange best practices in civic education and youth empowerment on a global scale.

References

Bakic, S., Bašić, S., Dudić, A., Hirkić, M., & Kapidžić, D. (2022). *Bosnia and Herzegovina—Meso-level drivers of radicalisation and violent extremism*. The European Institute of the Mediterranean (IEMED). Retrieved November 2024, from https://h2020connekt.eu/publications/bosnia-and-herzegovina-meso-level-drivers-of-radicalisation-and-violent-extremism/

Bieber, F., & Pollozhani, L. (2021). *Compared perspectives on radicalisation and violent extremism in MENA, the Balkans and the European Union*. The European Institute of the Mediterranean (IEMED). Retrieved September 2024, from https://h2020connekt.eu/publications/perspectives-on-radicalisation-and-violent-extremism-in-mena-the-balkans-and-the-european-union/

Bieber, F., & Pollozhani, L. (2023). *Regional report: Meso approaches to the study of radicalisation and violent extremism in MENA and the Balkans*. The European Institute of the Mediterranean (IEMED). Retrieved September 2024, from https://h2020connekt.eu/publications/report-on-meso-level-drivers-of-radicalisation-in-mena-and-the-balkans/

Bieber, F., & Pollozhani, L. (2024a). *Cross-regional study on radicalisation in Mena and Balkans*. The European Institute of the Mediterranean (IEMED). Retrieved September 2024, from https://h2020connekt.eu/publications/cross-regional-study-on-radicalisation-in-mena-and-balkans/

Bieber, F., & Pollozhani, L. (2024b). *Prevention measures in Mena and Balkans*. The European Institute of the Mediterranean (IEMED). Retrieved September 2024, from https://h2020connekt.eu/publications/prevention-measures-against-violent-extremism-and-radicalisation-in-the-mena-and-balkans/

Bogdanova, V. (2024). *Tackling radicalisation risks in the Balkans: Multi-level complexities and policy solutions*. The European Institute of the Mediterranean (IEMED). Retrieved September 2024, from https://h2020connekt.eu/publications/tackling-radicalisation-risks-in-the-balkans-multi-level-complexities-and-policy-solutions/

Chirchi, T. (2022). *CONNEKT country papers on meso-level drivers in MENA and the Balkans*. The European Institute of the Mediterranean (IEMED). Retrieved September 2024, from https://h2020connekt.eu/publications/country-paper-on-meso-level-drivers/

Chirchi, T. (2024a). *Joint study on drivers of radicalisation in MENA*. The European Institute of the Mediterranean (IEMED). Retrieved September 2024, from https://h2020connekt.eu/publications/joint-study-on-drivers-of-radicalisation-in-mena/

Chirchi, T. (2024b). *Addressing violent extremism in the MENA region*. The European Institute of the Mediterranean (IEMED). Retrieved September 2024, from https://h2020connekt.eu/publications/addressing-violent-extremism-in-the-mena-region/

Chirchi, T., & Ghribi, K. (2023). *Meso approaches to the study of radicalisation and violent extremism: A view from the MENA region*. The European Institute of the Mediterranean (IEMED). Retrieved September 2024, from https://h2020connekt.eu/publications/meso-approaches-to-the-study-of-radicalisation-andviolent-extremism-a-view-from-the-mena-region/

Freedom House. (2023). *Global freedom status/map*. Retrieved September 2024, from https://freedomhouse.org/explore-the-map?type=fiw&year=2023

Hirkic, M., Dudić-Sijamija, A., & Bakić, S. (2024). *Policy paper on countering and preventing meso-level drivers in Mena and Balkans*. The European Institute of the Mediterranean (IEMED). Retrieved November 2024, from https://h2020connekt.eu/publications/policy-paper-on-countering-and-preventing-meso-level-drivers-of-radicalisation-and-violent-extremism-in-mena-and-balkans/

Kapidžić, D., Hirkić, M., Dudić, A., Turčalo, S., Bašić, S., & Bakić, S. (2021). Bosnia and Herzegovina. In D. Kapidzic (Ed.), *Country papers on macro-level drivers: Drivers of radicalisation and violent extremism in the light of state dynamics in MENA and the Balkans*. IEMED Publications.

Kapidžić, D., Hirkić, M., Bakić, S., & Dudić, A. (2023). *Meso approaches to the study of radicalisation and violent extremism: A view from the Balkans region*. The European Institute of the Mediterranean (IEMED). Retrieved November 2024, from https://h2020connekt.eu/publications/meso-approaches-to-the-study-of-radicalisation-andviolent-extremism-a-view-from-the-balkans-region/

Mhadeen, B., Bint Feisal, A., & Štikovac Clark, J. (2021). *Jordan - Macro-drivers of radicalisation and violent extremism*. The European Institute of the Mediterranean (IEMED). Retrieved November 2024, from https://h2020connekt.eu/publications/mapping-the-drivers-of-radicalisation-in-the-light-of-state-dynamics-in-jordan/

Mouna, K., & Er-Rifaiy, A. (2021). *CONNEKT Regional report on macro approaches to the study of radicalisation and violent extremism: A view from the MENA region*. Barcelona: The European Institute of the Mediterranean (IEMED). Available at: https://h2020connekt.eu/publications/mena_macro_approaches_to_the_study_of_radicalisatio_and_violent_extremism/

Peci, L., & Demjaha, A. (2022). *Kosovo - Meso-level drivers of radicalisation and violent extremism*. The European Institute of the Mediterranean (IEMED). Retrieved November 2024, from https://h2020connekt.eu/publications/kosovo-meso-level-drivers-of-radicalisation-and-violent-extremism/

Ralchev, S., & Stoynova, N. (2022). *Drivers of radicalisation and violent extremism in the light of community dynamics in MENA and the Balkans: Bulgaria*. The European Institute of the Mediterranean (IEMED). Retrieved November 2024, from https://h2020connekt.eu/publications/bulgaria-meso-level-drivers-of-radicalisation-and-violent-extremism/

The manufacturer's authorised representative in the EU is Springer Nature Customer Service Centre GmbH, Europaplatz 3, 69115 Heidelberg, Germany. If you have any concerns regarding our products, please contact ProductSafety@springernature.com

Printed and bound by CPI Group (UK) Ltd, Croydon, CR0 4YY

01/10/2026

02225950-0002